Dune and Philosophy

Popular Culture and Philosophy®
Series Editor: George A. Reisch

VOLUME 1
Seinfeld and Philosophy: A Book about Everything and Nothing (2000)

VOLUME 2
The Simpsons and Philosophy: The D'oh! of Homer (2001)

VOLUME 3
The Matrix and Philosophy: Welcome to the Desert of the Real (2002)

VOLUME 4
Buffy the Vampire Slayer and Philosophy: Fear and Trembling in Sunnydale (2003)

VOLUME 5
The Lord of the Rings and Philosophy: One Book to Rule Them All (2003)

VOLUME 9
Harry Potter and Philosophy: If Aristotle Ran Hogwarts (2004)

VOLUME 12
Star Wars and Philosophy: More Powerful than You Can Possibly Imagine (2005)

VOLUME 13
Superheroes and Philosophy: Truth, Justice, and the Socratic Way (2005)

VOLUME 17
Bob Dylan and Philosophy: It's Alright Ma (I'm Only Thinking) (2006)

VOLUME 18
Harley-Davidson and Philosophy: Full-Throttle Aristotle (2006)

VOLUME 19
Monty Python and Philosophy: Nudge Nudge, Think Think! (2006)

VOLUME 23
James Bond and Philosophy: Questions Are Forever (2006)

VOLUME 24
Bullshit and Philosophy: Guaranteed to Get Perfect Results Every Time (2006)

VOLUME 25
The Beatles and Philosophy: Nothing You Can Think that Can't Be Thunk (2006)

VOLUME 26
South Park and Philosophy: Bigger, Longer, and More Penetrating (2007) Edited by Richard Hanley

VOLUME 28
The Grateful Dead and Philosophy: Getting High Minded about Love and Haight (2007) Edited by Steven Gimbel

VOLUME 29
Quentin Tarantino and Philosophy: How to Philosophize with a Pair of Pliers and a Blowtorch (2007) Edited by Richard Greene and K. Silem Mohammad

VOLUME 30
Pink Floyd and Philosophy: Careful with that Axiom, Eugene! (2007) Edited by George A. Reisch

VOLUME 31
Johnny Cash and Philosophy: The Burning Ring of Truth (2008) Edited by John Huss and David Werther

VOLUME 32
Bruce Springsteen and Philosophy: Darkness on the Edge of Truth (2008) Edited by Randall E. Auxier and Doug Anderson

VOLUME 33
Battlestar Galactica and Philosophy: Mission Accomplished or Mission Frakked Up? (2008) Edited by Josef Steiff and Tristan D. Tamplin

VOLUME 34
iPod and Philosophy: iCon of an ePoch (2008) Edited by D.E. Wittkower

VOLUME 35
Star Trek and Philosophy: The Wrath of Kant (2008) Edited by Jason T. Eberl and Kevin S. Decker

VOLUME 36
The Legend of Zelda and Philosophy: I Link Therefore I Am (2008) Edited by Luke Cuddy

VOLUME 37
The Wizard of Oz and Philosophy: Wicked Wisdom of the West (2008) Edited by Randall E. Auxier and Phillip S. Seng

VOLUME 38
Radiohead and Philosophy: Fitter Happier More Deductive (2009) Edited by Brandon W. Forbes and George A. Reisch

VOLUME 39
Jimmy Buffett and Philosophy: The Porpoise Driven Life (2009) Edited by Erin McKenna and Scott L. Pratt

VOLUME 40
Transformers and Philosophy (2009) Edited by John Shook and Liz Stillwaggon Swan

VOLUME 41
Stephen Colbert and Philosophy: I Am Philosophy (And So Can You!) (2009) Edited by Aaron Allen Schiller

VOLUME 42
Supervillains and Philosophy: Sometimes, Evil Is Its Own Reward (2009) Edited by Ben Dyer

VOLUME 43
The Golden Compass and Philosophy: God Bites the Dust (2009) Edited by Richard Greene and Rachel Robison

VOLUME 44
Led Zeppelin and Philosophy: All Will Be Revealed (2009) Edited by Scott Calef

VOLUME 45
World of Warcraft and Philosophy: Wrath of the Philosopher King (2009) Edited by Luke Cuddy and John Nordlinger

Volume 46
Mr. Monk and Philosophy: The Curious Case of the Defective Detective (2010) Edited by D.E. Wittkower

Volume 47
Anime and Philosophy: Wide Eyed Wonder (2010) Edited by Josef Steiff and Tristan D. Tamplin

VOLUME 48
The Red Sox and Philosophy: Green Monster Meditations (2010) Edited by Michael Macomber

VOLUME 49
Zombies, Vampires, and Philosophy: New Life for the Undead (2010) Edited by Richard Greene and K. Silem Mohammad

VOLUME 50
Facebook and Philosophy: What's on Your Mind? (2010) Edited by D.E. Wittkower

VOLUME 51
Soccer and Philosophy: Beautiful Thoughts on the Beautiful Game (2010) Edited by Ted Richards

VOLUME 52
Manga and Philosophy: Fullmetal Metaphysician (2010) Edited by Josef Steiff and Adam Barkman

VOLUME 53
Martial Arts and Philosophy: Beating and Nothingness (2010) Edited by Graham Priest and Damon Young

VOLUME 54
The Onion and Philosophy: Fake News Story True, Alleges Indignant Area Professor (2010) Edited by Sharon M. Kaye

VOLUME 55
Doctor Who and Philosophy: Bigger on the Inside (2010) Edited by Courtland Lewis and Paula Smithka

VOLUME 56
Dune and Philosophy: Weirding Way of the Mentat (2011) Edited by Jeffery Nicholas

IN PREPARATION:

Rush and Philosophy (2011) Edited by Jim Berti and Durrell Bowman

Dexter and Philosophy (2011) Edited by Richard Greene, George A. Reisch, and Rachel Robison

Halo and Philosophy (2011) Edited by Luke Cuddy

Sherlock Holmes and Philosophy (2011) Edited by Josef Steiff

Philip K. Dick and Philosophy (2011) Edited by D.E. Wittkower

Spongebob Squarepants and Philosophy (2011) Edited by Joseph Foy

Inception and Philosophy (2011) Edited by Thorsten Botz-Bornstein

Breaking Bad and Philosophy (2012) Edited by David R. Koepsell

Curb Your Enthusiasm and Philosophy (2012) Edited by Mark Ralkowski

The Rolling Stones and Philosophy (2012) Edited by Luke Dick and George A. Reisch

For full details of all Popular Culture and Philosophy® books, visit www.opencourtbooks.com.

Popular Culture and Philosophy®

Dune and Philosophy

Weirding Way of the Mentat

Edited by
JEFFERY NICHOLAS

OPEN COURT
Chicago and La Salle, Illinois

Volume 56 in the series, Popular Culture and Philosophy®,
edited by George A. Reisch

To order books from Open Court, call toll-free 1-800-815-2280, or visit our website at www.opencourtbooks.com.

Open Court Publishing Company is a division of Carus Publishing Company.

Library of Congress Cataloging-in-Publication Data

Dune and philosophy : weirding way of the mentat / edited by Jeffery Nicholas.
     p. cm. — (Popular culture and philosophy ; v. 56)
     Includes bibliographical references and index.
     ISBN 978-0-8126-9715-5 (trade paper : alk. paper)
     1. Herbert, Frank. Dune series. 2. Herbert, Frank—Philosophy.
  3. Dune (Imaginary place)—Philosophy. 4. Philosophy in literature.
  5. Philosophy in motion pictures. 6. Dune (Motion picture)
  I. Nicholas, Jeffery, 1969-
     PS3558.E63Z65 2011
     813'.54—dc22

                   2010052001

Contents

Invitation

In 20217 A.G., Gaus Andaud delivered his famous peroration on Leto II, celebrating the ten thousandth anniversary of Leto II's transformation into a sandworm-human hybrid—into the God Emperor. While Andaud's speech received wide renown, particularly as promoted in the histories of the Bene Gesserit known as *Heretics of Dune*, his was not the only speech delivered at that august celebration. In fact, his peroration, while the most momentous since the demise of the God-Emperor, amounts to only one of many such speeches.

This volume collects together, for the first, many similar speeches given in honor of the God-Emperor as well as key addresses delivered at the anniversary whereat Gaus Andaud spoke. Many of these have been found only after long sifting through the Bene Gesserit Archives. The editors of this volume would like to extend a thorough thank you to the Sisterhood for opening up their archives. We hope this will be the first of many joint endeavors with the Sisterhood. I, for one, would be much interested in examining their archives covering the period of the so-named Scattering.

Other such essays we found at Dar-es-Balat II. These were a choice find, and many of our archaeologists are busy sorting through the papers and other items found there. As you know, the location of Dar-es-Balat remains a secret, and only Guild navigators know its true source. It's protected by no-globes and no-ships as well as covered by those carrying the Siona-gene. Thus, material trickles out at a slow pace. But we'd like to extend a thank you to the Guild for alerting us to the material so that we could include some of the choicest in this volume.

When selecting speeches to include in this volume we had a cornucopia of material so vast as to defy any easy categorization. I, along with my colleagues, decided to provide a sampling of some of the thematic issues that arise in study of Leto II and the "Dune-times," as they've become known. We selected essays that we thought expressed a . . . well, academics don't like to admit it . . . but a love for the subject. All the essays gathered here, whether they look favorably on the Dune-times or not, are authored by those fascinated with those times. They are truly inspired. And they examine, not only Leto II's life, but that of his father, Paul Muad'Did, his ghola-Mentat Duncan Idaho, and life on Arrakis-Dune itself.

What we found really intriguing were the number of speeches that looked back to ancient human times and those legendary philosophies we rarely see anything of now. . . .

Well, I'd rather not speak for the chapters in this volume. In fact, I can't—they speak for themselves, and I imagine that this book vibrates in your hand the way it does in mine.

Open up and enjoy!

Ecology of Muad'Dib

Facing the Gom Jabbar Test

We Bene Gesserit sift people to find the humans.

—Reverend Mother Gaius Helen Mohiam

I'm standing on the mezzanine at the mall, Christmas time, waiting to just grab a burger and get back to shopping. The new girl behind the counter can't seem to figure out how to work her radio-device to deliver orders to the cooks. It's not a cell-phone. I turn up my iPod. *Why can't she just hurry up?*

A sneering voice from behind says, "Who do you think you are?" I perk up my head and look around to see an ancient face, eyes beady, staring at me. She must be talking to someone else. Raising my eyebrows, I glance left and right, but there's only my grumbling stomach and me.

Then she says something even more remarkable.

"You're not even human!"

"'Scuse me?"

A long, gnarled, big-knuckled finger points out at me, almost touching my chest. "You're not even human!" she repeats.

She's crazy, touched somehow, maybe had too much to drink, though I don't smell anything but an overly spiced latte on her breath. She's a street person, obviously, wearing that baggy, black dress. Then I look at the dress closer. *What is this woman doing at my mall in that dress? I don't have time for this.*

Before I can think or do anything else, the woman raises her other hand. In it, she holds a little green box with a black opening. Then my pulse starts to race. I know where this is going, right? Been here before—not me personally, but I know who the old, wrinkled woman is now—Gaius Mohiam. Reverend Mother Gaius Helen Mohiam, and she wants to see if I'm human.

'Course, I know I'm human. *Look at me.* I've got the basic body of a human, maybe a little taller or a little heavier, maybe red-headed or green-eyed. I look back up, and . . . wait, there's that box again. The green one, almost glowing, with the blackness that my eyes sink into. I want to run, right? I know there's pain in that box and I don't know if I can withstand the pain. Oh, I know the pain will end, if I wait long enough. Still, it's pain, and I'm hungry already, plus shopping to do, and then later the bar, sing some karaoke, have some brews, eat a large cheeseburger and fries.

Still, I know I'm human, that's why I don't want to put my hand in the box, why I don't want to take that test. What would it prove?

Paul Atreides, son of a duke and a Bene Gesserit, trained by the best fighters in the universe, trained by the Warrior-Mentat Thufir Hawat—he stood before Reverend Mother Mohiam too. How dare she suggest that Paul was an animal. The gall of this woman. She sent his mother—Lady Jessica, concubine of Duke Leto, lady of the house—out into the hall to wait for her command.

"Let's say, I suggest you're human," she says, breaking my reverie.

Ah, yes, animal versus human. The Bene Gesserit sift people to find the humans. The rest, merely animals. And here I stand, order placed, credit card out, being told that I'm not human. Which means I'm an animal. Which means . . .

Why do the Bene Gesserit search for humans? How do they test?

Paul inserts his hand into the green box.

The pain begins. A tingling sensation, an annoyance really, gives way to a burning sensation. Paul tries to remove his hand, but a sharp command from Reverend Mother stops him. At his neck, he sees the thumb needle. Reverend Mother assures him and the reader that the needle is poisoned and will kill him with just a prick. Only now has the real test begun. The Gom Jabbar kills only animals. Paul, like most of us, is insulted. Are we animals? The Gom Jabbar test isn't to show that we're animals. Rather, it's to prove that we're human beings.

The Reverend Mother Speaks: "You've heard of animals chewing a leg to escape a trap? There's an animal kind of trick. A human would remain in the trap, endure the pain, feigning death that he might kill the trapper and remove the threat to his kind."

My stomach turns, feeling queasy. I'm thinking about the animal I'm about to eat—chicken now, later cow. I don't need to be thinking about chewing off a leg or some animal coming after me when I've trapped it. Do we even trap animals anymore? And why is this woman still in my face? I have shopping to do. I start to say something but look at the box again.

To be human is to withstand the pain. More, really. To be human is to turn the trap onto the trapper, to capture the trapper, even if it means feigning death. And then, to kill the trapper and remove the threat from humanity – from his kind, the species.

Am I ready to put my hand in the box yet?

He Who Can Destroy a Thing Controls It

The story of *Dune* really is the story of Paul sacrificing himself to save humanity. The continuing story of Dune in *Dune Messiah* and *Children of Dune* shows how both he and later his children sacrifice their lives to save humanity from extinction. Human beings are on a roll: there's a species instinct driving them to death, to nothingness.

Paul must use the trap on Arrakis to claim victory over the Harkonnens. He does so well that he's able to surmount even a greater victory by defeating the Padishah Emperor, CHOAM, the Space Guild, and the Bene Gesserit.

We can call to mind, then, the idea that drives Paul's plan of revenge. Once he discovers how to destroy the spice, he knows that he holds all the cards. CHOAM's profits, the Emperor's authority, and the Bene Gesserit and the Space Guild's future-telling depend on the spice. Paul depends on the spice as well, though. He needs it to be able to see the future in the particular way he does, but he needs it simply for life as well. Spice becomes an addiction, and if the spice is taken away, death follows. All of these aspects of the spice feed into why it's a perfect allegory for water, but that is a different story. What we have here, in this case, is the way that, as human, Paul can take the death of spice and use it for ultimate victory. Death leads to life.

Soon after the Gom Jabber test, he senses a terrible purpose in the words of the Reverend Mother. He's sensed this terrible purpose before. Terrible purposes drive against all odds and have their own necessity. Once Paul experiences the poison of the water and awakens to being the Kwisatz Haderach, the terrible purpose drives him. But not in the way that one might naturally think. Paul tries to save humanity from the terrible purpose. He wants to protect people from the jihad that his being will give rise to.

He attempts with each choice to lessen the impact of that jihad and to lessen the effects of that terrible purpose within him. So he walks into the trap to control the trap so it does not close on him. Or on humanity.

We see further evidence of this in *Dune Messiah*. There, Paul knows that he walks into a trap set up by the Bene Gesserit and the Tleilaxu. He goes so far as to allow himself to be blinded by a nuclear blast. He knows, further, that the ghola, Hayt, is a trap. He could send the trap away, but he keeps it close by. Only by keeping it close, he thinks, can he free himself from the trap and also free humanity from further destruction at the hands of the jihad or, conversely, the hands of the sisterhood and the Tleilaxu. Rather than let the trap serve the purposes of others, he manages the trap—at some considerable harm to himself – to free himself and his species.

Because Paul, and later Leto II, can see the future through their prescience, they know what awaits humanity—the slow decline to nothing. Paul tries to prevent it by bringing on jihad. It will forestall the end for a long time, but not forever. Leto II, by becoming the God-Emperor and sacrificing his very humanity, will remove the possibility of inevitable decline.

Both of them pass the Gom Jabbar test. They pass it so well that they sacrifice everything about themselves to save humanity. This trait is fundamental to the noble Atreides line – self-sacrifice for others. It's also why they claim such loyalty from their followers. It's also what makes them human.

Am I human? Atreides?

Thou Shalt Not Make a Machine in the Likeness of a Man's Mind

The Bene Gesserit Gom Jabbar test for humanity must be understood in light of the Butlerian Jihad. By looking at that jihad, we see how the notion of freedom goes hand-in-hand with the notion of humanity in Herbert's thought.

Return to the original Gom Jabbar test of Paul. He asks Reverend Mother, Why do the Bene Gesserit test for humans? Her answer: "To set you free."

The prehistory of Paul's universe includes the Butlerian Jihad. Humanity had enslaved itself to thinking machines. It took a religious war to release humanity from that enslavement. But why had humanity turned their minds over to machines in the first place? The Reverend Mother tells us that humanity sought to free itself by letting the thinking machines have power. What happened any student of the human mind could guess: other humans with other machines took advantage of the situation and enslaved all of humanity.

Thus, the Butlerian Jihad founded itself on a principle written in the Orange Catholic Bible: "Thou shalt not make a machine in the likeness of a man's mind." Reverend Mother, however, thinks the principle should be reformulated. "Thou shalt not make a machine to counterfeit a *human* mind." Why the difference?

To counterfeit is to make in the image of so as to pass off as. We counterfeit money in order to use the counterfeit as if it were the real thing—the real dollar. Reverend Mother warns us, then, not to counterfeit the human mind. Don't make a machine to pass it off as the real mind. That way lies slavery.

While discussing this, the reverend mother changes topics, asking Paul if he has studied the Mentat. Paul, notice, immediately corrects her and says that he has studied *with* Thufir Hawat. Paul doesn't use Thufir. Paul could never manipulate people in such a fashion. He hasn't studied Thufir as a tool to be examined; he's studied with Thufir as someone to learn from. It testifies to Paul's real concern with freeing humanity as opposed to the sisterhood's desire to free humanity in order to control it. They study people but not with people. The Gom Jabbar test shows that the Bene Gesserit and the Reverend Mother in particular aren't immune to using people. The whole system of genetics that the Bene Gesserit controls is a form of manipulation to bring about their Kwisatz Haderach—so that they can control this person when he emerges. Because he won't allow them to control him, the Bene Gesserit don't celebrate Paul's existence but plot against him. He has escaped from their bondage by the very trap they laid down for him.

But why bring up the Mentat at all when discussing machines? Because Thufir Hawat and his kind are an example of why one shouldn't counterfeit a human mind. The Butlerian Jihad took away the crutch of the thinking machine. Consider our current times.

That girl behind the counter can't deal with the radio to make orders because it's not like her phone. Have you ever been to a store when the computers break down? They close up shop . . . go home.

We have Blackberries and iPhones to remember dates. Our PDA's contain the contacts of our most intimate relations so that we don't have to. Our computers organize our finances for us. Herbert, in writing about computers, is prescient, but he has a history from which to work. That is, what he says about the computers taking over human functions wasn't as true when he wrote as it is today. There were no grammar and spell-checkers for Herbert, no Blackberries, and certainly no cell-phones. The complaints he levels at thinking machines, however, arise out of previous complaints about paper. If we use paper to keep notes, our memories will dwindle. Most of us have never lived in an oral culture. Can you imagine what it would have been like to have a mind so trained as to remember the whole of *The Iliad* or *The Odyssey?* The computer and its children have further reduced the need for our memories.

Hawat, on the other hand, outshines the computer because he doesn't have that crutch. The Great Revolt took away that crutch. In taking away the crutch, the revolt—the jihad, mind you—"forced *human* minds to develop," in the words of the Reverend Mother. To train these human talents, schools began. Only two remain at the time of *Dune*: the Spacing Guild, focused on mathematics, and the Bene Gesserit, focused on politics.

Mohiam's answer mirrors that of the ancient philosophers, especially Plato and Aristotle. Both held that contemplation was essential to human happiness. Can you imagine that—contemplation and not shopping? Aristotle put as much emphasis on politics, however. He did not mean the politics we know of today—the politics of bureaucracy where you have to cut through red tape to accomplish anything.

Rather, Aristotle thought that the politics of community constituted the highest form of the good life. Here, we work together to define and attain the common good. This was an activity for equals, and a way to exercise our particularly human talent for practical reasoning, what Aristotle called *phronesis*.

Aristotle did not think that politics was possible for everyone. Someone had to work, someone had to grow food and work in the market—like that woman behind the counter taking my orders and the guy behind her flipping burgers (probably has a PhD in Philosophy or English). Yet, here I stand waiting for that burger, not practicing politics. I'm the lucky one, according to Aristotle. We, living in the twentieth century, with our machines—vacuums and dish washers—have the time to practice the politics of the common good and to contemplate—to think.

Then Alannis Morriset asks, "Why are you so petrified of silence? Here can you handle this?"

Am I still holding the credit card? Still in line? Still hooked up to my iPod?

Humans Must Never Submit to Animals

Animal consciousness does not extend beyond the given moment nor into the idea that its victims may become extinct . . . the animal destroys and does not produce . . . animal pleasures remain close to sensation levels and avoid the perceptual . . . the human requires a background grid through which to see his universe . . . focused consciousness by choice, this forms your grid . . . bodily integrity follows nerve-blood flow according to the deepest awareness of cell needs . . . all things/cells/beings are impermanent . . . strive for flow-permanence within.

The problem is that we people of the twenty-first century remain animals, caught up in our own desires, tortured by our limited consciousness, unable to hold off the attainment of a thing when we desire it.

Environmental issues inspired Herbert's writing of *Dune*. Not only does the planet Arrakis lack sufficient water for its population, but melange also serves as a scarce resource that gives and extends life. It symbolizes water, just as much as the lack of water on Arrakis symbolizes the plight that threatens the world.

Already, many places suffer from lack of clean, fresh water. As the icecap melts and ocean levels rise, human demand on fresh water in the twenty-first century will deplete water resources before the century is out. Scientists have already mapped out the places that will be without fresh water by 2050. Earth might not turn into Arrakis, but without cheap technology to convert salt water to drinking water, it may very well feel like Arrakis.

Imagine our future: a world in which toilets don't flush because there's not enough water. A world in which we can't shower weekly or even monthly. A world in which people kill over water the way they kill over food . . . or oil . . . today. A world in which crops don't grow, starvation rises, and we'll look back fondly on the days when only one in six suffered malnutrition worldwide.

But we people of the European world—America, England, France, Germany—continue like Baron Vladimir Harkonnen, carried along by our suspensors, oblivious to the prophet on Arrakis. "Let them have their religion." The United States accounts for about five percent of the world's population, yet, we consume sixty percent of the world's resources. The amount of meat we consume testifies against us.

Conservative estimates from cattle-ranchers suggest it takes almost a thousand gallons of water to produce one pound of beef (http://www.earthsave.org/environment/water.htm). So when you go to McDonald's and eat a quarter pounder with cheese, you've just used 250 gallons of water. Good restaurants, however, usually have half-pound burgers, which would account for 500 gallons of water—on conservative estimates. More realistic estimates from scientists suggest it takes 2,500 gallons of water to produce one pound of beef. We could give a hundred people enough water to last twenty-five days if we didn't produce that one pound of beef. Would that be putting our hand in the box, so that our species can escape the trap? A trap we've built?

Yet, like Baron Harkonnen, we eat, not worrying about what others have and don't have.

In this sense, we are not human. We are animals. We cannot escape the trap of the imminent and immanent environmental collapse because we are the trap. We refuse to sacrifice now to live tomorrow, and we especially refuse to look for some way to turn the trap back on the one who created the trap. We've created the trap with our rampant desires.

Now we must wait: wait for our own Muad'Did who will save us from ourselves and show us how to be human.

Am I Muad'Dib?

Humans Live Best when Each Has His Own Place, when Each Knows where He Belongs in the Scheme of Things

If we're to be free to grow our potential, to develop our talents, then we must begin by recognizing where we belong in the scheme of things. The Lakota Sioux have a saying: *mitakuye oyas'in*—we are all related. This idea carries forth in the Gom Jabbar test and in our daily lives as we choose to live as humans or as animals. If we're caught in the trap, we escape the trap to capture the trapper to protect our species. We do this because we recognize a fundamental level at which we are all related. If we are animals, gnawing a leg off constitutes an action of the individual, the self concerned only with the self.

Perhaps we continue to ignore the Gom Jabbar because we don't know where we fit in the universe. In a sense, the idea of place unites the warnings from the Gom Jabbar test in *Dune* with the over-protective ship of humanity in *Wall-E*. Those "people" are our descendants. They've run from a planet that is nothing but a waste-bin now. They float around on carts—suspensors, just like Baron Harkonnen—and drink—drink!—their food and play virtual golf. They have no place in the universe, and what's funny is that they don't know it. They do not develop human talents.

Yet, the threat the Butlerian Jihad banished looms before us: will we develop human talents?

Herbert's philosophy of the human warns against two things: being animal and being a slave. As animals, we may be enslaved to our animal desires, but there's a different slavery—being a slave to the machine. The Butlerian Jihad freed humanity. It freed human beings from enslavement to machines. And it freed us to develop our human talents.

Herbert isn't asking us to abandon our favorite play things—iPod, computer, and game system. He's challenging us to find out how to use those toys to live a human life. The warning is not to stagnate.

The End of the Story

I continue to stare at the old lady, random thoughts about *Dune*, the Butlerian Jihad, and what I'm eating running through my mind. There's a trap here, I realize. The trap is one I've created and walked into. The carrot that gets me into the trap is the ease of my modern life. I mean, look at me. Look at us! We stand in line during the holidays, impatient for food that we didn't trap, rushing about from one store to the next. What talents do we develop here? Not talents for hunting and stalking prey, but so what? Are there other talents that I develop in their place with all the time I save?

Reverend Mother Gaius Helen Mohiam suggests there are two talents humans should develop: math and politics. But I'm not so sure those are interesting to me. I'd much rather grab my burger, slip on my iPod, and go back to shopping.

But there's that damnable green box of emptiness and pain! The old lady staring at me—why me? I walk away from the fast food and slip my hand into the box.

Oh, the pain of humanity! The pain of our species!

BENE GESSERIT ARCHIVES
Compiled by: Reverend Mother Belionda
Date: circa 14050 A.G.

The Golden Path of Eugenics

Humankind periodically goes through a speedup of its affairs, thereby experiencing the race between the renewable vitality of the living and the beckoning vitiation of decadence. In this periodic race, any pause becomes luxury. Only then can one reflect that all is permitted: all is possible.

—The Apocrypha of Muad'Dib, *Children of Dune*

Eugenics is at the heart of the Dune stories. 'Eugenics' is one of those words that frightens us. It means the controlled breeding of humans in order to achieve desirable traits in future generations.

The idea of eugenics goes back to Socrates's discussion of Kallipolis, the ideal city, in Plato's *Republic*. The ideal city, as Socrates explains it, includes three classes, two that guard the city and its constitution (the ruling guardians and the military guardians) and one that produces the material goods the citizens need. Famously, Socrates says that the the Guardians, the ruling class, should be denied all personal property and share everything in common. Socrates proposed that the traditional concept of private homes and family life should be abandoned in favor of a system where the Guardians live together as a large single-family unit.

Socrates insists that the city should cultivate the highest quality of offspring for this class, since they will grow up to become the leaders of the city. He proposes that the men and women of the ruling class will breed and rear their children in common in a manner not unlike the breeding of domestic animals. Adult Guardians are not permitted to breed on the basis of their affection for others. Instead, their sexual unions must be conducted under strict surveillance by the rulers. Moreover, the children should be raised communally and are not to be permitted to know their biological parents so that family loyalties can be eradicated from the class of rulers altogether. *Dune* fans will recognize striking similarities between the Guardian class of the Republic and the Bene Gesserit.

Mention of eugenics calls forth Huxleyan visions of genetic meritocracies as well as utopian fantasies of human perfection. The prospect of a rigorous eugenics was taken seriously in the first half of the twentieth century and was largely abandoned with the end of World War II—because of its connections to Nazi war crimes. The most developed eugenics programs involve pseudo-scientific schemes of racial supremacy and racial purity. Since the postwar period, both popular discussions and the scientific community have associated eugenics with Nazi abuses, such as enforced racial hygiene, human experimentation, and the extermination of undesired population groups. However, recent accomplishments in genetic, genomic, and reproductive technologies have raised many new and important questions about what exactly constitutes the field of eugenics, and what it ought, or ought not, to pursue.

Alarm about eugenics ranges from academic philosophy to wild doomsday prophecies. Examples cited in these responses are often thought to belong only to the world of science fiction: human clones and other genetic derivatives, various machine-human combinations, hyper-humans who are better than current members of the species *Homo sapiens* (who are more intelligent, fit, or longer lived), humans, who evolve beyond the scope of *Homo sapiens* into one or several new species, a world divided into a genetically enhanced elite and a genetically underdeveloped proletariat, among many, many others.

When ethics intersects with science on these questions, widespread concerns arise about the preservation of humanity, the meaning of human life, of doctors and scientists "playing God" by interfering with nature, and of being unconcerned or ignorant of the social consequences of their research. Not surprisingly, science fiction has created an arena for far-reaching speculation in the broad area that we refer to with the word 'eugenics'. In its long and storied relationship with the concept of eugenics, authors such as H.G. Wells, H.P. Lovecraft, Isaac Asimov, Arthur C. Clarke, and, of course, Frank Herbert, have delved into the possibilities inherent in a program of genetic manipulation in human beings.

Frank Herbert's interest in the possibilities and ethical consequences of genetic manipulation of humans is apparent in all his works (most notably in *Hellstrom's Hive*, *The Santaroga Barrier*, and *The Dosadi Experiment*, as well as the short story *Seed Stock*), including the *Dune* novels. In the *Dune* novels, Herbert shows us three long-term eugenics programs, each with a different ethical stance—that of the Bene Gesserit, the God-Emperor Leto II, and the Bene Tleilax. He also mentions other kinds of genetic 'products' in passing, such as the creation of gholas and twisted Mentats by the Bene Tleilax, the Ixian creation of Hwi Noree as the ambassador to Leto II, and genetic manipulations of non-human animals, such as thorses and chairdogs. A single idea anchors his interest in eugenics: the capability of planning that transcends the span of a few lifetimes, a direct result of Herbert's interest in ecology in the large scale.

What he shows us is that even with the longest possible view (up to and including that of the robot Erasmus, whose scope covers at least thirty thousand years), eugenics still presents pitfalls, both moral and practical. Despite these problems, some of Herbert's dramatic devices suggest there might be good reasons to pursue human breeding, but that all moral systems can fail when it comes to making long-term plans in order to better the human condition.

Nature Groomed: The Bene Gesserit

The order of the Bene Gesserit functions as one of the principal characters in the *Dune* saga. Herbert presents the Bene Gesserit as one of the forces that shape the Duniverse—albeit one that prefers to stay behind the scenes. The social, religious, and political machinations of the Bene Gesserit usually veil them in extreme secrecy and subterfuge—not limited to the organization itself, as the 'need to know' protocol often applies even to high-ranking Reverend Mothers.

The Bene Gesserit order comprises a secretive sorority whose members undergo an extremely rigorous educational program, both physical and mental. After years of physical and mental conditioning, those who excel are chosen to undergo the "Spice Agony," in which they ingest the poisonous essence of the spice melange. The powerful awareness-enhancement of the poison causes the successful sister to neutralize the poison with her body chemistry, as well as gain access to the memory of the other Bene Gesserit ancestors.

The connection between current sisters and their ancestors through genetic memory allows for the Bene Gesserit to make plans that transcend the span of a few generations. The power of their education, training and access to genetic memory results in powers and abilities, ascribable both to each sister personally, and to the order as a whole, that seem other-worldly and magical to outsiders. Their contact with outsiders is often itself fraught with subterfuge. Bene Gesserit Reverend Mothers were often hired as Truthsayers, and young women with Bene Gesserit educations were often solicited as companions. These interactions put Bene Gesserit operatives in strategic locations where they could influence events, and most importantly, breed with carefully selected (and often unwitting) sires. The fact that outsiders, from the Houses Major, CHOAM, and the Guild, call them witches indicates the conflicting responses of fear and awe that they inspire. Their secrecy and capacity to view time in terms longer than human lifetimes allowed for the hatching of a centuries-long genetic program.

Up to the end of the novel *Dune*, the Bene Gesserit Sisterhood aims to ultimately create the Kwisatz Haderach, a male equivalent of a Bene Gesserit Reverend Mother. One of the reasons the Bene Gesserit wish to breed a Kwisatz Haderach is to have access to the male side of the human psyche. As Reverend Mother Gaius Helen Mohiam tells the young Paul Atreides, "Yet, there's a place where no Truthsayer can see. We are repelled by it, terrorized. It is said a man will come one day and find in the gift of the drug his inward eye. He will look where we cannot—into both feminine and masculine pasts."

The Sisterhood needed a male with the ability to look into the Other Memory of the male ancestors, and also be able to withstand the onslaught of those memories. In short, confronting these memories terrified the Reverend Mothers. The man who could "be in all places at once," the meaning of Kwisatz Haderach, could only be born through a carefully controlled breeding scheme involving the bloodlines of the Houses Major.

Since the time of their inception on the planet Rossak, the Bene Gesserit thought of themselves as the stewards of the most important genes. They 'secured' the genes by marrying to the royal families or by selected sexual encounters. The Kwisatz Haderach program comprises a massive human breeding program, conducted on the span of countless generations. By manipulating relationships and the gene carriers in the Houses Major (accomplished not only through careful selection of biological parentage, but also through the selection of the gender of children—as Bene Gesserits are capable of choosing the sex of the children they carry), the Bene Gesserit control and monitor the predominant bloodlines through the ages.

The Kwisatz Haderach, with access to both male and female lines in Other Memory, was desired so that he could be the power figure in the Bene Gesserit's manipulations, thrust upon the universe as a Messiah, secured by the *Missionaria Protectiva,* the religious engineering project of the Bene Gesserit.

As the events of *Dune* begin to unfold, the Bene Gesserit design the Kwisatz Haderach breeding scheme to culminate in the union of an Atreides daughter, born of the Lady Jessica and the Duke Leto Atreides, and the na-Baron Feyd-Rautha Harkonnen, nephew of the Siridar-Baron Vladimir Harkonnen. The desired traits in the Harkonnen genes are reinforced by the lineage of Jessica: Vladimir Harkonnen is the natural father of the Lady Jessica, a fact unknown to her until she confronts the Spice Agony. The Kwisatz Haderach program was disrupted when, out of her love for Duke Leto, Jessica chose to conceive an Atreides son rather than the daughter the Sisterhood had ordered her to bear. This son proved to be the Kwisatz Haderach, a generation early. The birth of Paul Atreides crystallizes the fate of the Sisterhood, and eventually, the universe.

In terms of the eugenic designs of the Sisterhood, Paul is both a success and a failure. Paul constitutes a success because he is the male Bene Gesserit with all the powers of a Reverend Mother, unlike Count Hasimir Fenring, the man who came the closest to being the Kwisatz Haderach. However, Paul proved a failure for the Bene Gesserit because they couldn't control him. He had taken the mantle of Messiah and used it to his own ends, leaving the Sisterhood with a universe where they were to be subordinate to Paul and his progeny for millennia.

From the novel *Dune Messiah,* the Bene Gesserit are duly chastened by their hubris and shortsightedness. They realize that they compromised themselves in their pursuit of the Kwisatz Haderach. They're even more horrified when the Tleilaxu Master Scytale, as member of a conspiracy to destroy Paul Atreides, reveals that the Bene Tleilax had created, through their genetic modification and axolotl tanks, their own Kwisatz Haderachs.

The Tleilaxu Kwisatz is a particularly disturbing thought, because the Bene Gesserit always insisted on natural insemination and births, no artificial insemination, gene splicing, or surrogates were allowed. The Tleilaxu, on the other hand, used genetic materials in all manners. They treated the bits and pieces of humanity as raw materials, from which they could design any creatures they chose. Their Kwisatz Haderachs all destroyed themselves (this particular aspect of the story is developed further in the most recent book by Brian Herbert and Kevin J. Anderson, *Paul of Dune*) because they were morally one-dimensional. They were either entirely good or entirely evil, and they were destroyed by forcing them to become their opposites—of course Scytale suggests that the same might be done to Paul, the Emperor Muad'Dib. The conspiracy also serves to show the folly of the Bene Gesserit breeding program, since the Kwisatz Haderach appears to ascend to power through his prescience, but the power and control that springs from it also inexorably traps the prescient in a foreseen future that cannot be changed. The schemers found themselves ensnared in the scheme.

The penance of the Bene Gesserit continues in *God Emperor of Dune*: the God-Emperor, Leto II, has effectively taken over the Bene Gesserit breeding program for his own purposes. They are subject to thousands of years of privation—they have very little melange, very little control over their own programs, and absolutely no control over Leto II, who has as much claim as Paul to being a Kwisatz Haderach. A millennium later, in *Heretics of Dune*, the Bene Gesserit dreams of a superhuman to bring them to ascendancy have been crushed. Rather than breeding for a particular trait or individual, they focus instead on breeding to strengthen and secure certain human characteristics and preserve them.

This much more conservative approach reveals a lesson-learned on their part. They refrain from breeding to any one purpose again. In both *Heretics* and *Chapterhouse: Dune*, the Bene Gesserit prefer to think of themselves as stewards of humanity, gently making subtle improvements.

The ethical implications of the Bene Gesserit eugenics programs prove perhaps the clearest of the three considered here: the practice of breeding human beings for very specific purposes, as one might breed dogs or horses, leads to disastrous consequences. In addition to the problems that attend the Messiah phenomenon, the powers that were engendered in Paul Atreides endangered, not just the Bene Gesserit themselves, but the whole of humanity. The Bene Gesserit continue to monitor and keep breeding records all through the millennia between Paul's ascendance and the end of *Chapterhouse: Dune*. Herbert's conclusion seems to be that a general approach to a breeding program might not be a bad thing, so long as it does not aim at any particular goal. To echo the axiom of the Butlerian Jihad, the lesson the Bene Gesserit seem to have learned is *"Never seek to create a human being in any one image."*

Thus we see the Bene Gesserit shift from a consequentialist view, in which the outcome of breeding program defines its moral value, to a deontological approach, in which the acts of the breeding program determine its moral value. The Categorical Imperative of Immanuel Kant is perhaps the best-known example of a deontological view. Kant contends that morally laudable acts are determined by the moral value of the actions themselves, and not the outcomes of the actions. The Categorical Imperative entails that it's always morally unacceptable to use others as a means to our ends. The moral duty follows from our rationality.

In the case of the Bene Gesserit axiom, the duty implied by the command against an end-goal in breeding is to avoid trying to completely predict and control the outcome of human breeding (and human events—a matter for the ethics of prescience). As the Bene Gesserit progress through the *Dune* saga, we see them espouse this axiom in a general way, although, like the proscription against creating artificial intelligence, they come extremely close to violating it if the ends appear to them to justify the means. We might take Herbert to be suggesting through the Bene Gesserit example that eugenics cannot be guided by consequentalist ethics, simply because the outcomes of such programs cannot be known well enough to assess their moral value.

Nature Denatured: Leto II

In the wake of his universe-shaking ascendance, Paul Muad'Dib created an Empire through warfare and an economic monopoly on melange. After Paul's becoming blind, (both literally and figuratively, as his prescient visions cease) and going out into the desert in *Dune Messiah*, his sister Alia assumes the regency during the childhood of Paul's children, Leto and Ghanima. During the excesses of Alia's regency, which become more and more egregious as Alia is consumed by the specter of Baron Vladimir

Harkonnen, her maternal grandfather within her, Leto and Ghanima use their access to their Other Memories to create a plan to assume power and change the dangerous precedent that had been set by the religious zeal created by Paul's empire. Leto, during his spice trial in the desert, comes to formulate what he calls the Golden Path. His plan causes him to meld with sandtrout, ultimately making him into a human-sandworm hybrid. His transformation into a giant sandworm both enhances his physical strength and extends his lifespan to encompass 3,500 years.

The Golden Path is a term that refers to the strategy formulated by Leto II to prevent humanity's destruction and the destruction of the giant sandworms of Dune. The Golden Path proves so important in the novels that follow *Children of Dune*, it could be thought of as a principal character in its own right. (Brian Herbert and Kevin J. Anderson explore the Golden Path more in their sequels *Hunters of Dune* and *Sandworms of Dune*.) Both Paul Atreides and Leto II foresaw multiple futures in which humanity would become extinct.

Leto II, in particular, foresaw a threat to human existence, revealed in the later novels to be the computer empire of Omnius that had enslaved humanity tens of thousands of years in the past. Humanity could be tracked by prescience if it remained confined within the known universe of the Imperium. Leto II showed that mere abundance in population was not enough to protect the human race from complete annihilation—in his own regime, he demonstrated that humanity, by existing in an empire, could be controlled by a single interest. Throughout *God Emperor of Dune,* Leto II reflects on his rigid enforcement of a stable, peaceful society. The conflict between humanity's stated desire for peace and their actual need for volatility provides the central theme of the entire *Dune* series after the first. God Emperor Leto II states that he intends to "teach humanity a lesson that they will remember in their bones," that sheltered safety is tantamount to utter death, however long it might be delayed.

Leto II designs The Golden Path to make the human race follow multiple paths—rather than fall into a single sphere of influence. One aspect of this design consists in keeping the entire Imperium in a stranglehold of economic and political control to force them to create ways to thwart his rule. In doing so, Leto II acts as a predator, making humanity adapt by creating ways to hide from his prescience. Many adaptations arise from this predation, including Leto II's own eugenics program, which he wrests from the Bene Gesserit. It aims to make at least some humans invisible to prescient minds, like Paul's or Leto II's. The Atreides descendant Siona, who was the final product of this breeding program, could not be seen in Leto's prescient visions. Leto's political domination also brought out innovations in the Ixians, who created technology—no-rooms and eventually, no-ships—that could hide people and places from prescient minds.

The aftermath of his own death, however, proved to be the most prominent aspect of Leto II's plan. The centralization of the human government under his rule led to a complete collapse after his death. The collapse caused the Famine Times (since the economy Leto configured had collapsed), and the Scattering, in which human beings fled the mainstream Imperium, beyond the scope of the influence of the main powers—and therefore became more difficult to track. Herbert portrays Leto II's adherence to the Golden Path as a personal sacrifice, since Leto II forsakes his human nature in order to become half sandworm, allowing him to live long enough to achieve his goal, the preservation of the human species.

Leto II'S Golden Path includes at least two strands of genetic manipulation. He personally oversaw the first strand, the breeding program that began with his mating of his sister Ghanima to Farad'n Corrino. The addition of the Duncan Idaho gholas to his genetic design adds a layer of complexity—the gholas provide a control, showing Leto what he had started from in human evolution, and also allowing Leto to integrate and reinforce older traits, by mating the gholas with his newer subjects. In addition to the general enhancement of human attributes, both physical and mental, he also seeks to isolate and enhance the specific Atreides traits—particularly the element of prescience. He desires to enforce, not the prescience itself, but the invisibility that goes with it. He knew that a strong oracle made the future murky: the Guild navigators noticed this property with Paul, as he would later with the Navigator Edric. By constantly looking for the children in his breeding program, he could take the bloodlines that were the most difficult for him to see and breed them together. Ultimately he sought to create in humans a new mimetic defense—just as other animals create camouflage to elude their predators, he selected the adaptation that allowed human beings to hide in time from prescient minds.

There is also the aspect of Leto's acting as a predatory force on the entire human population. He seeks to make human beings resent his total command, making them forever averse to another charismatic leader with absolute power. The two strands are the direct plan that he conducts in reinforcing a genetic complexion in subjects he controls and breeds, and the other in (artificially) selecting traits in the entire human population by preying on them, and the traits of those who defy and oppose his rule are results he seeks.

Both aspects of Leto II's Golden Path take a decidedly consequentialist approach to the ethical relationship between Leto II and his plan in that the outcome of the action determines its moral value. On one view, he gives up his own interests for those of the entire race. This sacrifice could be seen as his weighing the interests of the trillions of members of the human race over his own. It might also be seen as making a distinction between individuals and entire species—that the needs of humanity as a species outweigh the needs of any one human, or group of humans.

This view strongly resembles utilitarianism, one of the most well-known forms of consequentialist ethics. Utilitarianism, whose most famous proponent is John Stuart Mill, maintained that the amount of pleasure (understood very broadly) an action produced determined its moral value. Thus, actions that result in happiness for many people are more valuable than those that create it for fewer people. Not only can pleasure be weighed by how many people are affected by an action, but pleasures can also be weighed by their natures, so that a mere sensory pleasure is inferior to an intellectual pleasure. Herbert shows Leto II sacrificing many profound pleasures so that humanity can survive as a species.

The other side of the ethical approach of Leto II is persistently Machiavellian. No matter how morally repellent the actions required to achieve the goal might be, the ends justify the means. Leto II believes that the end goal of his grand eugenics program is so important that any means to achieve it are morally justified. While Leto's own doubts surface relatively rarely, the heirs to his universe constantly question his decisions and motives. Siona, upon the death of Leto II, asserts that, despite the end result of the Golden Path, which Leto had revealed to her in the desert, he had no right to act as brutally and tyrannically as he did. Later, the Bene Gesserit, who see themselves as the heirs of the Golden Path, also question the ethical propriety of his actions—despite their own habit of acting from pure practical expedience.

At the end of the original novels, the Golden Path seems to be in danger: In *Heretics of Dune* Miles Teg, the Bene Gesserit Bashar, becomes able to see no-ships, leaving open speculation about who or what else might be able to do so. The fugitives from Chapterhouse in *Chapterhouse: Dune* are pursued by unknown assailants, only described as an aged couple, Daniel and Marty, who can intermittently spot the no-ship where they are hiding. In his portrayal of the Golden Path's creator Leto II, and his legacy, Frank Herbert gives us a mixed bag: surely it's most important to secure the survival of the human race; however, it might not be the case that any means are justified in the pursuit of that end. One might also see in the later novels a critique of Leto's eugenics plan similar to that we see of the Bene Gesserit—that imperfect knowledge, even that of Leto II—means that the best of intentions can still result in disaster. However, one could argue that even if Leto II did not secure the eternal survival of the human race, in trying to do so, he extended the trajectory of the species—a goal that Herbert presents as *prima facie* laudable.

Leto II is an example of the ultimate consequentialist in moral thinking—not just the life of one person, or one billion persons, but the very existence of human beings. Herbert presents the ultimate challenge: is the very existence of human beings enough to justify any means? Leto II commits atrocities on a galactic scale, all in the name of creating a human populace that will forever despise despotic rule, ensuring the continued survival of the species. Herbert might be giving us an example of the ultimate superiority of a consequentialist view, or else he might be showing us its limits. The fact that he depicts characters like Siona, who opine that even the goal of species survival for human beings cannot justify some actions, implies that he has his doubts about the totality of consequentialist ethics.

Nature Subverted: The Bene Tleilax

The Bene Tleilax, also called Tleilaxu, comprise a marginal society in the Duniverse. The first novels portray them as obscure beings with religious undertones and indicate that they are isolationist. Readers know, however, that they traffic in human products, they are known in *Dune* to create Twisted Mentats. In *Dune Messiah* they are also credited with the trade of metal replacement eyes and the first Duncan Idaho ghola, Hayt. In *God Emperor of Dune*, they engage Leto II throughout his reign by supplying him with countless Duncan Idaho gholas, while simultaneously plotting against him. We don't come to know them well until the events in *Heretics of Dune*, where they are shown to be genetic geniuses, who live in a merit-based theology loosely based on Sufi-Zensunni religion.

The Bene Tleilax masters believe that they are poised for ascendancy, and that by creating a universe in which the rest of humanity will be destroyed, they will be the only ones left to inherit the universe. At that point, they are still marginal and isolationist, but their power is comparable to a major house in the Imperium. They exclusively control several systems, but they claim the planet Tleilax as their homeworld, prohibiting most non-Tleilaxu (whom they call powindah) from setting foot there. The Tleilaxu deal in morally questionable but extremely desirable biological products, such as gholas and Twisted Mentats. They ultimately develop the technology to produce melange in axolotl tanks, breaking the monopoly on spice. Throughout the remnants of the Imperium, they are universally distrusted and profoundly disliked, but still influential.

In *Heretics of Dune,* Herbert reveals that the Tleilaxu deliberately cultivate universal dislike and revulsion. Their society is stratified into Masters and their Face Dancer servants. The Masters are the leaders and true core of the Bene Tleilax. Only they are privy to the secret language of their faith, Islamiyat. They think of their mission as a religious one, where their ascendance is foretold by their prophet. The genetic code is a mystical thing that they call "the language of God." Thus, only the Masters have access to the genetic expertise cultivated and developed over the centuries. They learn, after the Hayt ghola is reawakened in *Dune Messiah*, that they have the ability to regain their genetic memory with ease, allowing them to live seemingly forever, using the axlotl tanks to create gholas of themselves.

Heretics of Dune makes clear that their genetic plans are not natural breeding programs. Their plan is a genetic design for immortality and supremacy. The immortality of the Masters is secured by creating gholas of themselves in axolotl tanks; their supremacy is attempted by the creation of Face Dancers—their shape-shifting subordinates who can mimic the appearance of anyone, and who can also absorb their memories. In general the Tleilaxu Masters control their creations by implanting controls at the genetic level. Thus Face Dancers are designed to serve the Masters.

The ethical stance portrayed in the genetic designs of the Tleilaxu might be best described as myopic—the Masters see only one possible goal for their genetic pursuits—their own furtherance through growing their gholas and the creation of Face Dancer servants. Mores and customs of the mainstream Imperium are disdained as irreligious. Women are subjugated to becoming axolotl tanks, and they are never seen nor heard of off Tleilax. Their absolute certainty of the correctness of their religion blinds them in their view of the universe. Thus, they never question the ethical implications of their genetic manipulations.

The outcome of their myopia proves catastrophic: in *Heretics of Dune*, Master Waff attempts to control his perfectly mimicked Face Dancer copy of High Priest Tuek with a humming language, but fails due to the Face Dancer's complete change into its new form. Thus the new Face Dancers are too good at their mimicry. By absorbing all the memories of the person they replace, they effectively become that person. The Tleilaxu creation of a huge Face Dancer population and their subjugation of their female populace bring about their ruin. The sequels, *Hunters of Dune* and *Sandworms of Dune*, show that the Face Dancers, in their constantly connected hive mind, have a plan to overthrow the Tleilaxu. They also plan to overthrow their computer masters who elicited the new Face Dancer technology.

In *Chapterhouse: Dune*, the Honored Matres nearly annihilate the Bene Tleilax. The sequels reveal that the Honored Matres are descendants of Tleilaxu women who rebelled against their oppressive society. In both cases, the Bene Tleilax create monsters that they cannot control, regardless of their intentions. Ultimately, they bring about their own destruction through their genetic designs. The only one who survives is Scytale, who, ironically, is the ghola of the original Scytale of *Dune Messiah*. Scytale started as a Face Dancer too and went on to become a Master, ultimately, the only Master. The destruction and irony that befall the Tleilaxu result from their monomaniacal and closed-minded agenda.

While Herbert develops and explores several ideas with the Bene Tleilax, such as the intersection of religion and politics, the nature of the 'outsider' culture, and the ethical implications of alternative forms of reproduction, the chief aspect of the eugenics program of the Bene Tleilax is that of ascendance. They do not merely intervene in the process of reproduction, as we see with the Bene Gesserit, but they create an entirely artificial method by which human beings are created. The axolotl tank constitutes the logical terminus of in vitro fertilization, and the practice of reproducing oneself by creating gholas is far more literal than doing so by having biological children.

In creating this element of the Duniverse, Herbert challenges us to examine our mores: Why would it be morally preferable to have a child as opposed to creating an exact copy, and mental extension of oneself? The ethical system of the Tleilaxu is fanaticism—creating a combination of deontology, where there are moral axioms predicated on duty (in this case the precepts of the Tleilaxu religion), and consequentialism, in which the goals set out by the religion are paramount, and the pursuit of the end goal, in this case the ascendance and galactic rule of the Bene Tleilax Masters, justifies any act. And Herbert creates spectacularly repugnant atrocities.

The (Single) Garden Path

Frank Herbert's examples of eugenics programs in *Dune* shows a complex ethical posture—it reveals that human genetic planning and engineering is potentially dangerous, but also that it might be beneficial, indeed, even necessary to the survival of the species. Perhaps what's most important in Herbert's contribution to the ethical discussion of eugenics is the inherent dangers in adopting absolutes: the Bene Gesserit fail because they sought a single person in their breeding scheme; Leto II seeks a single result, the survival of the species, and the Bene Tleilax follow a single religious and ethical agenda. As expressed in *Children of Dune*, "The most dangerous of all creations is a rigid code of *ethics*."

If this is what Herbert is telling us, we might take heed in our applied ethics: the more rigid the code, the more dangerous the application.

Even with the seemingly laudable goal of preserving the existence of humanity, Herbert gives us a person no less than Leto II to make the frightful decision to apply eugenics in the interest of human survival. Herbert's dramatic use of eugenics in the *Dune* saga, at the very least, should make us feel relieved that none of us has yet had to make any such decision. Even the Golden Path is a potential garden path—we should tread as carefully as possible.

With assistance from:
STEPHANIE SEMLER

Shifting Sand, Shifting Balance

A theme running throughout *Dune* and its sequels is the human race's need for strife and conflict. By going through that strife and conflict, the race is able to advance and evolve. Muad'Dib saw how the human race had grown stagnant and how the galactic jihad that would occur from leading the Fremen to reclaim Arrakis would result in a mixing of gene pools and move the human race forward ever so slightly.

Leto II also saw this—the true goal of the Golden Path comprised, not the peaceful empire that he created and oversaw for thousands of years, but the vast explosion of humanity that would occur after his death, the Scattering, as humankind began to look for new places in the universe to live and new forms to take to inhabit these new homes.

This conflict and strife can come in many forms—famine, disease, the sudden absence of a governance system, and war. All of these play some role within the *Dune* saga as a method of strife and conflict to advance the human race, but war perhaps plays the largest role. A cursory glance at the amount of space dedicated to describing fighting and battles shows that it's a small amount of the overall level of text. But creating page after page of battle scenes doesn't show the importance of an event; it's almost the lack of that description and the great detail that the books place about their after-effects that really highlight the importance of war in the series.

War entails more than just shooting people. War creates a relationship between the society that conducts the war, the military forces they use within the war, and the government that leads the society. Each element has a role to play, and, as the conflict unfolds, the balance between the elements must shift and adjust to ensure that, directly or indirectly, all elements work toward achieving the political goals the war is fought for. There are different types of war, but the basic nature of the relationships remains the same. *Dune* does a wonderful job of demonstrating how, even with differing types of conflicts, the balance between the elements of war can be maintained. Perhaps more importantly, *Dune* demonstrates the danger of significant unintended consequences when sufficient thought or balance isn't maintained. This lesson applies in the modern world when military force is considered a tool to achieve a political goal.

Making a Clausewitz Ghola

I'm not convinced that Frank Herbert's theme of war as a human need is correct. That line of thinking can lead down a trail that has a distinct temptation to militarism, and militarism can be very dangerous for a society. But, war has had a major impact on the shaping of history and the societies that we, as humans, have formed.

There have been several notable individuals to write about war in a theoretical light—Sun Tzu, Jomini, Mahan, T.E. Lawrence, and Liddell-Hart are just some examples. But for the granddaddy of the strategists, the Mentat of war theory Mentats if you will, you have to go with von Clausewitz and his examination of war as a part of the human experience.

It isn't the first point that most pick up about von Clausewitz's writings, but a foundational idea that leads to the others is that war constitutes a social activity—not in the cocktail party sense—unless your cocktail parties feature real land mines—but an activity in which societies engage. Nothing is more of a social activity than politics—the forming of a system of governance, regardless of what that form may be, such as representative democracy in much of the modern western world or a caste-based oligarchy of the Duniverse. Now, if we layer that with the most well-known piece of Clausewitzian thought, that war is just another form of political discourse and a method by which to achieve a political goal, we can say that war is a social activity engaged in by societies in an attempt to achieve an identified goal. The presence (or lack thereof) of cocktail parties within a given war will be variable.

Clausewitz's Trinity

Expanding on this concept of social activity, Clausewitz identifies three distinct but related factors that characterize war which he labels as the "remarkable trinity." He describes this trinity in rather flowery language as being composed of the "original violence of its elements, hatred and animosity, which may be looked upon as a blind instinct; of the play of probabilities and chance, which make it a free activity of the soul; and of the subordinate nature of a political instrument, by which it belongs purely to the reason." Traditionally, the "hatred and animosity" points out the support and willingness of the people of the state to participate in a war. The "play of probabilities and chance" refers to the capability of the military forces as they identify, mitigate, and accept risk on the battlefield. Finally, the "subordinate nature of a political instrument" links the military efforts to the political leadership of the state and the political goals established for the war.

For a successful war, these three elements must be balanced. Balance does not mean symmetry, but each must be addressed and emphasis placed properly based on the nature of the conflict and the state of the conflict as the war unfolds. Duke Leto appears to be quite the master of this balancing act. Before the Duke even arrives on Arrakis, he recognizes that he will face an unconventional warfare situation, as the Harkonnens will attempt to wage a conflict of sabotage and assassination against him, slyly supported by the Emperor.

Unconventional warfare, according to the US Department of Defense *Dictionary of Military and Associated Terms*, names "the broad spectrum of military and paramilitary operations, normally of long duration, predominantly conducted through, with, or by indigenous or surrogate forces who are organized, trained, equipped, supported, and directed in varying degrees by an external source." Leto II's government element is secure, being surrounded with sound and experienced advisors, and his military forces element is reasonably secure with the troops he brought from Caladan.

However, the population of Arrakis is likely at best ambivalent to the change of ruling houses, and this means that he must focus on the population element. If it would be possible to gain the support of the Fremen, then it would balance his trinity and allow him to stifle the threat of Harkonnen saboteurs left behind while also increasing his ability to govern and granting him a truly significant military force with which he could strike his corpulent cousin and repel the activities of a duplicitous Emperor. We see the Duke working towards this from early on—sending Thufir Hawat to begin early negotiations with the Fremen and meeting with Stilgar to begin efforts at achieving the needed balance of this element. Unfortunately, his strategy isn't given sufficient opportunity to come about before the Emperor and Baron Harkonnen strike. After that point, the nature of the conflict dramatically changes. So does the theory of the trinity remain valid?

Ernesto "Usul" Guevara

If the trinity theory and the nature of the conflict suffer a problem, it would probably come from the experiences of Clausewitz. We need, then, to place him, and his work, in context.

Clausewitz's experiences were based on the Napoleonic Wars, although his personal battlefield exposure wasn't very great. These wars involved massed formations of soldiers, horses, and cannons bringing havoc and destruction on each other. The use of irregular forces wasn't particularly in vogue and even when practiced, as in the Spanish guerrillas on the Iberian Peninsula or by the Tyrolian mountaineers, was seen as a strategic adjunct to the more formalized formations conducting conventional warfare—supporting the Anglo-Portuguese forces or creating opportunities for the Austrian army, respectively. This wasn't a new development, as a similar situation had occurred earlier in the New World, during the Seven Years War and the American Revolution.

You'll notice in all these examples, these conflicts were being played out within a political setting of state versus state or the irregular forces were closely linked to a state, such as the Tyrolian mountaineers. So Clausewitz is a very state-centric perspective, but that is understandable. After all, the political changes that swept Europe with the French Revolution and the eventual toppling of the Emperor Bonaparte were the most significant changes to the development of the modern state since the Peace of Westphalia following the end of the Thirty Years War, 167 years before. At this point in history, the state was all. Clausewitz's work reflects these two factors, where the role of irregular forces is relegated to unconventional warfare in support of a conventional force, which is the primary capability of a state to achieve its established goal.

But what happens when a state doesn't exist, or a non-state actor is in play? The conflict is no longer unconventional warfare, but irregular warfare, "the violent struggle against state and non-state actors for legitimacy and influence over the relevant population," not warfare that needs more fiber in its diet. The nature of the conflict is different as we shift from two forces (whether conventional or unconventional) facing each other to placing the influence of the population at the center of the efforts.

Clausewitz doesn't address irregular warfare, and from the historical context in which he wrote his work, this is no surprise. But this lack doesn't mean that the remarkable trinity is obsolete, just that the traditional labels of people, military forces, and government leadership need some tweaking. Even for a non-state actor, they must address the balance between the various demographic groups with which they must interact, their ability to conduct violence against their opponent, and ensuring they are working towards their eventual political goal if they're to be successful in their struggle. In the end, the concept of the state is just another grouping of political leadership; it's just the model that we've been living with for the past four hundred years. The underpinnings of the social activity remain the same.

This type of conflict is what Muad'Dib finds himself in, but he manipulates the social activity in just the same fashion as his father. He has no external support—the Atreides forces are defeated and the members of his father's formations are scattered or dead. Some, such as Gurney Halleck, do eventually find their way back to him, but that is merely coincidence. He has a formidable fighting force which is the same as his population—the millions of Fremen who have never been accounted for in the Imperial census. This, however, doesn't mean that two of the elements of the trinity are now fused. They still remain separate, despite the combat and warfare-centric nature of Fremen culture. And Muad'Dib, at least in one snapshot in time, demonstrates a great ability to balance the remarkable trinity in book three of *Dune* when he must deal with the traditions of Fremen culture that require an almost cannibalistic changing of leadership mantles.

By this point, the Fremen insurgency is in full swing and the tribes are anxious to continue their attacks on Harkonnen forces, Muad'Dib's influence across the Fremen is growing, and Stilgar recognizes him as the rightful Duke of Arrakis. Accordingly, Fremen tradition would dictate that Muad'Dib and Stilgar duel for control of

Tabr Sietch and leadership of all the tribes. To take this course would address the support of the people, but would seriously hamper both his military forces and his political leadership. Despite his growing prescience, Muad'Dib still needed the experience and skill of Stilgar on the battlefield to minimize the "play of probabilities and chance," as well as within the sietches to govern the people on the day-to-day needs that a government must provide. For this moment in time, Muad'Dib holds the trinity in a nice balance—he creates change within the people's traditions, effectively reducing the influence of that element of the trinity so that he can maintain the strength of the other two elements, despite the fact that the military and population elements derive from the same source, the actual Fremen population.

We can suggest that in an irregular warfare situation the trinity does heavily shift toward the people element. Of course, there is a lot of room for nuance here—you could be ensuring you have the support of a particular demographic, or you may simply be ensuring that a gap remains between your opponent and a demographic from which he's trying to secure support. So a leader, military or civilian, must dedicate a large amount of effort to this aspect of the remarkable trinity, but that doesn't mean that the other two elements are obsolete. The social activity of war remains the same—it's just the techniques and some parameters may differ slightly.

In for a Ducal Seat, in for an Imperial Throne

We've talked about the element of the trinity that deals with the political control over the war—the political-strategic leadership that ensures that wartime efforts are pointed in a direction which will result in the achievement of the political goal. Achieving that political goal comprises the reason for starting the war in the first place. So, perhaps a great deal of attention should be placed on what that goal will be before war even begins.

The difficulty of irregular warfare and political goals is that it's difficult to say when you have achieved those goals. For a conventional war, it's easy—conquer this piece of land, destroy this particular fighting force, or force your opponent to lower those tariffs. For unconventional, it gets a bit murkier, but a goal can be pinned down. After all, based on our definitions there is an external, more conventional source which will have more conventional political goals—some links can be made. And of course, the conflict itself may shift into a more conventional model as the time passes, as in Guevara's guerrilla warfare model.

But in an irregular war, how can you tell when the goal is achieved? If you are the non-state element seeking a change have you achieved it when the state has been completely destroyed, or when you take the place of your opponent and become the state? The difficulty is that now you have just switched positions with your opponent and you still are in an irregular war, just on opposite sides of the equation. Or is the goal simply not being destroyed as you conduct the struggle? In which case, how long do you have to survive before you can declare you have achieved your goal? This is the true problem of irregular warfare—not that the trinity doesn't fit, but that it's extremely difficult to manage the trinity when the three elements rest on a very loose, unrealistic, or perhaps even non-existent goal.

Duke Leto set two political goals—to meet the spice quotas in an honest and fair fashion, and demonstrate to the other great houses the duplicity of the Emperor's conniving with the Harkonnens on spice supply. To achieve the first goal, he would seek to gain the support of the Fremen to secure his population's support and bolster his military capability. To achieve the second, if pushed out of Arrakeen by force or treachery, he would use the skills and strength the desert gave the Fremen to gain the evidence needed to unite the Landsraad against the Lion Throne and secure his fiefdom. These goals are rather modest, and if not for the treachery of Dr. Yueh, perhaps they may have been achievable.

We can't say the same for Muad'Dib's goals, or more specifically how he matches that goal to his balancing of the trinity. His initial goal also appears rather modest—to restore the Atreides family to its place as ruler of Arrakis, specifically with him as the new Duke. But how he goes about attempting to achieve it is another matter. We've already talked about that one instance with Stilgar where he did balance out the trinity nicely so as not to damage his efforts, and force a small change on Fremen culture. But on several other occasions, either consciously or unconsciously (one of the drawbacks of being the Kwisatz Haderach), he manipulates Fremen culture and religion to achieve his goal of restoration of the fiefdom. But these things he manipulates talk about much grander goals—goals of vengeance for injustices experienced thousands of years ago and of messianic salvation. This pushes the population element of the trinity away from the

control of the government element and then out of synchroniza-
tion with the political goal.

The results of resting an unbalanced trinity on a less-than-firm
goal are dramatic unintended consequences. After the Battle of
Arrakeen, the galaxy experiences a Fremen jihad as the legions of
Fremen soldiers spill off the planet to spread the story and rule of
their messianic Muad'Dib. Billions are killed. Because of prescience, Muad'Dib knew this would come. He even sought ways to
halt or control it. However, even with his ability to see the future
he couldn't. For those of us who are nowhere close to being a
Kwisatz Haderach, the ability to forecast or limit the effects of such
events is even less and should stand as an important warning.

From the Deserts of Arrakis to the Deserts of Earth

Even today, the unintended consequences of having a poorly
defined or non-existent goal, when entering into an irregular warfare situation are readily evident. As I write this chapter, NATO has
been involved in an irregular conflict in Afghanistan for nine years
without establishing a goal that all NATO members agree is clear or
achievable. The result is continuing and increasing violence within
that country. Post-Saddam Hussein Iraq provides another example—while the initial goal seemed rather clear, the removal of the
Hussein regime, the inability of the American government to fully
understand and establish a post-conflict political plan resulted in
another irregular war which has lasted for over six years, although
now solely in the hands of the Iraq government to wage. In both
cases, the poor or non-existent goal and inability of the government element of the trinity to properly focus war efforts tied to the
population element has led to unintended consequences of significant loss of life and treasure from combatants and non-combatants
on all sides of the conflicts. Unless you have the future sight of a
Kwisatz Haderach, the long term outcome of these adventures is in
flux and the extent of the unintended consequences is unknown.

Humans are social creatures, and so we partake in social activities. One of the most basic is that of political activity. Throughout
history, one political activity we have repeatedly engaged in and
expended many resources on is warfare. We are likely to continue
to do so into the future, and in the Duniverse, it's an activity that
continues to consume a lot of human energy. As such, it's worth-

while to make sure we understand this activity, this force, so that we can minimize the unintended consequences. Regardless of the type of political system in which people live, Clausewitz's remarkable trinity highlights the relationship between population, the government, and the military capability that will be wielded in a war and provides a framework for understanding the force of this activity. Without a proper balance within this relationship and a realistic, achievable goal on which this relationship can rest, the utility of war for political purposes is highly questionable and the results may not be pleasant. Just ask Muad'Dib about his attempt to regain a ducal seat that results in becoming emperor at the expense of thousands of planets and billions of lives. There's a warning lesson for those of us in the modern world about ensuring we have full understanding of what we wish to achieve before utilizing military force for a political end.

FROM DAR-ES-BALAT
Possible Author: Leto II
Date: 12333 A.G.

Curse of the Golden Path

When God hath ordained a creature to die in a particular place, He causeth that creature's wants to direct him to that place.

—The Orange Catholic Bible (*Dune*)

The Trap of Prescience

Oracle—the visionary power of foreknowledge of the future—has long been thought to hold very special dangers. It's double-edged, both gift and curse. If you can see the future, and know that what you see is true, then the future will be as you have seen it. Oracular vision severely impinges, maybe destroys, our sense of having free will to make our future different by making different decisions. It's called the paradox of foreknowledge.

Frank Herbert explains clearly how prescience functions in the Duniverse. Powerful oracles like Paul-Muad'Dib and Leto II see many possible futures. Should these futures be possible and plural—possible futures—then it would appear the future is not really fixed after all. The future's history is open. For that matter, Leto reveals that, for him at least, because the oracle manifests his oracular power at a particular present point in time, prescience affects what's contained in the future possibilities oracles see. In two ways, then, it appears in Herbert's Duniverse that the future is open to be made.

Frank Herbert? Smart, smart fellow; Mentat smart. Seemingly, Herbert establishes that Paul's and Leto's prescience functions in a way that avoids the paradox of foreknowledge. His characters' free will remains unthreatened. So it might seem. First impressions

37

mislead, for Herbert's version of prescience threatens free will. Herbert wants to show us why, if Atreides oracles have any free will, it's a strange free will. Powerful though it may be, paradox runs through it and limits it. It's not much different from our own free will.

Paul Atreides: Kwisatz Haderach?

The Bene Gesserit understood that the Kwisatz Haderach would see all possible future threads of time. He would be able to pick between them, much like the three Fates of classical Greek mythology. Herbert leaves unclear whether Paul fulfills or surpasses the expectations of the Sisterhood's long-awaited Kwisatz Haderach.

For one thing, he can't see all the threads of time. Paul's oracular vision has its limits. Princess Irulan in *Arrakis Awakening* reports that "Muad'Dib could indeed see the Future, but you must understand the limits of this power. Think of sight. You have eyes, yet cannot see without light. If you are on the floor of a valley, you cannot see beyond your valley. Just so, Muad'Dib could not always choose to look across the mysterious terrain" (*Dune*).

"Abysses," periods where Paul's prescient vision isn't available to him, arise where he can't see how or which of the possible futures he has seen lead from this right-now moment. This blindness happens to him twice in *Dune*, in his knife-fights with the Fremen Jamis and later the Harkonnen Feyd.

Also, Paul can't see certain people: Count Fenring never appears in any of his visions. Paul wonders if that's because Fenring is the man who will kill him. (I suspect this is Herbert's first clue in the *Dune* saga that some people may be genetically predisposed to be invisible to prescience.) Significantly, Paul also can't see what other oracles have seen or have done, such as the Spacing Guild's Navigators who have their own constrained form of prescience. However, he's a much more powerful oracle than they; he sees much more, much farther.

In *Children of Dune*, Leto says "The joy of living, its beauty, is all bound up in the fact that life can surprise you." This is as much a lament as a piece of wisdom, because for oracles, surprise may be a rare joy. Surprise visits us as the unexpected; for an oracle, with the power of true foresight, potentially everything that happens is entirely expected. After all, they have foreseen it. *All of it.*

Do the Atreides oracles spring the trap of the paradox of fore-knowledge? Or, because Frank Herbert stipulates that the power of oracle works in a special way in the Duniverse, do they slip the trap? It's poor form to answer questions with a question, but I reckon these questions really amount to, What do the Atreides oracles know about the future and how well do they know it? To answer this question, we need to talk about fate, God, the future, and possibility. We also need to talk about knowledge.

Belief, Justified, True

First then, briefly, knowledge. How could knowing the future threaten free will?

Epistemology names the philosophical study of knowledge, belief, justification, and reason. Plato, the ancient Greek philosopher, gave the first philosophical understanding of knowledge: justified true belief. You know P if and only if 1. you believe that P, 2. P is true, and 3. you hold your belief that P on the basis of some justification. The justified true belief theory is pretty simplistic. However, as a theory of knowledge, it usefully distinguishes knowledge from opinion and mere belief. Opinion can be (and typically is) arrived at without proper justification, whereas justification comprises a necessary condition for knowledge. And beliefs? Well, they can sometimes be false. Plato's theory respects a key, often unspoken condition of knowledge: factivity. A necessary condition of knowledge is that knowledge is always and only of the truth. You can't know something false. Know is a success verb.

Knowledge's factivity contributes to the paradox of foreknowledge. As a type of knowledge, foreknowledge entails that the object of knowledge is true. Thus, for foreknowledge, the future has factivity—there is a fact of the matter what will happen in the future, even though it hasn't happened yet. Foreknowledge implies that there is one truth of the matter as to what happens in the future. Being true, the future can't be altered or revised. Individuals change, situations change, times change, but the truth about what they were like at those times does not change.

To know something means to be in an especially strong epistemic position towards it. It implies, not only that something is true, but that it was knowable. Consider the prescient dream Paul has while still on Caladan about his first meeting with his future beloved Chani, the Fremen. Paul Atreides sees in his oracular

dream-vision a first meeting that will occur. A necessary condition
of its being foreknowledge—the knowledge of the future—is that
there's a truth about the future to which he somehow has direct
access (as we realize, presciently). Since something is known, then
it must be knowable. In the case of the future, there must be truths
about it before it happens for it to be foreknown. Paul's seemingly
lucky meeting with Stilgar and his tribe, including Chani, in the
desert was true of that very place and that very time. True—and
inevitable for the moment of Paul's dream on Caladan months
beforehand, inevitable since forever.

The future's knowability threatens free will because it invites the
claim that all events are fated to occur in one way and no other,
inevitably, unavoidably. You can't choose to make events go
another way than they must. Even choice isn't free: the act of
apparent free choice is just one more inevitable event.

Oracles present a double-threat to free will. An oracle's existence also implies that the future is known to them, making freely-
willed choice for the oracle themselves close to hopelessly
paradoxical. The existence of a power of oracle implies that the
future is knowable, which threatens free will for everybody, oracle
and other people alike, because it invites the possibility of fatalism.
The existence of an oracle threatens everybody's free will in the
Known Universe because the oracle knows the future history of the
universe, which encompasses the actions of citizens of the
Imperium. *All of it.*

The Paradox of Foreknowledge

Usually we think of knowledge as liberating. The more you know,
the better you can judge your courses of action and decide on the
best one. The paradox of foreknowledge is that because an oracle
knows what is going to happen in the future, they are no longer
free to change what happens. Prescient foreknowledge threatens
free will because it traps the oracle into enacting the future foreseen. If this understanding of foreknowledge is correct, then Paul
isn't free. Neither are you or I. Paul has one meager advantage over
us: he realizes the illusory nature of free will.

Some advantage! The oracle himself can't think of his choices as
freely-willed at all because he knows what they will be. Consider
that when he first gains his future-vision, Paul presciently foresees
a jihad. He foresees a holy war will erupt as fanatic legions of

Fremen under the Atreides banner sweep out across the universe. Paul sees many possible futures leading from that time, but except for some faint and closing gaps, all lead to the holy war; whatever he chooses "he could still sense the green and black Atreides banner waving . . . somewhere ahead . . . still see the jihad's bloody swords and fanatic legions" (*Dune*). Paul tells himself: I will not let it be. He tries to steer the course of history in another direction as he experiments with his powers of oracle. It may be why he calls Feyd-Rautha out in the Great Hall. He doesn't do it just in the same devil-may-care spirit of his grandfather, Paulus, facing down the bull that killed him, or to honor his father's challenge of kanly against the Harkonnens. He senses the time-winds boiling in those moments like a storm. Paul may secretly hope that if he dies on Feyd's blade, his death would not become a martyr's death which would inspire the jihad anyway.

And yet—Paul realizes that no matter whether he kills or is killed, he sees "how futile were any efforts of his to change any smallest bit of this. He had thought to oppose the jihad within himself, but the jihad would be" (*Dune*).

Paul appears trapped in paradox if he believes he can make any change to something he knows will happen. Freedom is predicated on the idea that something happens such that it could happen one way or the other. Choices, as we mere mortals as well as oracles make them, are predicated by their limits. Paul's attempts to oppose the jihad are not merely insignificant and unsuccessful: they are futile. Choosing that he change how he knows the future will happen is about as futile as trying to make it a choice that Feyd is rushing at him with a knife. That's no choice: Feyd's knife and murderous glare is a fact which limits his choices: dodge, parry, thrust, roll. A fact once known can be forgotten, denied, contradicted, disbelieved, but it can't be made untrue.

Paul's foreknowledge means that his will is his own, but he is no longer free to will choices that he knows have this ultimate limit: they shall never happen. The paradox for the oracle is that his visions trap him. His vision lays out a path into the future. It's a high-walled path where, as the nightmarishly slow-dawning ineluctability of Paul's life plays out in *Dune Messiah*, there's no turning back and no turning aside. Path . . . or roller-coaster . . . or sluice. Paul doesn't even have the luxury of pretending he's free. Even entertaining the thought that he isn't free is unfree; the very thought too was an element of the foreseen future.

I Am the Book of Fate

The Fremen have a saying they attribute to Shai-hulud, Old Father Eternity: "Be prepared to appreciate what you meet." On hearing arguments for fatalism, you might be happy to accept fatalism, that our every action is inevitable, that nothing could happen otherwise than it does. You would be in good company, the company of ancient Roman Stoics, Zen Buddhists, believers in karma, and Fremen, who recommend fatalism as bringing a calm acceptance of what the future holds. Fatalism replaces surprise with a kind of expectation of fittingness. Be prepared to appreciate what you meet in time as it approaches from the future, because eventually there it will be in the present, unavoidably.

In the meantime, you might also be appalled. You must protest, search for the mistake in the argument, the break in the Shield Wall. Maybe knowing the logical possibility of future events doesn't threaten our sense of free will. Free will is a precious idea, you feel, underwriting our genuine responsibility to do right and wrong such that we can be praised or shamed for freely doing it! Free will also underwrites our hope that we have any creative, individual contribution to make in the theatre of life! That we aren't just puppets dancing on the strings of fate!

Possibly Paul and Leto's power of oracle is not the kind of knowledge that threatens freedom, or, maybe, they don't foreknow enough to make their foreknowledge a trap. Let's shave the "edge of mystery" off Paul's prescient awareness and view it as he initially views it, a computation of the most probable futures. In that case, what the Atreides oracles do is predict. Prediction, however, seems a much less epistemically strong position than knowledge. It seems fallible and indirect. "Fallible and indirect" seems a lot less . . . God-like.

God's Knowledge and Free Will

Does the foreknowledge of the Atreides oracles compare to God's knowledge of the future? Christian theologians concerned themselves greatly with resolving the tension between God's foreknowledge and human free will. Without free will, then we can't be rewarded for our faith or punished for our sins, by human or God, unless human or God is unjust. Yet, to deny God foreknowledge is to put a limit on God's power and a limit on God's knowledge. Supposedly one of God's aspects is that He is omniscient. He knows everything that it's possible to know. Another of God's supposed aspects is that He is perfect, which means either that He is perfectly successful and does not make mistakes—hence, His infallible knowledge—or that He is perfectly immutable, in other words, unchangeable, particularly, unable to change for the better. Does God's knowledge increase every time a point in time solidifies from flux into just one of its possibilities? If so, then God can change, which suggests his perfection grows from less to more, but is certainly less that an absolute perfection.

Absolute free will implies that every time we choose, we choose between possible actions in such a way that we could have freely chosen any of them. The implication is that any choice is possible and that whichever choice we happen to make of our own free will was, before we made it, indistinguishable as just one possible choice among the many. Free of will, Yueh could have not fired the dart. God, watching over him, couldn't have known with absolute certainty what Yueh would do. Before we choose, what we are yet to choose is in the future, a contingent and undecided fact; choosing and acting decides and fixes the future possibility into the sequentially next present moment of time.

Mere mortals have no God-like perspective. Assume the decision to betray is Yueh's to make. Baron Harkonnen and his twisted Mentat Piter de Vries may well have found a method by which to subvert Dr. Yueh's Suk training. However, they haven't rigged him with a hypnotic compulsion. Yueh isn't somehow psychologically addicted to betrayal. From the Baron and Piter's perspective, probably Yueh shall act according to their plan of attack. Finally, they can't know for certain. (As the Baron and Piter soon learn. Yueh does betray his Duke—not without betrayals within his betrayal, helping Paul and Jessica escape the Harkonnens and arming Duke Leto with a poisoned tooth to revenge on the Harkonnens.)

If God foreknows how Yueh shall decide to act, how may Yueh's choice still be freely willed? Boëthius, a sixth-century Roman statesman and philosopher, was accused of conspiracy with the Byzantines and sent to prison. Around 524 A.D., while awaiting his sentence of death, he wrote a book called the *Consolation of Philosophy*. "If God foresees all things and cannot in anything be mistaken," Boëthius writes, "that, which His Providence sees will happen, must result" (p. 131). According to Boethius, "God has a condition of ever-present eternity. His knowledge, which passes over every change of time, embracing infinite lengths of past and future, views in its own direct comprehension everything as though it were taking place in the present" (p.144).

St. Thomas Aquinas, arguably Roman Catholicism's greatest philosopher, proposed a variation on Boëthius's theme. In his *Summa Theologica*, Aquinas argues that God knows the succession of time *sub specie aeternitatis*, "under the aspect of eternity." God stands above or outside of time. "Just as he who goes along the road does not see those who come after him; whereas he who sees the whole road from a height sees at once all those traveling on it" (p. 156).

In other words, delete the "fore" from in front of foreknowledge. God doesn't know beforehand Yueh's freely-willed choice to betray his Duke. Notions like "before," "during," and "after" make no sense in relation to a being who is outside time. God sees all of the events of Yueh's betrayal, every event leading up to it and away from it, at the same time. The Baron's choice to subvert a Suk doctor, Yueh's choice to become a traitor, his choice also to save his Duke's son and concubine and to try to kill the Baron; each was freely willed, might have happened otherwise than they did, but of course only happened one way—and God sees the single line of time stretched out before him, from beginning to Yueh's betrayal to the end. God is sometimes called the Divine Author. On this picture, He is the Divine Reader.

God's foreknowledge isn't a prediction but something like perception. God's foreknowledge becomes something like unmediated access to every actual event across the whole of time. So we should hope that God's perceptive foreknowledge on the same scene is not only superior to the Baron's and Piter's, but also to that of the Atreides Oracles. God's foreknowledge is direct and infallible, where the Atreides's foreknowledge, being predictive, is indirect and much less reliable.

Demons of Prediction

All of which is fine and dandy as a solution to the paradox of foreknowledge . . . if you're God.

Sadly, there are clear disanalogies between Paul-Muad'Dib and his son Leto II and God. Paul and Leto aren't beings magically outside of time but very much creatures in time. They also lack God's aspects of omniscience and perfection. Frank Herbert gives no suggestion that the Atreides oracles are in fact prophets, divinely inspired and blessed with access to God's perspective on time and the foreknowledge it brings.

Suppose instead (as I think Herbert wants us to) that Paul and Leto's oracular vision isn't divinely inspired. Paul and Leto's prescience represents a power brought on by a complex reaction between ingestion of the spice melange, which heightens psychic capabilities, and dormant abilities lying in wait in their Atreides genes. Whatever prescience is, it's on a level with special powers such as Truthsaying, Guild Navigators' folding space, and Bene Gesserit sharing. Insofar as they are woven into the pattern of reality in the Duniverse, they aren't magical or supernatural powers. They are strange, mysterious only because Herbert keeps them mysterious. A metaphysical or scientific explanation simply happens not to be offered for them.

Maybe Paul and Leto's prescience isn't much different from other, super-computing functions of a Mentat's mind like prime computations and first approximations, just future-oriented and colossally powerful in scope and range. In which case, their foreknowledge ranks as no more superior than would be the Baron's or Piter's or anybody else's. It's a powerful yet still fallible and indirect form of knowledge, and, in being fallible and indirect, doesn't completely threaten free will.

This possible escape route misunderstands the nature of prediction. As knowledge is to belief, so too prediction is to uninformed guesswork. Prediction can still make for a freedom-threatening kind of foreknowledge. Pierre-Simon de Laplace, seventeeth-century French physicist, mathematician and astronomer, offered two reasons why absolute prediction threatens absolute freedom. He theorized that a being of supreme intelligence, suitably informed about the laws of physics and of the state of the universe at a given time, could predict the entire future of the universe. "For it, nothing would be uncertain and the future, as the past, would be present to its eyes" (*Philosophical Essay on Probabilities*, p. 4). Known as Laplace's Demon, his thought-experiment assumes causal determinism: all events are rendered predetermined because of the necessary connection between causes and effects. Every particular event must have a preceding situation which caused it. The relationship is such that if the past situation had been different then so would the future event—and vice versa.

The late, famous twentieth-century American metaphysician Richard Taylor might butt in here. Taylor supported the philosophy of fatalism. Fatalism is the thesis that whatever happens is inevitable; it is or always was going to happen. Fatalism is often fatally misunderstood. Taylor points out that fatalism doesn't claim that what happens is inevitable no matter what. It isn't as though what happens necessarily must happen that one way by fiat or something mysterious like destiny. There has to be a reason why what inevitably happens, happens inevitably.

For most of us, when we talk about the future we aren't talking about a logically-guaranteed eventuality. Talk of "the future" is almost nonsensical; there is no future yet happening to be referred to, no set of events to be spoken of. For example, consider the two or three pages of *Dune* where it all starts to go badly for House Atreides: Yueh's act of betrayal.

Imagine that it's right now in the present moment when Yueh fires the dart that immobilizes and tranquilizes Duke Leto. As he now fires the dart, Yueh's sabotaging the house generators and killing the Shadout Mapes is in the past. We don't think of the future as at all like reading *Dune*, where the next event of plugging the tooth is right there already on the next page, waiting for us to turn to it. We believe that the future comprises just a stretch of time somehow or other abstractly empty of concrete events. The future is time laid out waiting to be filled in by one more event in the present (just at a later time than the last). Our choices partly decide how the future turns out. Yueh could think again, reconsider his intention to follow through with the rest of his betrayal, call for help, surrender himself. Plugging the poison gas tooth into Duke Leto's mouth, as he intends to do next, isn't an event out there in the future, concrete, realized, waiting for the now to move a bit later in history, like our eye across the page, so that the tooth-plugging changes from being future-tensed to present-tensed. Yueh could choose otherwise and write a new page into the chapter.

Taylor and Laplace are of the same mind. Laplace imagined a demon which could, from the state of affairs at Laplace's birth in 1749 A.D., predict absolutely that Laplace would die in 1827 A.D., and that a novel called *Dune* would win the Hugo and Nebula Awards in 1966 A.D., and (assuming the fictional Duniverse is on the same, real timeline as us) that in around about 10,191 A.G. Yueh Wellington would fire a dart in betrayal of his beloved Duke. The argument concludes that the future is inevitable because an unbreakable, logically necessary chain of cause and effect predetermines it.

Here is a straightforward reason why what inevitably happens, happens inevitably. We understand that effects necessarily follow from their causes. If a cause-event such as Yueh's firing the dart had been different, the effect-event of his betrayal overall would have been different too. However, he couldn't have done otherwise, because his firing the dart was the effect of a previous cause, the events leading up to that moment which necessitate only one act. Causal determinists must also be fatalists, on pain of self-contradiction. The future may well be yet empty, but it will fill with whatever single line of particular events necessarily, indeed, inevitably, follow one from each other in a single chain of cause and effect.

On the Balancing of Probabilities

We might care to believe that the future's openness confirms our belief in our free will. Quite the opposite, Taylor suspects. Our belief in our free will is consonant with a belief in the future's openness. Consonance proves nothing. It's just like semuta music to our ears. "Metaphysics and logic are weak indeed in the face of an opinion nourished by invincible pride, and most men would sooner lose their souls than be divested of that dignity which they imagine rests upon their freedom of will," Taylor writes (*Metaphysics*, p. 71). I would add, lose their souls or their rationality.

Laplace's description of absolute predictive knowledge does accord with the descriptions of prescience for Paul and Leto II. Prescience seems like a super-attunement to the present instant of time that brings with it a super-awareness of the possibilities for the future potential in the present instant.

The same disanalogies between the Atreides oracles and God also apply between the Atreides oracles and the Laplacean demon. Unlike Laplace's demon, Paul and Leto foresee many possible futures, not just one single future. Also, presumably unlike God and Laplace's demon both, Paul and Leto cannot reliably discriminate between all the possible futures they envision which is the one possible future that will actually happen. Paul and Leto may not be so utterly trapped by their powerful foresight because it may be they don't foreknow enough to make their foreknowledge a trap. There are spans of future time which they apparently don't or can't see into with their future-vision. Maybe they are freed in will in these brief "abysses"?

No, sorry, I think, maybe not. Feyd Rautha and Paul clash on the floor of the Great Hall, knives crossed. Paul's vision is obscured by a storm nexus in the time-winds at this cataclysmic point in history. Feyd is more than a match for him; Paul will kill or be killed. Paul has already seen, though, before he steps into the ring just what the future holds, every possibility leading to the jihad. If Paul dies here, "they'll say I sacrificed myself that my spirit might lead them." If Paul survives, "they'll say nothing can oppose Muad'Dib" (*Dune*).

"This is the climax," is Paul's thought, "From here, the future will open, the clouds part on to a kind of glory." In the metaphor of the abysses, although Paul is in a valley, he has seen across the plain before it dropped as it has temporarily out of sight. He has seen the on-coming flood. Even were Paul to throw himself willingly on Feyd's knife, it would be a free choice in name only. Free will is predicated on acting such that you could have done otherwise. Doing otherwise is done in the expectation that you shall achieve something otherwise than what would have been. Paul's suicide would be pitifully futile, changing nothing. A mitigated freedom.

Intending the Way Out

I think what Frank Herbert is trying to do in the *Dune* saga is carve out for the Atreides oracles a sort of freedom unthreatened even by their own power of oracle. They do slip the trap of the paradox of foreknowledge.

Paul and Leto foreknow much more than anybody else. Some things they foresee they absolutely know are inevitable: the jihad, then Krazilec, the Typhoon Struggle at the end of the universe. Krazilec, the Typhoon-Struggle, provides a clue to how much freedom prescience allows in the Duniverse. Paul and Leto both foresee the battle at the end of the universe. Of every future timeline in the set of possible futures they see in their visions, there is Krazilec at the end of the line.

Paul and Leto are attuned to the weight of probability each possible future timeline has. Possible future timelines can become less and less probable, and even disappear from the prescient's vision altogether when the probability of them occurring reaches 0. An example of this is in *Dune*, where Paul loses sight of the possibility he might somehow ally with the Baron Harkonnen.

Possible future events, segments of timelines, can be seen along some timelines but not others. Some possible future events, such as Krazilec, can be seen along every timeline. Present in every vision, the jihad and its sequel the Typhoon-Struggle, have a probability of 1. Some events, if not all events, are inevitable. Many of the future possibilities they see in their oracular vision remain just that: mere possibilities. As Paul and Leto act and make decisions just like everybody else, they can presciently foresee that their actions change the balance of probabilities within the set of future possible timelines they envision.

"Why" has to do with intention. Elizabeth Anscombe, a British analytic philosopher, wrote a book on just that topic: *Intention*. When you follow through on an intention to act you have a special form of knowledge, which she dubs "practical knowledge." Anscombe borrows the phrase from Aquinas's wording for God's knowledge of His Creation. The world is God's Creation, too, so He knows what the world is like because the world is just as He intended it.

Intentional action is simultaneously creative and determinative in just this fashion. To be the author of an event, as God is, entails that your knowledge of the event forms because you are its cause rather than because you perceive its effects. Paul and Leto, as they in their visions foresee the possibilities for the future—see futures—and the spectacularly magnified consequences of their every minute action in the present, see a terrific responsibility. Seeing this and being the noble Atreides they are, they can't escape the further realization that the chances of the future happening one way or the other are chances decided pretty much as though they intended it, because they are in a position to decide. A most unenviable position.

Discovered By:
Sam Gates-Scovelle

Politics of Muad'Dib

The American Fremen

Not long after the 2003 invasion of Iraq, US soldiers captured an American citizen in Afghanistan carrying a weapon and wearing the dress of a Taliban soldier. Heralded by the news media as the "American Taliban," he became a spectacle, bound, gagged, naked and blindfolded on a stretcher in a photo taken soon after his capture.

The story of how the homeschooled twenty-year-old from a middle-class Northern California family became an enemy combatant in the Afghani desert piqued the popular imagination. After converting to Islam, he went to Yemen, learned Arabic, returned home and then left again to attend a madrassa (Islamic religious school) before receiving training at an Al-Qaeda training camp in Afghanistan. Some Americans reacted to the young man's story with wonder; others with loathing.

How did this youth stray from the values that most Americans hold dear? In fact, he didn't. Similar to Paul Muad'Dib who, at the end of *Dune Messiah*, wandered into the desert a blind holy man, the American Taliban had acted in accordance with values that most Americans prize: self-reliance, ingenuity, spirituality, and practical know-how. It's widely believed that the Fremen culture derives from their religion, *Zensunni*, an imaginative blending of Zen Buddhism and Sunni Muslim beliefs. However, a closer look reveals that the Fremen (similar to the American Taliban) were shockingly American in their core values.

The Weirdness of Dune's Fremen

"The Fremen are civil, educated and ignorant," Scytale said. "They're not mad. They're trained to believe, not to know. Belief can be manipulated. Only knowledge is dangerous."

—*Dune Messiah*

The weirdness of Dune, its man-eating sandworms, water-starved environs, and hostile colonizers (who cultivate the prized spice or melange), explains the weirdness and wildness of its indigenous desert population, the Fremen. The prologue to *Dune Messiah*, titled "The Weird of Dune," begins with a short description of the planet and its original inhabitants:

> Dune is the planet Arrakis, an arid world of great deserts where life survives against terrifying odds. The semi-nomadic Fremen of Dune base all their customs on water scarcity and face the deserts in stillsuits which recover all moisture. Gigantic sand worms and savage storms are a constant menace to them. Dune's only resource is the melange, an addictive drug produced by the worm.

Subject to Dune's harsh conditions, the Fremen had to adapt to their environment if they wished to survive. They wear special water-recycling clothing (stillsuits), fight with immense ferocity against their rivals, and ride the great sandworms across wide expanses of the open desert. Thus, it's unsurprising that they would become the hardened and brutal shock-troops for Paul Muad'Dib, the prophet who would inspire them to fight in the jihad to subjugate the known universe and prepare the way for the God-Emperor.

What is the Fremen religion? The Indigenous people of Arrakis revere the sandworm, Maker, or Shai-Hulud as a deity. The Fremen acolytes become Reverend Mothers by drinking the poisonous "Water of Life," the spice essence or concentrated melange produced by the sandworm's lifecycle. They thereby render it harmless and access the memories of previous Reverend Mothers.

According to one source, "Dune mentions the religion of the Zensunni, presumably a combination of 'Zen' [Buddhism] and 'Sunni' [Islam]" (Moongadget). Following this widely-accepted view, the Fremen have a syncretic religion (that is, a product of synthesizing two other religions). The Fremen would have adopted elements of both in their wanderings from planet to planet (indeed, they were originally called "Zensunni Wanderers"): i. as slaves taken to the planet Poritrin (where they revolted and escaped); ii. to Salusa Secundus (where they were also enslaved); iii. to Bela Tegeuse, their "third stopping place"; iv–v. two other planets that are unmentioned; vi; Harmonthep, the "sixth stop"; and vii. finally, to Arrakis, Dune, desert planet ("Terminology of the Imperium," *Dune*). While the *Zensunni* faith shares much in common with the mysticism of Zen Buddhism and Sunni Islam, this isn't the entire story.

Neither Sunni Islam nor Zen Buddhism embodies a liberation theology. Neither would have inspired the beliefs of a long enslaved people. Orthodox Islam condones slavery (though the Qu'ran allows a slave-holder to release slaves as a way to atone for a sin). Buddhism doesn't explicitly ban slavery (though it would seem to violate the Eightfold Path's prohibition against human trafficking).

Once Paul Muad'Dib became Emperor of Dune, the Fremen religion commingled with Catholicism, thereby becoming another syncretic faith: "Zensunni Catholicism." Catholicism is a liberation theology typically embraced by former slaves and colonized peoples. Citing the Fremen ritual of recalling their enslaved condition ("We will never forgive and we will never forget"), Julia List argues that the values of the Fremen are similar to those of Protestants in 1960s American society (p. 40). Therefore, it's likely that, from its very beginning, the *Zensunni* faith more closely resembled Catholicism or Protestantism than Sunni Islam or Zen Buddhism. Indeed, the Orange Catholic Bible, created shortly after the war between humans and thinking machines, is the authoritative religious text for Zensunni Catholics.

The problems apparent in the widely-held view impart a critically important lesson: it's best to avoid conceiving the Fremen way of life, culture, and beliefs as solely derived from the Fremen religion. The values of the Fremen come from many other sources, including their history as an enslaved people and the harsh environment they endured on Arrakis. In reacting and adapting to demanding conditions, the Fremen outlook imitates the frontier mentality and values that manifested in the American psyche during the nineteenth-century: resourceful, self-reliant, spiritual and pragmatic.

Imagine having grown up in a sietch in a rocky outcropping of the desert world Dune, hardened by the harsh conditions that you have known your entire life. Every day you walk into the desert, wearing a stillsuit that recycles your bodily moisture (a permanent mark beside your mouth and beard formed from the stillsuit drinking tube), riding the massive worms over the wide expanses of desert, praying to Shai-Hulud, and awaiting the prophet's coming. Since the most standing water you have ever seen is contained within a cistern, the thought of an ocean, water as far as the eye can see, is unimaginable. Yet, when the prophet Paul Muad'Dib arrives and calls you to fight in the off-world jihad, you take your crysknife and lasgun, board a heighliner space-ship, and fight for years in the service of your God-Emperor on fantastic ocean-covered planets. Such an extended period of time away from your home world causes you to reflect: Who are you? Why are you here? What principles form your character? What beliefs are at the core of your very being, your soul? Two American philosophers can provide guidance in the quest to define Fremen character and values.

Emerson's Self-Reliance

In his essay "Self-Reliance" (1841), the American philosopher Ralph Waldo Emerson (1803–1882) characterized the virtue, or excellence of character, of self-reliance. For Emerson, self-reliance means, not only material, but also spiritual self-sufficiency. It's the ability to follow one's own instincts and avoid dull conformity; to be a leader and not a follower. The self-reliant person steers his own course, sees his own ideas as universal truths, rejects soulless logic, and embraces a liberating spirituality that transcends earthly experience. In Emerson's words,

> Every true man is a cause, a country, and an age; requires infinite spaces and numbers and time fully to accomplish his design; —and posterity seem to follow his steps as a train of clients. All history resolves itself very easily into the biography of a few stout and earnest persons. (p. 61)

Self-reliance also entails that a person trusts herself or himself as having the wisdom to make good choices, to project their spirituality within to the world without. Americans tend to be among the "few stout and earnest persons" who exemplify the virtue of self-reliance. Those who possess it in the highest degree are poets and prophets; in the least, politicians and bureaucrats.

Self-reliance is a virtue familiar to the Fremen people. Though the Fremen are a nomadic people—mostly scavengers, hired spice harvesters, and soldiers—they have a deep-seated spirituality (faith in Shai-Hulud, the Maker), a cause (to follow their prophet, convert Dune into a green paradise, and spread the jihad to other worlds), a country (Arrakis), and an uncompromising belief that they're the chosen people of their age. Formed by the harsh conditions of Dune, the character of the Fremen people epitomizes the spiritual self-sufficiency that Emerson so eloquently praised in the American people.

In "Self-Reliance," he writes: "A man should learn to detect and watch that gleam of light which flashes across his mind from within" (p. 62). Peculiar to the Fremen is this self-reliant capacity to find and project one's internal strength, one's (in Emerson's words) "gleam of light." Furthermore, self-reliance involves practicing tremendous self-control. According to Princess Irulan, "The Fremen were supreme in that quality the ancients called 'Spannungsbogen'—which is the self-imposed delay between desire for a thing and the act of reaching out to grasp that thing" (*Dune*). Only a self-reliant people could survive prolonged enslavement, centuries of wandering the universe and, eventually, the process of adapting to the harsh desert conditions of Dune. The Fremen ability to persevere in the face of extreme hardship is what makes them self-reliant—and American.

Dewey's Democracy as a Way of Life

For another American philosopher, John Dewey, democracy resembles a method for realizing an ideal: social and political equality. Dewey writes: "Democracy is a way of life controlled by a working faith in the possibilities of human nature" (*Later Works* 14, p. 226). One interpretation of this statement is that only in a democracy can citizens hope that the conditions of their individual and collective lives (political freedoms, economic opportunities, quality of life) will improve. While this is part of what Dewey means, it's only the proverbial tip of the iceberg. Still deeper is the idea that democratic citizens must genuinely believe that they and their fellow citizens are equal. Though they might not all be descriptively equal (having the same strength or I.Q.), they are morally equal in each other's eyes and formally equal before the law. Dewey writes:

Belief in the Common Man is a familiar article in the democratic creed. That belief is without basis and significance save as it means faith in the potentialities of human nature as that nature is exhibited in every human being irrespective of race, color, sex, birth and family, of material or cultural wealth. This faith may be enacted in statutes, but it is only on paper unless it is put in force in the attitudes which human beings display to one another in all the incidents and relations of daily life. (p. 226)

In other words, equality has a pseudo-religious quality in a democracy, a quality that permeates all spheres of social life, not merely the political. To realize democracy as a way of life, citizens must flatten hierarchical (social, political and economic) structures, work as equals to solve common problems and, thereby, generate "a freer and more humane experience in which all share and to which all contribute" (p. 229).

Although the Fremen don't embrace political democracy, they do see each other as equals in the light of Shai-Hulud. One of the primary goals of the jihad is to liberate humanity from rule by the royal families and Great Houses. By undertaking the bloody twelve-year-long religious war, their prophet, Paul Muad'Dib, believed that the relations of humans would be cleansed and transformed into relations between relative equals, not masters and slaves.

However, *Dune*'s creator, Frank Herbert, thought that the effort to democratize human experience was bound to turn out badly. "In fact, I believe attempts to create some abstract equalization create a morass of injustices that rebound on the equalizers. Equal justice and equal opportunity are ideals we should seek, but we should recognize that humans administer the ideals and that humans do not have equal ability" ("Dune Genesis"). Indeed, the eventual reign of the God-Emperor, Leto II, is no democratic utopia!

The Fremen as Pragmatic Americans

"Alia is right, Mother," Paul said, not looking at either his sister or Jessica. "While we manage the business of war, we are also in the business of creating a myth. It is the only way we can accomplish what is necessary. . . ."

"You are cynical, Usul." Chani sounded disturbed. . . .

"My brother is pragmatic," Alia countered.

—*Paul of Dune*

The power of myth-making is notorious. For instance, there's the myth that we, Americans, are a chosen people, exceptional, moral exemplars and world leaders. There's also the countervailing myth that America is an evil empire, jingoistic, imperialistic and exploitive of other nations and peoples. Myth-making is pragmatically valuable—it works! It brings people together around a common set of values and beliefs.

Indeed, Frank Herbert acknowledged that the observation of the human craving for myths informed his creation of the Duniverse: "People tend to give over every decision-making capacity to any leader who can wrap himself in the myth fabric of the society" ("Dune Genesis"). Paul Muad'Dib's sister, Alia, correctly insisted that her brother "is pragmatic" in his use of a myth to motivate the Fremen. Similar to the American people, the Fremen saw themselves as an exceptional and chosen people, tasked to accomplish a special calling at a propitious time in human history. They were chosen to liberate humanity by fighting a jihad.

As Princess Irulan notes in her history of Paul Muad'Dib, "God created Arrakis to train the faithful" (*Dune*). One could add that God created the fanatical Fremen to successfully prosecute a war against the known universe. And one might even go so far as to say that God created Fremen in the image of a truly pragmatic and self-reliant people, that is, in the image of Americans.

Emerson's transcendentalism and Dewey's pragmatism equally capture the rich meaning of our uniquely American ideals. So it's no surprise that the Fremen would appear quintessentially American. Or do they? After all, the Fremen people were the foot-soldiers who spread violent holy war across the Imperium, not the freedom-loving American corpsmen who rushed the beaches of Normandy and Iwo Jima to make the world unsafe for tyranny. According to one historical account, "Muad'Dib's Quizarate missionaries carried their religious war across space in a jihad whose major impetus endured only twelve standard years, but in that time, religious colonialism brought all but a fraction of the human universe under one rule" (*Dune Messiah*). So, who were the Fremen? Were they the agents of religious tyranny? Or did they embody the American spirit?

The Jihadist Way of Life

He [Paul] remembered his earliest visions of the Jihad-to-be, the terror and revulsion he'd experienced. Now, of course, he knew visions of greater terrors. He had lived with real violence. He had seen his Fremen, charged with mystical strength, sweep all before them in the religious war. The Jihad gained a new perspective. It was finite, of course, a brief spasm when measured against eternity, but beyond lay horrors to overshadow anything in the past.

—*Dune Messiah*

With the power of prescience, the prophet, Paul Muad'Dib, could foresee the terrible bloodshed of the jihad. Nevertheless, he led the heroic Fremen people to expand the religious war throughout the known universe, subduing those people and colonizing those worlds that opposed them. Jihad became a way of life, a method of razing the hierarchical structure of the Great Houses and reconstructing the relations of humans on a more equal basis. While the human race wouldn't become a race of Fremen (recall Emerson's remark that the self-reliant include only a "few stout and earnest persons"), such an exceptional people were needed to liberate the rest, to give them the gift of greater equality, first through force and then through a millennia-long peace under the rule of the prophet's son, the God-Emperor.

The American Taliban is strikingly similar to Dune's Fremen. Traveling from a Northern California suburb to Yemen to the desert battlefield of Afghanistan, his studies and conversion to Islam led him down the dangerous path to jihad, as well as eventual capture and imprisonment by US forces. Still, he was aptly named, for he's first and foremost an American and only secondarily an associate of the Taliban.

This isn't to state the trivially true point that his citizenship is American. Though most Americans didn't consider him a patriot (and some insisted that he should no longer be an American citizen), he showed himself to be enterprising, self-reliant, spiritual, pragmatic, and, therefore, quintessentially American in his values and character. In many ways, he was no different than Paul Muad'Dib, who in the conclusion of *Dune Messiah* is doubly transformed into a blind man, with eyes burnt out by an atomic weapon and his inner vision, his prescience, lost. Following the Fremen custom, Paul travels into the Arrakeen desert, walking without a trace upon his own holy path: "We say of Muad'Dib that he has gone on a journey into that land where we walk without footprints" (*Dune Messiah*).

Re-recorded by:
SHANE RALSTON

What's Wrong with Politics in the Duniverse?

In the *Dune* saga, Frank Herbert relates a story about imperial instability. Throughout the several thousands of years depicted in the chronicle, characters use different strategies to gain and uphold power, and all ultimately fail. The Corrino rule ends with Paul Atreides's rise to the throne, but the first period of Atreides rule is war-ridden and increasingly brutal. As the God Emperor, Leto II rules with an iron fist for three and a half thousand years, creating a yearning for freedom that eventually leads to his assassination. Finally, the period following the reign of the God Emperor destabilizes, and the original series ends in uncertainty about what the future holds.

Frank Herbert, in his essay "Dune Genesis," suggests that he wrote *Dune* to show how our reliance on heroes makes us vulnerable and our societies politically unstable. We should trust, not heroes, but our own judgment. We don't believe that this is the main explanation for the instability and the political failures of the *Dune* societies. Instead, by looking at how stability relates to legitimacy, in particular to democratic legitimacy, we claim that the reason is that the rule-makers of the Duniverse do not create the appropriate paths for the people in terms of political participation in rule-making.

The Politics of *Dune*

Politics consists of social relations involving power and authority. It commonly refers to a process by which a group of individuals makes decisions and regulates a political organization or society.

The group of people in a society, who hold political power, control and administer all public resources, for example, wealth, labor, and law. When we study politics we examine the acquisition and use of such power. Indeed, the *Dune* saga recounts a story about political power struggle, making the Latin word for political power, 'imperium', quite fitting.

As a body of fiction, its complexity and creative imagination far surpasses "mere" entertainment. Already in *Dune,* we confront a fascinating, vast future society, highly advanced yet neo-feudalistic, with an emperor and an assembly of noble houses (the *Landsraad*) as the body of government. The society is technologically advanced far beyond our own current levels, and the future depicted differs dramatically from what we would normally imagine of our own future. For example, the Duniverse has been shaped by substantial social conventions, such as those prohibiting computers and any form of artificial intelligence. These conventions have severely limited the technological systems of the Duniverse and thus induced the need for other means of human advancement, a significant portion of which has emerged through specialized groups.

The *Spacing Guild*, for instance, develops means of navigating through space without the assistance of computers and holds a monopoly on interstellar travel. The female sect of *Bene Gesserit* trains their adepts into gaining mental and physical skills well beyond those of the normal human being and plays an important part as advisors to the noble houses (in addition to their own political agenda, their secret breeding program). The *Mentats,* people trained from infancy to become "human computers," also play an important advisory role. Further, the secretive societies of *Tleilaxu* and *Ixians* provide vital products and, as a consequence, play central political roles—the former as experts on biological and genetically engineered products, the latter as technological innovators pushing the limits of the prohibitions against thinking machines. Thus, all these specialized groups in different ways obtain possession of political power.

In the original novel, *Dune*, we follow the rulers of the House Atreides upon entering their new fiefdom, the planet Arrakis, with the immensely important task of harvesting the most valuable commodity in the universe, melange, the "spice" that enhances awareness and vitality, ultimately prolonging the life of its user. House Atreides is the good protagonist of the story. Its rule is conceived as fair and benevolent. Furthermore, its ruler, Duke Leto Atreides, remains popular among the other Houses of the Landsraad, even figuring as a spokesman for some of them. The good House Atreides contrasts mainly with the brutal and decadent House Harkonnen.

The cruel Baron Vladimir Harkonnen leads House Harkonnen, oppressive rulers of the dark and heavily industrialized planet Giedi Prime. Like his fellow Harkonnen noblemen, he treats the life of others as merely one commodity among many. Herbert depicts him as a sadist who enjoys killing, a theme exemplified throughout *Dune.* He seldom misses a chance to torment both opponents and collaborators and goes to great lengths to catch Duke Leto alive merely to gloat over his victory. Moreover, he punishes his sex-addicted nephew Feyd by forcing him to kill all his lovers.

The Houses Harkonnen and Atreides are long sworn enemies, and their struggle provides a major theme in the novel. Whereas Herbert depicts the Emperor's hostilities directed at Atreides, not as intentional acts against Atreides *per se,* but as logical consequences of his current rule, the fight between Atreides and Harkonnen reflects their mutual disdain for one another. And the struggle between them could rightfully be described as the struggle between good and evil. However, while the fairness of Atreides and the cruelty and unfairness of Harkonnen are significant differences, when looked at from the question of stability and instability in relation to legitimacy and rightful authority, these differences become almost irrelevant. Focusing on this question, House Atreides and the House Harkonnen, along with the other main actors in the *Dune* saga (such as the Bene Gesserit, the Tleilaxu, the Ixians, and later the Honored Matres), act and organize their political communities in very similar ways.

This similarity between opposing factions explains the political failures of the Dune societies and draws attention to the pervading theme of human development in Frank Herbert's works.

Strategic Action in the Duniverse

In the *Dune* miniseries, one of the first lessons that Duke Leto teaches Paul upon moving to Arrakis is that "in the world we live in, self-interest governs all." This statement reveals much, for strategic action dominates decision-making and rulemaking in the Duniverse. Strategic action is goal-oriented action that aims at achieving a desired end. Rather than being particularly good or bad in himself, the Emperor Shaddam Corrino IV embodies a profoundly strategic actor. His actions depend, not on moral considerations or even more explicitly feudalistic considerations such as loyalty, but on intriguing strategic considerations alone. In several places he acts reluctantly, yet with a sense of obligation towards what strategy demands. In *Dune*, we're told that the Emperor admired the Duke "and disliked the political necessities that made them enemies." So while he admitted to disliking the circumstances, it is in no way relevant to his action.

Moreover, Baron Harkonnen represents another archetypical strategist who plans to gain power through ruthlessness. His obsession with bloodline and the strategic means to secure it shines through in almost every act. "The Baron could see the path ahead of him. One day, a Harkonnen would be Emperor. Not himself, and no spawn of his loins. But a Harkonnen. . . . There was a sharpness to young Feyd-Rautha that the Baron enjoyed . . . a ferocity. *A lovely boy*, the Baron thought. *A year or two more—say, by the time he's seventeen, I'll know for certain whether he's the tool that House Harkonnen requires to gain the throne.*"

However, strategic action characterizes, not only the antagonists in *Dune,* but also the protagonists. Duke Leto's view that self-interest governs all shows an analysis of the external constraints to which the House Atreides had to adapt. But when House Atreides comes to power, self-interest still seems to govern. In a typical example, after Paul's takeover, the Atreides council discusses the Landsraad demand for a constitution. The council doesn't touch upon the substantial issue of whether a constitution would be a legitimate demand. Instead, they discuss only strategic actions, such as consort Irulan's suggestion that measures should be taken to give the appearance of a constitution. As Princess Irulan states in *Children of Dune*, "Deceit, after all, is a legitimate tool of statecraft." Later when Paul is gone and Alia assumes the throne, the strategic pattern continues. House Corrino suggests a marriage between Paul's daughter Ghanima and Farad'n of House Corrino. Alia succumbs, but points out, "Make it clear: Atreides's interest will dominate."

Political philosophers commonly distinguish strategic action from communicative action. The influential German philosopher Jürgen Habermas first made this distinction in *The Theory of Communicative Action*. Rather than drawing pessimistic conclusions about the loss of meaning, freedom, and solidarity in the modern technocratic-capitalist world, in which self-interest has become the guiding principle, Habermas illustrates that modernization proves an ambivalent process that also opens the door for the possibility of social and moral learning as well as for increased human liberation. As opposed to viewing rationality solely as strategic, Habermas makes room for a complementary idea of rationality, that of communicative action. To act communicatively means to be oriented towards mutual understanding with others. While in strategic action, the actor defines her desired end before the interaction, in communicative action, an actor defines her ends in a cooperative process through interaction with others.

Habermas develops the idea that strategic action even drives technology and capitalism. A society can't be held together by such action alone, however. In the end, we, as social beings, invent these strategic processes through a web of shared understandings. Indeed, the moment everybody would agree that money is toilet paper, we wouldn't be able to buy anything with it. Through communicative action we have agreed that money is pieces of paper that we can use as currency for buying and selling things. However, this agreement is not strategic but is reached through a common understanding. Of course, we often *use* money strategically, but this is a different matter. In fact, we wouldn't even understand a strategic action unless we first possessed the capability to reach understanding through language, to act communicatively.

Take the treacherous Baron Harkonnen or the strategic Corrino Emperor, where we get the impression that they mostly tell lies. This impression is based on just looking at their willingness to deceive others when it suits them, not on all their communications. How would they be able to make their collaborators and servants understand their orders, or even deceive other people, if all they did was lie? The Corrino Emperor's power over the other Houses could not be upheld unless most of what he did was aimed at telling the truth. For this reason, Habermas argues that the basic action in our everyday life remains communicative, action that holds society together. A social order couldn't be sustained without it.

In *Dune* rulemaking, moral norms, laws, and principles are formulated and decided upon by strategic action, for example, by letting a leader define what is right or wrong, just or unjust, and make the people under his or her rule accept these norms as valid, typically through the threat of sanctions. But defining morality purely through strategic action would mean that people would have good reasons to go against moral norms as soon as they gained something by doing so. Strategic action means that, whenever I have a goal and action can help me achieve that goal, I act accordingly. In the *Dune* miniseries, Paul and his Fremen warriors capture a Spacing Guild representative who claims that he is protected by Imperial treaties. Paul refuses to acknowledge the legitimacy of such treaties: "Imperial law is void where Muad'Dib stands."

Stability and Rightful Authority in the Duniverse

In a political context, social order is often discussed in terms of stability, a concept that is central for every society in the Duniverse. In the wake of the Butlerian Jihad, the sense of peril for humankind seems imminent, as reflected in the prohibitions of the Great Convention and the subsequent developments in the *Dune* series. The quest for stability characterizes the neo-feudal structure of the Corrino Imperium as well as the Atreides reign through Arrakis. With the rise of the God Emperor the stakes mount even higher: the fear that the human race will become extinct motivates Leto II to embark on the harsh and despotic path that Paul himself feared choosing—the *Golden Path*.

Independently of whether Herbert depicts the ruler as good or evil, authority in *Dune* consists in the ability to enforce law through coercion, threats, and sanctions, in other words through strategic action. Political theorists often describe strategic decision-making as hierarchical political steering, which means that rule-makers direct rule-followers, the people, to act the way it wants in order to achieve desired ends. By exercising authority in this way, the rulers of the various Duniverse societies create stability. However, this stability depends on security and order upheld by physical means such as threats and sanctions. The problem, as we are well aware today, is that no modern state or state-like political organization can rely entirely on hierarchical political steering to enforce the law.

A political system consists of two parts, a political authority (rule-makers) and a group of people subject to this authority (rule-followers). To say that such a system has authority is to say that its rule-makers and its rule-followers have a certain kind of relationship. In political philosophy the concept of *legitimacy* is used to describe the moral aspects of this relationship. Thus, legitimacy refers to a rightful authority. Today, philosophers consider democratic legitimacy a morally attractive kind of rightful authority. A democratic system requires that those who are subject to law are simultaneously made authors of law. In order for a political authority to uphold its democratic legitimacy or rightfulness, the people must, directly or indirectly, give their approval. From a democratic perspective, even the most perfectly structured hierarchical political system will eventually become unstable.

Not only in the Duniverse but also in international politics today, stability is commonly characterized in physical terms. Following in the footsteps of Habermas, however, we argue that stability and legitimacy are intimately connected. More to the point, stability must be understood *in terms of* legitimacy. Without such legitimacy, we assume that political orders sooner or later become unstable. The failures of the *Dune* empires bears ample witness to the fact that physical stability proves a fragile basis for a social order. Physical stability differs significantly from normative stability, which refers to a social order held together by common norms and rules regarded as fair and legitimate. Democracy ensures normative stability because democracy primarily aims to create common norms and rules considered legitimate by those who have to abide by them.

How could the recurrent political fiascos of the Duniverse societies have been avoided? We don't agree that they failed to maintain stability because rulers eventually became too obsessed by power and made mistakes, as Frank Herbert argued in "Dune Genesis," or even because they became decadent and excessive, as a classical explanation of imperial declines has emphasized.

Rather, the *Dune* empires failed because strategic power was *allowed* to dominate and was viewed as *the* accepted form of authority. To be sure, independent of whether a society is ruled by an omnipotent enforcer who does not have to rely on others—and not even the God Emperor Leto II is such an omnipotent being—any political authority depends on constraints, on rules and conventions that are upheld by being *treated* as in some sense legitimate. Otherwise they wouldn't be obeyed. And we're not strangers to such conventions in the Duniverse.

As noted earlier, social conventions banned computers and other thinking artifacts (after the Butlerian Jihad), and atomic weapons were uniformly prohibited (the Great Convention). These conventions receive, not only lip service, but actual enforcement, which demonstrates that in the Duniverse binding rules are possible.

Whereas these conventions remain in the *technological* domain, the normative-political framework remains severely undeveloped.

Democracy stays an almost invisible idea in the Duniverse. When referred to, it is mainly as an unstable, unwanted system of government. For example, in the *Children of Dune* miniseries, when confronted with a suggestion of participation on a small, local scale, Alia cries out: "Atreides power must never be marginalized by the chaos of democracy."

Nonetheless we believe that democracy provides the remedy to Herbert's worries about obsessed rulers and the solution for the *Dune* empires, mainly because democracy means exactly the opposite of power in the hands of the few. It means that every citizen has equal power and through egalitarian democratic decision-making can remove corrupt leaders from office. As long as authority arises from hierarchical steering mechanisms, creating physical stability, this *two-way* story of democracy—where everyday citizens legitimize the leaders—converts into a *one-way* story of dictatorship. Even a compassionate dictator, who rules in the interest of the governed, tells a one-way story. Democracy isn't solely government *for* the people, existing for the sake of the people and ruling in the interest of the governed, but also and more importantly the rule *by* the people.

Sometimes democracy can be described as a "chaotic" political system, as Alia says. She seems to think that people in a democracy disagree and that conflicts of interests will inevitably arise under democratic rule. And to eliminate it, one merely lets a ruler decide what is right and wrong, true and false, and so on. However, if we define "chaotic" in this way, then chaos would be a good thing from a democratic point of view. Even if collective decision-making in a pluralistic democratic society can often be a serpentine exercise, such a society remains healthy precisely because it's capable, not only of accommodating disagreement and conflicts of interest within the institutional framework of the law, but also of transforming it to a politically creative force.

When looking at the many fiascos of the political rule-makers and power-holders in the Duniverse, the advantage of democracy as a political system hinges on the fact that legitimate authority is *at the same time* an answer to instability. Thus, from a democratic perspective, physical stability is reached *through* normative stability rather than the other way around.

The House Atreides's rule is perhaps the closest we get to an example of normative stability in the Duniverse. While not being democratic, their rule is perceived as wise and fair by the people, making it internally stable. Still, in the long run, after becoming the ruling House in the Empire, they fail to uphold this stability, which is in our view far from surprising in light of their attitude towards the democratic process as chaotic and their reluctance to "give away" or divide political power.

Similarly, in the Fremen society that becomes Paul's means of regaining power, reliance on force and leaders' physical skills threatens stability. The custom of physically challenging the current leader in man-to-man combat destabilizes the Fremen people. This ultimate display of physical power as a means of gaining authority, however, is far from being exercised in the Fremen tribal culture alone but echoes throughout the Empire, in the *kanly* challenge for power that forms the final battle in *Dune* as well as in the rituals of the Honored Matres in the later novels. With such a dependence on physical stability and strategic action as the basic bricks in the political architecture, normative stability remains unreachable for the Dune rulers; instability is never far away.

The equal distribution of power and thus the inherent "safety" mechanism against tyranny is not the only stabilizing effect of democratic legitimacy. Exercising civil and political rights also plays a vital part for human life and well-being. The participation in the political life of one's community is in this sense of *final value*, a way for people to feel empowered. Related to this is the *instrumental value* of getting one's voice heard and being able to express one's values and preferences, without which we would be deprived of the possibility of being recognized as an equal.

If we view the analysis of the political structures of *Dune* in a historical perspective and take a closer look at the development of modern statehood, we see that the relationship between state and power has changed drastically since the Middle Ages. Right up to the Renaissance, separation of state and power didn't exist because states were seen as tantamount to their rulers. Only after the creation of the nation-state following the French revolution, do we see the starting-point of modern statehood. The institutionalized separation of state and power comprises one feature of this statehood. The state is no longer identified with either the sum of its members (citizens) or a personal ruler. From now on the state is viewed as a *locus* for the exercise of authority, on the one hand, established by citizens, and on the other, placed over and above them as a guarantor for their individual and collective security. This means that a "gap" appeared between rule-makers (those in power) and rule-followers (the members of the political community), now constituting two fundamental elements *within* the locus of the state.

Earlier, we called the societies of *Dune* neo-feudal in the sense that the main power constellation consists of nobility—the noble houses—that controls land and the means of production through fiefdoms and pays allegiance to the ruling Emperor. Our brief historical sketch suggests yet another way in which the Duniverse societies could reasonably be depicted as medieval, in spite of its advanced technological state. It displays the same lack of institutionalized separation of state and power. The people in the Duniverse societies almost never become more than a shadow in the background, neither before nor after Paul Atreides ascends the throne. Perhaps the Fremen mass gathering called to form the solution to the Fremen leadership between Paul and Stilgar provides the most evident exception. But this stands out as an exception rather than a permanent inclusion of the people in the decision-making process. In particular for the noble houses, the *bloodline*, not the citizens, establishes the authority. In this sense, the states *are* the noble houses, and the reigning nobleman is the House personified. This is true for the evil House Harkonnen and the Imperial House Corrino as well as for the good House Atreides.

In the *Children of Dune* miniseries, Leto II asks Gurney Halleck to abandon Alia and her oppressive rule. Halleck reluctantly replies, "My loyalty is to House Atreides." Alia belongs to House Atreides, and House Atreides is the power, no matter how oppressive. Leto retorts "I *am* House Atreides," settling the matter. Being Paul's son, Leto is the rightful heir to the throne. Hence, he is the House personified. Nothing more, nothing less.

Leto's Not So Golden Path

So far we have based our analysis mainly on what we called the first era of the *Dune Chronicles*, the period surrounding the life of Paul Atreides. But what happened next? Unfortunately, it seems that the subsequent strategies for stability—indeed, for survival—of the human race fail to address the basic problems of the Duniverse. The problem remains an overemphasis on strategic rather than communicative action and the corresponding deficiency in democratic legitimacy.

At the end of *Children of Dune*, Paul and Alia are both dead, and Leto II, transformed into a hybrid of man and sandworm, has taken the throne. In his new hybrid state, Leto is almost immortal and reins for 3,500 years, profoundly reshaping the Imperium through his *Golden Path*. He is convinced that the old paths—the old neo-feudal Imperium as well as Paul's reign with the religious fanaticism and bureaucracy that followed—would lead to the extinction of the human race. The old Imperium had stagnated, looking only inward rather than evolving. Furthermore, it depended on spice production and superhuman skills performed by specific groups, such as the Spacing Guild and the Bene Gesserit. Leto determines that the solution is to induce humanity to expand into unknown space and continue to evolve.

In Leto's view, the Golden Path provides the only viable means to this end of human evolution and survival. As a deliberately oppressive and despotic ruler, Leto enforces the Golden Path, creating peace in the known universe through extensive control of all its citizens. His rule circumscribes the old power structures. The Landsraad ceases to exist and only a few of the old Houses remain. While the Spacing Guild and the Bene Gesserit survive, he keeps them under tight control. Moreover, he establishes his own powerful force of fanatical warriors, the *Fish Speakers*, and embarks on his own breeding program, mixing Atreides and Bene Gesserit in order to create a human being with the best of both—the Atreideses' noble passion and the Bene Gesserit's physical and mental abilities.

Leto's oppressive rule and tight control over humanity, space navigation and melange, forces the remaining groups to become inventive in ways they never thought possible, eventually creating navigational devices (Ixian) and artificial spice (Tleilaxu). More important still, it demonstrates to humanity that non-autonomous, oppressive peace is not a viable option and that humans must evolve to survive as an autonomous species. He thus deliberately brings about his eventual assassination and the following *Scattering*, the abandonment of the safe confinements of known space.

Leto's analysis of the problems and necessary solutions of the human condition couldn't be further away from our own analysis of what is wrong with the Duniverse societies. He takes history as well as his own rule as proof of the ultimate wrongness of humanity to be "confined" to the known physical limits of space. While within these limits it was possible for a single interest to rule, he believes that sufficient physical expansion will make it impossible. Furthermore, just as the Bene Gesserit before him, Leto believes that breeding programs, mixing gene-pools with desired characteristics, provide part of the solution of human evolvement. Similarly, his "breeding" of the *Fish Speakers* into fanatical warriors resembles strategies employed by the Atreides rule of the first era (utilizing the Fremen) as well as the earlier Corrino rule (utilizing the Sardaukar). Hence, for all his precognition and desire to find a way out for humanity, Leto puts his trust in deterrence in the social domain and breeding programs in the biological one. In his own words from the *Children of Dune* miniseries, "to make a world where humankind can create its own future from moment to moment, free of one man's vision, free from the perversion of the prophet's words, and free of future predetermined."

As should now be clear, scaring humanity into physical expansion and trying to breed specific talents into humanity seem to us to deeply understate the deliberative potential already present in humanity. In fact, as Leto II realized, it *wasn't* possible in the long run for either the feudal old empire, religious fanaticism under Paul's command, or his own despotism to rule the known universe. They could control it for a while (admittedly a long while by our standards), but such control resulted from strategic action using physical rather than legitimate means to sustain stability. That Leto returned to the breeding programs of the Bene Gesserit rather than turning toward communicative action aimed at reaching understanding can only be described as ironic.

Indeed, in the years following Leto's rule, depicted in *Heretics of Dune* and *Chapterhouse Dune*, the Bene Gesserit continue their breeding programs and the strategic planning of taking control over anticipated powerful actors (notably the prophesized "sand rider") as well as regain control over religious forces. Their strategy includes imprisoning those who they see as key actors in order to use them as tools for the salvation of humankind, but yet again they fail to realize that this strategic reasoning remains fundamentally flawed. In the story, the prisoners react and become uncooperative. However, even if they had cooperated, as most people undoubtedly cooperated with Leto's oppressive rule, this mode of thinking and acting doesn't take advantage of the true human potential of communicative action, which explains why the Duniverse empires remain unstable.

When looking at the Duniverse with a political-philosophical eye, the question of what we mean and ought to mean by *human* development becomes unavoidable. It's a question all the more timely in our era of increasingly sophisticated warfare, information technologies, and genetic engineering. Generally speaking, while development implies both an aim and a change in relation to that aim, it doesn't include an evaluation of this change. Biologists, for instance, often view development as evolution, a transformation of hereditary characteristics over time. By contrast, theorists in the humanities and social sciences assume that development flows from a more undifferentiated state to a higher and more differentiated (better) one. And in this kind of reasoning, evaluations are at least implicitly brought into the analysis.

Thus, human development is a positively loaded concept, in our view foremost concerned with social and moral learning. From this perspective, our analysis of *Dune* suggests that one should be careful about equating technological development (indeed even biological development) with human development without further examination. If we go back to Habermas's analysis of modernization as a process opening the door for the possibility of social and moral learning through communicative action, we can't help wondering how the technologically advanced Duniverse societies could possess the characteristic features of hierarchical and centralized power found in Medieval societies. Perhaps part of the answer lies in the fact that human development remains first and foremost a social and moral development, for which technology might be of assistance . . . but again . . . it might not.

With Assistance from:
EVA ERMAN
NIKLAS MÖLLER

FROM DAR-ES-BALAT II
From: Conference on the Meaning of Spice
Date: 18150 A.G.

A Universe of Bastards

Law always chooses sides on the basis of enforcement power. Morality and legal niceties have little to do with it when the real question is: Who has the clout?

—Bene Gesserit Council Proceedings (*Heretics of Dune*)

Maybe tyranny isn't so bad. While this idea may seem foreign or bizarre, there's something to it. More than one thinker has tied government to human nature—the nicer we are to each other, the less government we need, creating a spectrum of theories from anarchism for the nice folks to authoritarianism for the bastards.

The universe of Frank Herbert's *Dune* comprises, to put it mildly, a universe of bastards, running the gamut of personal vices from overtly manipulative to lethally hedonistic. While some people occasionally inspire loyalty or confidence and are set up as examples of the best human qualities, most characters appear morally grey, possessing flaws at a conscious and unconscious level. Sometimes these characters know their weaknesses, while the weaknesses of others remain hidden.

Because of this ambiguity and uncertainty, we're left with few clear heroes. The novels aren't necessarily bleak, but they do paint a picture of a bent and cynical humanity. The collision path our nature demands constitutes one of the biggest concerns. Herbert portrays humanity as constantly in struggle, with groups vying against each other in a constant drive for supremacy and influence. This self-destructive conflict arises from the human drive for self-preservation. This universe of conflict reflects the political theory of Thomas Hobbes, in which rational agents vie with each other for power and the means for their own survival.

We recognize the inherently dangerous nature of people left to fend for themselves in a world of limited resources, compounded by split claims to power and authority. We end up in factions, fighting amongst ourselves until utterly exhausted, or, more accurately, extinct. This violence spurs us on in mutual war until someone emerges with the power and authority to force peace upon us. Hobbes calls this figure the Leviathan. Herbert portrays him most elegantly as Leto II. Literally, the term "Leviathan" names a sea monster in the Bible, and Leto II becomes a large monster—half human, half sandworm, all GOD. This mortal god, whether Leviathan or Leto II, awes us all and serves as the nexus of political power and authority. In the Duniverse, Leto II, called "Tyrant" and "God Emperor," prevents our mutual destruction and enforces peace, preserving humanity.

The Players in the Duniverse

". . . the Imperial Household balanced against the Federated Great Houses of the Landsraad, and between them, the Guild with its damnable monopoly on interstellar transport. In politics, the tripod is the most unstable of all structures."

—Reverend Mother Helen Gaius Mohiam to Lady Jessica (*Dune*)

So who are the morally grey characters of the Duniverse? Herbert's universe expands across a vast area. The individual characters that occur (and recur) represent much larger archetypes and trends. Very few characters recur in more than one or two of Herbert's six core novels, and their impact is significant. Further, the political spectrum changes over time. This fluidity serves essentially to destabilize. Because the centers of power shift so frequently, it becomes difficult to establish a clear authority. In Hobbes's state of nature, power is fleeting, surviving only so long as the strength and intelligence of the person who wields it. Likewise, in the Duniverse, we can split the political factions into a few key positions and groups, with some internal power shifts.

The Emperor

The institution of the Emperor changes dramatically over the course of the novels. In *Dune*, Herbert first presents to us Shaddam IV of House Corrino, who wields, apparently, supreme authority through his Sardaukar, legions of highly trained and lethal warriors. His power shifts to Paul Atreides (Paul Muad'Dib), establishing Paul as Emperor, a title he holds until the end of *Dune Messiah*. Alia rules as regent in *Children of Dune*, paving the way for Leto II, who fuses his body with sandtrout (the early stage of sandworm), transforming himself into an incredibly long-lived entity who rules as emperor for well over three thousand years in *God Emperor of Dune*. Following Leto's death and dissolution, the position of Emperor fades, and the political landscape revolves around different factions vying for power in *Heretics of Dune* and *Chapterhouse: Dune* (the Tleilaxu, the Bene Gesserit, and the Reverend Matres).

The Landsraad

The second leg of the early Duniverse is the Landsraad, a political body made up of the Great Houses (Atreides, Harkonnen, and others). It exists as a potential foil to the power of the throne, and the interaction and sparring between these houses sets the ball rolling. Collectively, the Landsraad can put pressure on the Emperor, but they're more often too involved in conflicts between each other to do so.

Dune introduces us to Houses who are motivated by pure self-interest and self-preservation with few stand-out families. Shaddam IV is of House Corrino, whose desire for power is seen most keenly in *Dune* and *Children of Dune*. House Atreides comprises our shining beacon of loyalty (an idea that becomes more ironic and bitter as the series progresses), and the Harkonnens embody self-indulgent and vicious amorality—sex and death constitute pleasures to be enjoyed frequently, with occasional stops for lunch.

The major houses accept formal war—kanly—as a means to resolve disputes. Their equal possession of nuclear weapons prevents kanly from deteriorating into total annihilation. In this regard, the Landsraad mirrors the system of mutually assured destruction that characterized the cold war between the former Soviet Union and the United States. A key difference, however, is that there is no NATO or Warsaw Pact—if one house used its nuclear weapons, then all the other houses would band together to destroy the aggressor. In *Dune*, the reassignment of spice production from House Harkonnen to House Atreides provides the catalyst for war, which provides the Imperial throne and House Harkonnen the chance to eliminate the entirety of the Atreides line. The Great

Houses are relevant during the first three novels—by *God Emperor of Dune*, the family lines exist, but their political power has been stripped away.

The Spice Guild

The Spice Guild has a parasitic relationship with political power. The Guild itself never rules—it's not willing to risk any interruption of the spice flow that gives its navigators their ability to steer their ships through the universe. They have political teeth, however, and they establish this clearly in the final battle of *Dune* by noting that Shaddam IV serves at their leisure, not his, and that their only *real* loyalty is to the spice. If he were to disrupt that, he would be removed, as death is a casual occurrence in Herbert's world—more about this later.

The Bene Gesserit

The Bene Gesserit Sisterhood is an interesting creature. The witches manipulate those around them masterfully, but like the Spice Guild, they never rule directly. They initially hope to control the Empire through the Kwisatz Haderach (a male version of their Reverend Mothers). The plan backfires, which requires them to change their plans permanently. As eugenicists, they manipulate royal bloodlines to preserve particular traits. Like the Guild, they are kingmakers and serve as background players.

The Tleilaxu

Herbert introduces the Tleilaxu in *Dune Messiah*, but they only become significant in later novels. They possess axlotl tanks, which produce both gholas (bodies created from the tissue of dead people and the means of continuity for several characters in the novels) and a temporary new source of spice in *Heretics of Dune*. Driven by religious fervor, the Tleilaxu aspire to galactic dominance. Just as manipulative as the Bene Gesserit, they act more overtly; they kill and replace key political and religious figures with their own agents.

The Honored Matres

The Honored Matres are descended from the Bene Gesserit, Fish Speakers, and Tleilaxu who branched off on their own following the end of Leto II's reign (when the Old Empire functionally dissolved and people spread out to different corners of the galaxy in search of spice). The Honored Matres dominate men through sex and violence, but not in a cool way. The experience is likened to drug addiction, which can produce almost the same love-hate relationship seen in many heroin addicts. Like the Tleilaxu, they seek to conquer the galaxy. The Honored Matres are only introduced as a force in *Heretics of Dune* and *Chapterhouse: Dune*.

Fringe Players

Many other groups are fringe players in galactic politics (the Fremen, the Fish Dancers, the Ixians, various cults, and so on), but these typically end up being tools used by those in power. Paul and Alia use the Fremen (and their religious fervor) to conquer the galaxy; Leto II uses the Fish Dancers to spread his governmental religion; the Ixians provide technology that assists the Guild during the spice famine.

The political structure in Dune is clearly rickety. Many players all stake out their particular territory and seek to survive in a volatile universe. So how do they stake their claims? By violence, coercion, blackmail, and force, creating a life that is, in many cases, solitary, poor, nasty, brutish, and short. In fact, this system proves ultimately untenable; it's destined to tear itself apart. So long as individuals recognize no authority aside from their own, nothing can hold this aggression in check. This, in turn, guarantees a state of constant conflict, as each faction seeks to impose its will on the others, threatening utter destruction for all involved. It requires the presence of a strong authority capable of reigning in individual power grabs and exerting dominance over the different factions; in short, it requires a tyrant, a savior, a Leviathan.

It's Like Fighting over the Last Beer

The "universe of bastards" looks a lot like a model proposed in 1651 by Thomas Hobbes in his *Leviathan*. Hobbes establishes a theoretical state of existence in which there is no centralized authority, but rather a collection of individuals looking out for their own interests. These individuals fight amongst each other (both between and within groups), producing conflicts at both individual and societal levels. These conflicts threaten the overall existence of everyone involved.

Philosophers have a marvelous ability to reflect the culture of their times in their writing. Hobbes wrote during the English Civil War (1642–1651), literally a war "of all, against all" (Hobbes, p. 88). Peter Gaunt estimates that ten percent of the population aged sixteen to sixty was directly involved in fighting between 1643 and 1645, and that twenty-five percent of all males took up arms at some point during the war (p. 8). In all, about two hundred thousand people died. While historians have proposed several potential divisive factors (religious, economic, and cultural differences), strong evidence suggests that religious extremism was the major force in the split. The Protestant Reformation produced factions of Puritans who rallied against "Papists," or Catholics (Gaunt, pp. 26–27). Hobbes fled this culture (he left England in 1640, afraid of being implicated in an early partisan attack), which would affect him deeply. He looked back at classical ideas on human nature and contrasted them with how history played itself out. This gave him insight into how humans behave, both towards themselves and others.

So what does Hobbes have to say about us? His discussion occurs in Chapter 13 of the *Leviathan*, from which the following analysis comes. We are all driven by self-interest—which he defines as an interest in our own preservation and in our own esteem (both self-esteem and how we are perceived by others). We want others to see us as positively as we see ourselves. Further, we recognize that we do not have all that we want or need to live—we have a drive to seek out the goods we believe necessary for our existence. Vladimir Harkonnen seeks sex and food, while Paul Atreides searches to avenge his father's death and claim his rightful fiefdom. Satisfying their own wants and desires serves as first priority. Hobbes's position does not entail that we act like animals, only that civilization, if it exists, rests on the self-interests of individuals.

Hobbes proposes that our basis for acting as we do results from our reasoning process: we recognize that there aren't enough goods to go around, so we fight for what we want—scarcity produces violence. Two individuals can't both have the same object, and neither one of us has any inherent or trumping right to it, so it just comes down to who wants it more, that is, who wields the club mostly deftly in the smacking of another's head. Sometimes this violence takes physical form and other times psychological form. I can trick you out of goods just as easily as killing you for them. Paul, for example, uses force in the form of Fremen against Emperor Shaddam IV but uses psychology against the Space Guild, threatening to destroy the spice.

Why do we resort to violence? It's actually quite simple—this is *rational* violence. My rational nature motivates me to preserve my own health and well-being by seeking out the means of survival. Without any authority (either a monarch or other form of ruling body), Hobbes claims that each individual has a right to preserve him- or herself, and that each individual has a right to the means of that preservation. It would be irrational to say that I had no right to preserve myself or to deny myself a good necessary for life.

But since everyone has the right to this means of self-preservation, I don't have a *greater* right to any particular good more so than anyone else, even if this good is in my hands. Consequently, it isn't unjust if someone takes my goods from me, nor for me to take someone else's goods. Justice in the sense of the protection of property rights or claims against other people only makes sense in a civil state. In the natural state, the only definition of "just" is what accords with reason. In effect, I justly kill someone when that person prevents me from getting what I need to survive. Hobbes notes that we are all capable of killing—differences between individuals in terms of strength or other necessary attributes can certainly be accommodated by joining forces or outwitting our opponents. Though our individual strengths may vary, overall the field has been leveled.

So long as we all fight each other, we can't enjoy the goods of life. We may stake out some small territory for ourselves, but it's ours only so long as we can hold it. If some other stronger force comes along, we're out of luck. This state can't be maintained forever—this "war of all against all" kills the species. We become the means of our own extinction. Our reason recognizes that we walk the path to destruction, which then causes us to seek peace with one another.

Consider, for instance, when the Fremen demand that Paul fight Stilgar, become leader of all Fremen, and lead them on their war against the Harkonnens. Paul, Stilgar, and Lady Jessica recognize the problem here: if the Fremen always seek to kill the strongest, then they will eventually weaken themselves so much that they can't defeat their enemies. Thus, Paul seeks peace first, so that he can secure victory over the Harkonnens. Thus, he refuses to kill Stilgar, effectively making Stilgar his vassal.

The realization that humanity walks this path of mutual destruction motivates Leto II's Golden Path. He fears that the path established by the Imperium-Landsraad-Guild balance of power produces human extinction. The balance of power is inherently unstable and will collapse into chaos and conflict. If humanity were to be allowed to continue on its path of power-grabbing, it would continue to fight itself, whittling down the population until none remain.

So in light of the natural conflict, we seek peace, and in doing so, we form communities and choose leadership or sovereignty. This formative and selective process is where things get fun and where Hobbes starts to create controversy (in Chapter 18 of *Leviathan*). Whatever government is selected serves as the representative of the people, and the people authorize the government to do whatever it needs to preserve peace.

As Hobbes describes it, we end up selecting leadership based on what we feel is best capable of preserving the peace, which impacts the size of government—how many people possess power. When all possess power, we get democracy, when only a few possess power, we get aristocracy, and when only one possesses power, we get a monarchy. Only monarchy unifies a position of political power—the monarch and sovereign are the same individual. The same cannot be said, obviously, in a system that divides power between different groups. The challenge for members of a democracy or aristocracy, therefore, is how to preserve peace in a system in which power is split.

Whenever we split power, we split authority, which increases the likelihood of us returning to that state of fighting amongst ourselves (*Leviathan*, p. 225). Just like the English government, split between the crown and Parliament, we end up fighting over who has what authority, property, goods and services, and so on, until someone eventually gets shot. Or, in the case of the *Dune Chronicles*, shot, poisoned, stabbed, incinerated, dismembered, eaten, crushed, drowned, beaten to death, beheaded, or left to die from exposure. A lot of people die in *Dune*—so many, in fact, that it's beyond our imagination. At one point, Paul Atreides estimates that he has "killed sixty-one billion, sterilized ninety planets," and "completely demoralized five hundred others" (*Dune Messiah*). Don't forget, *he's the good guy*.

A further area of concern for members of societies containing both political and religious institutions is the split between political and spiritual power—organized religions also make demands on followers and can have political influence. Hobbes has two pieces of advice—first, the Sovereign must control information. Hobbes establishes that the sovereign must be the ultimate judge of what material proves conducive to peace in society, and consequently, must control what ideas and opinions spread. The moment a controversial idea is tolerated and allowed to disseminate, the members of the community divide themselves into different competing factions based upon their agreement or disagreement with the controversial position. This conflict comes to a head when religious ideas are considered—witness the current debate about the role of religion in contemporary politics. The explicit challenge to peace is the establishment of a second Sovereign—a ruler of the spiritual world. This creates a division between the civil and spiritual sovereigns, which undermines the powerbase (and ultimate stability) of earthly governments (*Leviathan*, pp. 226–27). Just as political ideology produces factions and partisan sniping, doctrinal fundamentalism produces holy war.

The Imperial system of Paul, Shaddam IV, and their forebears ignored the threats to the Commonwealth which established a rickety framework, splitting real authority between two political institutions, a commercial institution, and the kingmaker witches. Even when Paul Muad'Dib spreads his jihad and unifies the galaxy under his politico-religious thumb, his reign is short-lived. His apparent death produces a power vacuum and conflict between his sister Alia, his children, and his mother. The temporary unification gives way to violence and intrigue. In essence, when understood from Hobbes's point of view, the old Imperial structure of Shaddam IV and Paul Muad'Dib was, by its very nature, doomed to failure.

When Leto II consolidates power, the shaky political landscape is stabilized. During his long reign (about three thousand five hundred years due to his metamorphosis), society stagnates but remains peaceful. The language used here provides an interesting insight to Herbert's thought. The title of the book detailing Leto's rule is *God Emperor of Dune*—an allusion to the theocratic rule modeled on the old pharaohs of Egypt, who ruled as living gods. Hobbes refers to his "Leviathan" as the "Mortal God" to which we owe our peace and defense (p. 120)—the being that keeps us in peace through awe and fear of punishment. Leto *is* a mortal god—his long life, superhuman prescience, and absolute oppression produce peace and defense throughout the galaxy. Leto *is* the Leviathan.

What kind of ruler is he? By all accounts, he's a tyrant, but as Hobbes notes, "tyranny" simply names a monarchy that we happen to dislike (p. 130). Spice production has stopped during Leto's reign—there are no sandworms to produce it. As such, he sits on a huge hoard, dispensing it as a reward and withholding it as a punishment. Because the Empire depends completely upon spice, they are quickly cowed. He writes histories, to ensure an accurate understanding of past events and his motives. He develops a religion, with himself as God-Emperor, and in spreading the net of its influence, secures absolute power and dominion over the known galaxy.

Again, power splits can occur both between civil governments as well as theocratic ones. By combining his material rule with a spiritual one, he turns breaking the law into a sin, unifying political and spiritual power, and preventing the civil-spiritual splitting of authority about which Hobbes warns us. This fusion of civil and spiritual authority prevents both the initial lawbreaking as well as the corruption that occurs when people are placed in positions of political power. Peace results. No doubt, Leto's rule oppresses and leads to the creation of rebels, but it still brings about peace, which satisfies Hobbes' first law of nature (*Leviathan*, p. 92).

Leto II refers to this as a necessary part of his "Golden Path"— a systemic approach to steer the future of humanity. The Golden Path proves austere, in that it forces conditions of scarcity on humanity. But it also nurtures, in that it forces a diaspora that will ensure the continuity of the species. Leto II perceived a threat to humanity's future in its dependence on spice and the limited range of its galactic occupation—the concentration of conflicting interests in a confined space over a common need served as a powder-keg waiting to explode. Many of the people Leto II places in positions of power were former rebels—by explaining the nature and purpose of the Golden Path to them, he wins their hearts and minds. The oppression becomes justified, even necessary, to preserve us all.

Leto II's death proves more insightful for understanding Hobbes and power. His assassination causes his body to fragment, creating new sandtrout and sandworms, with each possessing a small portion of his awareness. However, along with the new worms and a new source of spice, we also get the dissolution of the empire and new power factions emerging from people who scattered in the wake of Leto's regime. This scattering produces the Honored

Matres, the ultraviolent and unpredictable women who are the primary challenge to the Bene Gesserit in *Chapterhouse: Dune*. The upshot is that Leto's Peace is gone, and with this split of authority, the galaxy is once more consumed in violent grabs for power and influence—human nature reasserts itself, and violence becomes the means of acquiring the scarcest of scarce goods.

Spice as the Vehicle of Power

So what in the Duniverse is this scarce good? What has the power to produce lasting conflict and strife? What has the power to shape and destroy lives and governments? Spice—the rarest substance in the galaxy:

> Without melange to ignite the linear prescience of Guild Navigators, people cross the parsecs of space only at a snail's crawl. Without melange, the Bene Gesserit cannot endow Truthsayers or Reverend Mothers. Without the geriatric properties of melange, people live and die according to the ancient measure. (*God Emperor of Dune*)

Spice has produced a radical dependency, and consequently a strong desire to possess it. So agents are put into conflict—their needs are not compatible with a finite supply of this resource. (Admittedly, there is an abundance of spice in *Heretics of Dune*— the Tleilaxu axlotl tanks are capable of producing spice, but this only lasts until the Honored Matres exterminate the Tleilaxu, restoring scarce conditions.) These political bodies are all intelligent organizations; each is perfectly capable of producing the destruction of the other, which is in line with the agents in the state of nature.

In the Duniverse, the power conflicts arise largely between *groups of individuals*, rather than individuals in isolation (Hobbes concerns himself with *individual* conflicts, but the model still holds). While individual designs and plots pop up in the novels, the dominant conflicts center around collections of individuals. The Bene Gesserit lack physical might (they have no army like the Fremen or the Sardaukar), but they're very efficient at manipulation and poisons (in fact, we're introduced to them by a Reverend Mother who threatens to poison Paul Atreides in the opening chapters of *Dune*). The Spice Guild similarly has no army, but they provide the only means of rapid interplanetary travel—planets would become isolated and crippled without their transportation and trade. Further, given the lethally addictive nature of the spice itself, a refusal to transport it would be a death sentence for the affected population. The Emperor possesses his Sardaukar shock troops, but their physical might is not supreme, and we see that even the Imperial Throne reduces to a good in conflict. The subtle and overt power grabs that occur show that Shaddam only controls the Throne so long as the Sardaukar remain the strongest force and spice flow isn't threatened. By the end of *Dune*, both of these sources of power disappear, exposing the weakness at Shaddam's core. The Tleilaxu find alternate means of producing spice and possess Face Dancers, capable of replacing influential people with agents sympathetic to their religious cause. Many forces are at play, leveling the playing field—the natural position of Hobbes's agents in the state of nature.

The only time we establish peace and covenants (and thereby systems of justice) is when a power binds us all. This power must be supreme—it can't simply be another good open to us all, or else it just becomes another source of conflict. There must be one source of power that isn't limited; something that does ultimately carry trump power. In a state of nature, you and I are perfectly capable of making agreements, but nothing binds us to them; nothing prevents me from sticking a knife in your ribs once your part of the bargain is complete and your back is turned. Well, aside from the fact that I teach applied ethics, and philosophers are normally much more mild-mannered. Hobbes reminds us that words and promises alone don't carry power—we need something capable of forcing me to obey and fulfill my obligations (*Leviathan*, p. 96), punishing and rewarding me appropriately.

Paul Atreides ascends to power via control of the spice—he's perfectly willing to destroy it, which directly impacts nearly every facet of the Duniverse. As Paul notes, the power to destroy a thing is absolute control over it, and power over the spice is power over those who need it. Leto II has a similar approach to maintaining power. He recognizes that his prescience and long-life aren't sufficient to maintain power (he is, essentially, a longer-lived version of Paul Atreides). The nature of Leto II's power is even more extreme scarcity than we saw in Paul's time—the worms are gone, spice is no longer produced, and Leto has the largest supply at hand. Further, like Paul, he isn't afraid to destroy his remaining caches of spice—his ability to destroy the last remaining source of spice remains a key to his control, and essential to his ability to enforce peace and tranquility (*God Emperor of Dune*). This produces a shift in the conflicting factions in *Dune* (and the agents in conflict in Hobbes's political model)—their rational interest in self-preservation causes the various factions of the Duniverse to obey Leto's dictates. Hobbes's rational interest in self-preservation applies equally to preserving oneself from violence as well as preserving oneself from deprivation and withdrawal. The conditions of radical scarcity give Leto remarkable power, which he uses to preserve peace and avoid the lethal competition that marked the universe before his ascension to power.

Leto's Peace is forced stability—it serves to drive us towards peaceful coexistence (both through a fear of punishment as well as hatred of a common enemy), production of innovation (efforts to decrease dependency on the scarce resource), and avoidance of vulnerability (the population expands outward with a frontier mentality; this extension of humanity prevents us from being limited to a relatively small collection of worlds, and consequently increases our chances for survival as a species). This forced stability is, quite literally, the best thing to happen to mankind.

Herbert's six novels contain a number of references to events in our history—Genghis Kahn, Hitler, the pogroms against Judaism and the Diaspora, collective memories of the species back through and before recorded history. Our history is one of violence and of competition for scarce resources like land, oil, and in coming years, potable water. At some level, knowing that we can look forward to the Tyrant saving us from ourselves reassures us. Peace through control, control through power, power through spice. Leto's tyranny preserves the galaxy, preventing us from self-destruction.[1]

Possible Author:
MATTHEW A. BUTKUS

---

[1] Much thanks to Hanno Bulhof for offering feedback and clarification regarding Hobbes in this manuscript.

Ethics of Muad'Dib

Power Mongers and Worm Riders

It's hot. The sun's rising. You welcome the light because you can see across the sand, but the temperature's starting to rise. It won't take much longer before you need to find shelter, to hide from the light. You shift your weight as you try to get ready to spring into action. With each movement, the sand gives a little under your feet. You can't quite get the stance you want. You always feel a little off balance, a little too far forward or too far backwards. You'd feel better standing on the rocks a few feet to your left, but you don't have any choice. You need to be on the sand if you're going to catch a ride on a worm.

The worms provide *Dune's* most enduring image. Frank Herbert gives us an interesting cast of characters, from the Harkonnens to the Atreideses, from the Bene Gesserit to the Fremen, but the image I always have in my mind is of the worms. There's something both majestic and frightening about these creatures that live and move in the ground. They burst onto the scene without warning, scattering the people, disrupting whatever they're doing. Everyone has to build their world around these worms' activities, but they aren't characters in the book. There's no personality there. No intentions, dreams or desires. They just do what they do, and everyone else has to adjust.

Looking at *Dune* philosophically seems a little odd. From beginning to end, urgency pervades *Dune*. Threats are everywhere. Everyone jumps from task to task, with barely enough time to take care of their needs. No one has time to breathe, much less think, much less think philosophically. If I'm going to reflect on the philosophical content of *Dune*, if anyone is going to do it, then it must be because our situation differs from their situation. We've got something they don't have: the leisure to think. We can take the time to step away from the endless pressures of our daily lives to wonder what we're doing and why we're doing it.

Thinking philosophically may require leisure, but it's no walk in the park. One can't just wander about thinking whatever, taking things as they come, and call oneself a philosopher. Philosophy is more like mining. (It can even kick up metaphorical dust!) When doing philosophy, we dig into ideas. We find out what lies underneath them. We extract all kinds of material, and filter and test to find the valuable parts. Thinking about the meaning of life proves especially difficult. It's hard to know where to start. Aristotle proposes that we should start by examining the views of the wise. We do our best to understand their ideas, investigating different views in turn, and modify our own with what we learn. In this case, I propose that we take a little of our leisure and think philosophically about the lives we find in *Dune*.

Whether Aristotle would have counted Herbert among "the wise," Herbert does give us some powerful life stories. Each of these lives appears to us as good, bad, or perhaps a bit more difficult to judge. Taking these stories seriously, mining them for what they might say about living a meaningful life, I think we find an interesting philosophical position. Of course, *Dune* doesn't contain a defense of this view. It's not a philosophical work itself. It does, however, give us something to think philosophically about. So, while it might be more typical to think of monks and nuns in prayer, Sisyphus pushing his rock up the hill, or, perhaps, for a select few, the number 42, those visions leave out something that *Dune* captures for us. They leave out the dynamic struggle that the worm-riders embody.

Let me set the table. Let me take you back from the desert, back from the sands. Let's go back to the dinner that the Duke Leto Atreides hosts when his family first arrives on Arrakis. Leto has invited bankers, merchants, politicians—anyone who's anyone on Arrakis and many with ties beyond. It's a far cry from the meals that most of us eat. Rather than a moment for reflection, a chance for conversation, or, increasingly commonly, a meal grabbed in front of the television, the Atreideses have much more. There's ceremony, opulence, poison-snoopers, and silver. The idea of a relaxed, social meal remains.

Lady Jessica insisted on the dinner party hoping to build closer social ties between the Atreideses and local bankers, smugglers, merchants, and politicians. Thufir Hawat saw nothing but danger in such a close encounter. Duke Leto hardly enjoys himself either. He changes ceremonies. He plots to manipulate guests. At one point, he even tests them by pouring out some of his water on the floor after a toast. Of course, the others must follow suit, but it strains them. They've been the upper-class on Arrakis for some time. They always had enough clean water, but pouring drinkable water on the floor proves more than some can take. All the while, Leto and Jessica watch and learn. They size up the character of each of their guests. They note the relationships between them, the love and the hate, the care and concern.

For Jessica and Leto, the night is about long-term planning. They're preparing and settling in. They're still sizing up their position and trying to figure out who they will be on this new world. They have some plans. They don't come empty-handed, but they've left a lot behind. They need this meal to get themselves back on their feet.

In this respect, their position isn't unlike ours. Not that most people attend dinner parties with poison-snoopers in great halls, but we do often find ourselves dislocated in similar ways. Whether it's a new job, a new city, a new family, or even all three, we're easily drawn into social situations where we must feel our way forward. We have a sense of what should happen and how things should go, but behind that sense, we know that it might not be shared. The ceremonies are unclear. The meanings are flexible. And usually, much like Leto and Jessica, we find ourselves needing to act in this world before we really know what's going on. Jessica and Leto have some time, though. They can have a dinner party, even if it's a little rushed. They can't enjoy it, though it's stunning how little pleasure comes into Herbert's discussion of the dinner or, really, into *Dune* at all. No one seems to enjoy themselves, or even worry that they aren't enjoying themselves. No one has that luxury. Nonetheless, Leto and Jessica are in a hurry, but they have a moment. They can start to figure out how to fit in. The Harkonnens will ruin all that.

The Harkonnens and Power

Before the sun comes up the day after the party, the Harkonnens have undermined the Atreides plans. Yueh carried out his mission but was torn apart in the process. The Harkonnens executed an ingenious plan, overriding Yueh's rigorous and powerful training that supposedly renders him incapable of causing harm. They identified a weakness that leaves Yueh vulnerable: his wife, Wanna.

The Harkonnens plot tells us a lot about them. It's not that they're cruel. There's nothing unnecessary or gratuitous about what they've done to Yueh and Wanna. There's no extra violence involved or reveling in the pain they've caused. Nor is there any regret that their plan requires them to take such drastic means. They perceive the threat Yueh faces and know that he won't enjoy being a pawn in their game, but they don't have any sympathy for him. For Yueh, capturing Leto and placing him at the mercy of the Harkonnens undermines his very sense of self. Who he was, what was expected of him, and where he was placed in the world. The Harkonnens step on that. They see him as an instrument to be used, a vulnerability to be exploited, as they move forward in their project of amassing power. Nothing suggests they ever struggled with their decision to undermine someone so thoroughly. What they do is so horrific that one is tempted to think that they just couldn't understand the damage they did to Yueh.

Looking at the Harkonnens more directly, we can get a deeper sense of what they live for. Baron Vladimir Harkonnens is fat. He needs suspensors to lift his great bulk. I take from this a two-fold picture. On the one hand, this great weight reeks of power. It's gravitas. It's importance made flesh. It speaks to more than just a natural desire for food or natural extension of their power. After all, everyone needs power. A long line of philosophers have recognized that power is necessary, that every creature must seek power or else give up all desires. Power provides the all-purpose means. Power gets you what you want, no matter what you want. We might all be different, we might all have different desires, but we all want power. And that's natural. It makes sense. There's nothing greedy or perverse about it. At least, nothing necessarily so.

With Baron Vladimir Harkonnen, though, we can see that it's all out of whack. He's gone beyond the natural desire to eat. He's fat. He can't move without help, and still he's unashamed of this bulk. Instead, it announces his heart's desire: power. Power beyond the natural. Power beyond their need for it. The Harkonnens gather power for its own sake, and so they take this opportunity to destroy House Atreides and destroy Yueh in the process. All in the name of their goal of collecting more power.

Ultimately, the Harkonnens are not a pretty picture. They're not the ones to emulate. They're the bad guys, a warning that stands at the edge of *Dune* and tells us how not to live. The Harkonnens, for all their weight, seem hollow. They lack any discernible identity. They lack any sentimental attachments. They even lack a sense of group cohesion. Vladimir sees the need for a follower, a protégé, because otherwise death ends his power, but he doesn't identify with the young man. Nor does Feyd-Rautha identify with the Baron. They need each other to gain more power. They're locked together by fortune and chance, so they can work together as long as it takes, but power is all that holds them.

If that's right, and we judge the Harkonnens to live worthless or diminished lives, what does that imply for our lives? In some respects, we're like them. We need power. At the same time, we'd have to believe that power has a purpose. Whether increasing our power improves our lives depends on what we do with it. Pursuing it as the Harkonnens do leaves them isolated from each other and the social world in a way that most of us find chilling and that points to the deeper lesson here as well. We recoil from their use of Yueh. Their use of him seems particularly destructive, not because it kills him or literally destroys his body, but because it undermines his identity. Therefore, we must think that identities contribute something to living life well.

From this picture, we can't see what they add. Instead, we're left with a kind of a warning. The Harkonnen elements in us can't be ignored, but it would comprise a horrible end if they prevailed. We'd lose something. The identities that keep the story interesting and our lives meaningful would become useful conceits meant to ensnare one's opponents.

The Fremen and Identity

The Fremen occupy the other end of this continuum, and their lives throw more light on the value of an identity. As a group, they might seek power but only because they need it. Internally, they have rigid rituals that convey a fixed, perfect, eternal sense of meaning. The Fremen never question how to proceed, they never need to think about who they are and what they're doing. They live on the earth, slowly transforming it, exerting their will and their power, but only to restore. They seek to restore Arrakis to what it was before their planet became the center of the spice trade.

As Paul soon finds out, life among the Fremen is full of rules and rituals. It's striking to me that no one ever questions these rules. Though they're clearly much more sympathetic figures than the Harkonnens, the Fremen are anti-philosophical. Every question about how to live and what to do has been answered for them. Every square inch of their earth has a name, a purpose, and an elaborate set of rules about who can do what with it. Though no one ever seriously questions these rules and meanings, Herbert gives us a few explanations about how the Fremen came to be this way.

The harsh climate plays the key role. With this sun at their backs and water sweating away every moment, the Fremen must work as a group. They've no time for debate and discussion. At the same time, though, the environment can't explain enough. They could've packed it in a long time ago. They could've given up, sold spice, made their money and moved on. If they lived for pleasure, surely they would have. If they lived for power, it seems inevitable. But they don't. Something else anchors the Fremen to Arrakis.

That something else is their identity. Herbert's explanations for Fremen rituals always harkens back to the past. We hear of ancient rituals and great leaders that set things on this path. We hear of prophets that predict the future and call for a great revival of Fremen culture. Through theses rules and regulations, through a strong sense of how they're related to each other and, especially, to their ancestors, the Fremen shape a meaningful life firmly in one direction. And no one seems dissatisfied.

The worms and the waters of life flow underneath the story of the Fremen. There's a lot here the Fremen don't really understand. They don't know where the spice comes from. They need it. They sell it, but they don't cultivate spice. They just gather what they're given. Likewise, they ride the worms and know enough about how to control them to get around, but they never try to tame them. The waters of life are crucial, but forbidden. They don't drink deeply from it. They don't dive into it. They leave the structures that shape their identity and their lives remain unknown and beyond their control. They act within the identity they've been given and never question it or seek to be something more.

Herbert gives us a strong sense of the attraction of this kind of life. Once Jessica and Paul move into life in the desert, they lose their jumpy sense of hidden enemies around every corner. They're much more confident that they know who they can trust. While there's an urgency in all the events that follow, living with the Fremen feels safer. Even if they face physical danger, and they face plenty, their lives mean something among these people.

Life for the Fremen can't stay this way. It's not a human way to live. While the strong rails of identity and tradition keep human power in check, this life suffocates. Individuality is fleeting as the dead are reabsorbed. Only a few manage to live on in the legends, and even there, their lives are absorbed into a greater story. They become just a necessary step.

What does this story tell us about living well? We get a more positive picture of identity here. It's not just a tool for the Fremen as it was for the Harkonnen. They take identity seriously and it keeps their natural desires for power in check. It gives their need for power shape. They have particular goals that they're pursuing, convinced of their value, and they even have rites, rituals, and stories that seem to accomplish these ends. If Herbert's view is correct, we need identity to give our choices a particular shape, to understand who we are, and only from there can we think about how we should live. At the same time, the Fremen seem suffocated. There's a lot about their own lives that they don't understand. Paul and Jessica are always curious about the reason behind the traditions, and, in this respect, they seem to be better models. So we're left with a model of identity that shows both it's value and it's limit. There's something good about it, but take it too seriously and it smothers something necessary for living well. If we see the Fremen's lives as preferable to the Harkonnens but still unsatisfactory, then we must look elsewhere to find what we're missing.

When joining the Fremen, Paul must change things, reinvent the ritual. Paul even acquires the ability to see into the future and gather meanings from events that haven't happened yet. His control is limited. His understanding of what he sees is limited but, unlike the rest of the Fremen, he's not required to look back all the time, which is why Paul will change everything for good.

He Will Take to the Ways of the Fremen as if He Were Born to Them

This study of the lives of the Harkonnens and the Fremen sets us up for a more realistic and a deeper way of understanding how humans can live meaningfully in this world. The Atreideses sit squarely between the Harkonnens and the Fremen. And it's the Atreideses that can teach us the most about how to live.

I could point to a number of events in *Dune* where the Atreideses make decisions that go beyond their identities and traditions, that seek power in service of other valuable ends, and therefore seem to be living especially well. Paul has to break the rules of the Fremen to survive in the desert. Lady Jessica follows and breaks with the Bene Gesserit. They both take power cautiously, with a keen awareness of what it can do to their lives and the universe; however, we can see how to live well most clearly at a moment of failure. The darkest moment for the House of Atreides: the dinner before the Harkonnens kidnap Leto.

In my opinion, it's at this point that Leto stumbles. While the story in no way suggests Leto's stumble, here is what gets him killed, it's where you can see his virtue best. Leto starts the meal by eliminating an old custom. Typically, guests dipped their hands in some water, splashed it on the floor, dried their hands and threw the towel on the floor with the water. During the meal, the soaking wet towels would be taken outside and given to beggars who came by. Leto reacts as many of us would react. He's horrified. He ends the ceremony. It insults the lower classes. Their poverty drives them to accept water others have thrown away. It seems clear enough. Leto steps above the local culture and ends a tradition. All in all, it looks like a good thing.

But it backfires. As soon as Leto's completed his order, he can read off a servant's face that he's undermined a local economy. The servant would take the towels out back and sell what she could. Leto senses her discomfort and insists that his order be carried out. He wants the water given away without being thrown on the floor. Inadvertently, he'd cut his servant's pay.

He didn't see how unjust customs develop an economy of their own. People come to depend on them. Customs give them money, at least, and many give people meaning. They understand themselves as servants and beggars. They know their places, and gather meaning from those places, even when an outsider might judge those roles unjust. Leto steps in to make a difference. He asserts his power and tried to do some good. He upsets a careful balance. His act of charity becomes a lot less clear.

Later in the evening, Leto would use water for his own ends. As I mentioned earlier, he spills some water on the floor at the end of his toast. He intends to test his guests. He wants to see how they respond. Power has gotten hold of him. He's using the water to his own ends, but not in a way that sustains his life. He's not drinking it. He's not washing with it. He uses it in a political game. This water could have been used by the beggars as well. He could have a more noble purpose, but he doesn't. It's a sign. Leto is not quite with it. His acts aren't appropriate to the moment. They don't quite connect with the context they work in. Leto uses their most precious resource to score political points.

What are we to make of these events? How should we judge Leto?

This is harder. I think the Fremen and Harkonnens provide much clearer cases. Perhaps our previous account can help. With the Harkonnens, we concluded that power is necessary for living well, but not enough. We found that what the Harkonnens did to Yueh proved especially vicious, and so we concluded that identities provide lives with some of their meaning. The Fremen point in the other direction. We need a little distance. Immersed in identities, traditions, and customs, we drown. What we see in Leto might be a bit of that space above the identities, traditions, and customs. He starts his visit by violating local culture.

At first glance, we might think that we admire Leto because he's morally better. When Leto ends the practice of giving discarded water to the poor, he does so out of compassion and a sense of justice. Even so, his first act seems clumsy and graceless, even if morally well-intentioned. The gracelessness lies in the broken bond he leaves behind. He undermines one tradition and set of meanings without connecting the people to something new. Later, when Leto spills the water, he learns about his guests, but he doesn't transform it into something more meaningful. We see in Leto a dynamic interplay between shifting meanings, attempts to do well and gain power, and old, traditional meanings that have shaped the life on Arrakis for ages. For lack of a better word, I'm going to say that Leto doesn't display virtue. He rises up, out of traditions in a way that the Fremen don't. He strives to be something greater, but he doesn't reconnect the people to the past in a way that can sustain any of his noble accomplishments.

Combining those two things—gracefully moving beyond the meanings of traditions but in a way that preserves those bonds and doesn't seek to amass power for it's own sake—requires a particular kind of skill. To do it, one must engage in a constant struggle, balancing concerns and thinking carefully about the appropriate action to take. There's no formula or safe set of rules to follow. Context and history matter, but they can't determine every action.

Events overtake Leto, but where he failed, Paul and Jessica succeed. They use the cultural resources they find in the desert to create a meaningful existence out of their seemingly ruined lives. They acquire power by skillfully breaking select cultural rules; each time, however, they repair the social bonds, show the Fremen a new way forward, and emerge with a stronger, more just society. They manage to change the rules, not merely at their will, but in a way that responds to the needs of the situation and leaves the Fremen intact. Paul plays back and forth between his sense of himself as an Atreides caught in a life-or-death power struggle with the Harkonnens and his new identity, the Muad'Dib. He glances forward, with a vision of a just meaningful world, one where Arrakis thrives covered in green foliage, where life is secure, and the people flourish. To get there, Paul must set himself above the cultural meanings he finds with the Fremen, but not give in and become power-mad like the Harkonnens. It's a struggle that has no rules. Instead, he's guided by visions, by vague ideals, which he enacts as best he can, always sensitive to the needs and understandings of those around him.

The Spice of Meaning

In the end, Paul and Jessica are infused with spice. Their eyes turn blue. It's an interesting idea. The eyes are the first thing you notice when you look at someone. To see them is to see their eyes, so this coloration is the image they give to the world. It's them as they appear to others.

At the same time, you see the world through your eyes. Spice permeates everything. It brings it to life, gives it meaning, and stands at the center of all this activity. While the people of Arrakis struggle to survive, while the Atreideses try to make a new home, while the Harkonnens try to control a new world, the spice is in the background. Some people are immersed in it, some stand outside trying to control it, and a couple, Paul and Jessica, try to do both. They try to live meaningful lives of virtue.

Virtue, as I've described it, is open-ended, and the way *Dune* ends leaves us with a sense of that ending. Paul is now thoroughly enmeshed in his role as the Muad'Dib but his battles with the Emperor brings back his old identity. He is outed as an Atreides and now must balance both identities at once. I'm not convinced he manages it well. At the end of the book, Paul has ascended to the Emperor's throne. He's reshaped power in the universe. By Harkonnen standards, he's living extremely well.

Nonetheless, I'm left uncomfortable. The way he achieved his victory threatened everything on Arrakis and, really, the universe. We're left worrying that his need for power overshadowed everything in the end. Even if it was necessary, we can't shake the uncomfortable feeling. At the same time, Muad'Dib's identity has taken on a life of its own with the Fremen. Paul must prepare to confront himself, and it's not at all clear that the outcome will be for the best.

At this point, the book ends. We don't get resolution. In some ways, that ending is powerful. It catches something important about how we experience our lives. Any balance we find, any moments where we're able to rise above the traditions and identities that shape us, and move forward in a way that maintains our connection with the past, prove temporary. It' worked *so far*. The struggle for living well must continue. None of the previous steps guarantee future success.

So the image I'm left contemplating after I've read *Dune* is the worm rider. They're in a desert, shifting sand under their feet, trying to catch a ride on a worm. The worms aren't cars. They don't just go where you want them to go. They aren't even horses. The worms live underground, out of sight most of the time. They mysteriously create the spice which explodes onto the surface. They can be called, but never completely controlled. All the worm-rider can do is take stock of the situation, plant her feet in the shifting sands as best she can, and struggle to ride the worm to where she should go. They remain above. They're not pulled into the earth. They're not entirely part of the earth, but they aren't disconnected either. They struggle to remain in-between. That's an image of the struggle for meaning that's worth contemplating for a while, since, unlike any of the characters in *Dune*, we have the leisure necessary to think philosophically.

FINDING FROM GUILD LOST AND FOUND
Author: Unknown (possibly an Honored Matre)
Date: The Scattering

Just What Do You Do with the Entire Human Race Anyway?

A young Fremen was once complaining to an old Fremen about the Imperium. "All the Corrino care about is money and power. They rule all of humanity but what have they ever done to make our lives better?" The old naib answered "Better? Hard work has given you strength, desert life has given you endurance, and adversity has given you courage. What else is worth having?" The young Fremen stared wistfully at the horizon and said "a cup of water the size of a worm."

—From *Philosophical Jokes of Old Arrakis* by Princess Irulan[1]

What would you do if you controlled the entire human race? That's probably not a problem you'll ever have to face, but it's all part of the job for the galactic emperors of the *Dune Chronicles*. Dictators like the Padishah Emperor Shaddam IV, Paul Atreides, Alia Atreides, and Leto Atreides II have all of humanity under their control and are responsible for planning humanity's future. Of course, the emperor is not the only power trying to plan everyone's fate. The Bene Gesserit sisterhood schemes to breed a messiah, House Harkonnen schemes to seize the throne, prophets wander in from the desert to manipulate politics, while the Spacing Guild and the Bene Tleilax hatch even more complicated plots of their own, all for the sake of power over humanity. If the characters from the *Dune Chronicles* share a trait, it's a dedication to exerting control over other people. Even control over Arrakis and the spice is just a means to that end.

---

[1] All quotes at the beginning of sections are from the author's imagination. If Frank Herbert can invent books just for the pleasure of quoting them, then so can I.

Why do they all want power so badly? It all comes down to wanting to make life better. Some, like Baron Harkonnen, want to make life better for themselves. Other characters want to make life better for everyone. Paul Atreides takes power only in order to help humanity, believing that it needs him to save it, while Leto II endures centuries of absolute authority for the same altruistic reason. While it's never clear exactly what the ultimate agenda of the Bene Gesserit is, they, too, seem to have humanity's interests at heart. They conduct their breeding programs to produce the Kwisatz Haderach because they, too, want humans to have a better future.

However, before you can arrange a better future, for yourself or for all of humanity, you need to have an idea of what sort of future is better for people, and that requires having an idea of what sort of life is good for a human being. The characters of the *Dune Chronicles* often agonize over the human condition *especially when they are thinking in italics*. We readers have to think about this issue too; we all have a life to live, and so we all must decide what sort of life is a good one.

In this chapter, I'll ask how the Ancient Greek philosophers Socrates and Aristotle would rate the lives of the protagonists and populations of the Duniverse. Like the old Fremen, these two philosophers came from a harsh land where life was difficult and poverty widespread. Like Paul and so many others in the *Dune Chronicles*, they thought hard about how people should live, at a time when political dissent could get you killed. But let's begin with the most popular conception of the "good life."

Water in Your Stillsuit and Spice in the Bank

In all honesty, Baron Harkonnen lived the best life I ever saw. He wanted many things and got most of them. He gained intense pleasure from food, sex, money, and power. He was wonderful company.

—From *Count Hasimir Tells All* by Count Hasimir Fenring

The popular conception of what it is to live well may be vague, but its basic form is as familiar to us as it would have been to Socrates and Aristotle. In Ancient Greece, a good life, as popularly conceived, consisted in things like being rich, influential, healthy, capable, and well-respected—and this still pretty well describes what most people call "living well" or "being successful in life" today. On this view, Duke Leto and Lady Jessica live the good life at the beginning of *Dune*, just because they are rich and respected, ruling, as they do, the entire planet of Caladan. Baron Harkonnen lives the good life too. He may not be healthy and not everyone respects him, but he's fantastically rich and powerful, and he has a great time. In fact, most of the familiar characters from the *Dune Chronicles* live the good life in this sense—they are movers and shakers and never have to worry about where their next drink of water is going to come from.

Others are not so lucky. In *Dune*, life for the average Fremen on Arrakis is incredibly harsh, so bad that an inscription over the gate for departing travelers reads *"O you who know what we suffer here, do not forget us in your prayers,"* so bad that the locals all get tougher than the Emperor's elite Sardaukar troops just by living there. The Fremen get so little to drink that even tears are considered wasteful, and Baron Harkonnen can attract beggars just by throwing wet hand-towels on the ground. These people, on the popular conception, do not live good lives, just because their material conditions are so awful.

This popular conception of the good life would be very familiar to the characters of the *Dune Chronicles*. Even Baron Harkonnen, who cares nothing for humanity in general, seeks the good life for himself, and he sees it in terms of wealth, power and status. The same seems to be true of most of the nobility, probably including the emperor Shaddam IV of Corrino and Duke Leto Atreides. Even if Duke Leto aspires to higher ideals than his rival, the Baron, he isn't above ruling planets as dictator while plotting to advance himself and his family. The Fremen seem to recognize this notion of living well too. For all their concern with religion, their main project in *Dune* aims to improve their standard of living by irrigating Arrakis.

Judged from this perspective, the saga of the Atreides family in *Dune, Dune Messiah, Children of Dune* and *God-Emperor of Dune* presents a tale of human triumph. To humanity in general, Atreides rule brings three and a half thousand years of peace and stability. To the people of Arrakis, it means the transformation of their planet from a desert hell where a human can be worth less than the water in their body, to a lush world at the heart of a rich empire.

Something certainly appears attractive about this popular notion of the good life. Who wouldn't rather be rich instead of poor, respected instead of hated, healthy instead of sick? Having said that, might other things have value apart from such worldly "success"? Paul and Leto II seem to think so, because they both hated the empire they created, even though it brought peace and security. But if something other than worldly success matters, what is it?

A Sandworm Can't Hurt You Because It Can't Make You Morally Worse

Socrates? The man was executed by the people of Athens! Taking advice on how to live from a man who got himself executed is like taking advice on personnel screening from Duke Leto.

—From *Collected Rants* by Baron Vladimir Harkonnen.

Socrates emphatically rejected this popular conception of what it is to live the good life and criticized his fellow Athenians for their obsession with wealth and glory rather than the condition of their souls. Socrates believed that living the good life consisted in living virtuously. Goods like money and glory, even health, prove worthless or even harmful if you aren't a virtuous person. We should direct our attention towards improving ourselves morally rather than chasing worldly success. Socrates said that even survival itself should not concern us—only whether we act with justice.

Let's hope so for his sake because, like Duke Leto, his political enemies had him put to death. Even while on trial for his life, Socrates thought that he couldn't be harmed, because the court couldn't damage his moral character. Just like troublemakers in the Duniverse, Socrates was put to death with poison.

Before we can live a life of virtue, as Socrates suggests, we need to know what sort of behavior is virtuous. Different people have very different moral ideas, and a life that seems virtuous to one person may seem wicked to another. Socrates never states exactly what the good life of virtue requires, although he gives us clues. In particular, in the *Euthydemus*, he lists four virtues essential to living the good life: justice, courage, temperance, and wisdom.

A person living the good life is a just person. They are courageous in the face of danger and temperate in the face of temptation. Most importantly, a person living the good life is a wise person, because wisdom allows us to distinguish right from wrong. Conversely, in the *Apology*, Socrates gives examples of unjust behavior that is not compatible with living the good life. One who lives the good life does not steal, break promises, betray friends or commit adultery. How do people's lives in the Duniverse rate by those standards? Are people living the good life?

Socrates Boards a Guild Highliner

The great thing about Arrakeen is that you can find a philosophical debate on any street corner. Of course, some Fremen can get a little worked up.

—From *Doubt and Disorientation in Arrakeen* by SOCRATES (ed. Plato)

Let's start with the easy one: Socrates wouldn't think that Baron Vladimir Harkonnen lives the good life at all. He cares nothing for justice, happily "squeezing" the poor people of Arrakis to reach economic and political goals. Nor does he know the meaning of temperance, being a slave to food, lust, and greed. He enthusiastically steals, breaks promises, and betrays friends. He steals Arrakis from the Atreideses; he breaks his promise to Doctor Yueh to reunite him with his wife; and he plans to betray his Mentat, Piter De Vries, just because he has "outlived his usefulness." On the other hand, he is courageous in pursuit of his goals, since he is not deterred by assassination attempts or the potential for political disaster.

Emperor Shaddam IV probably wouldn't rate much more highly. We get less insight into his life than that of the Baron, but he seems the same sort of corrupt and dishonest dictator, if a little less susceptible to the pleasures of the flesh. We certainly don't see him show much interest in anything other than protecting his own position, and he's perfectly willing to ally with House Harkonnen behind the backs of the Landsraad in order to betray and destroy House Atreides. He may have "disliked the political necessities that made them enemies," as Irulan puts it (*Dune*), but that doesn't stop him from trying to wipe out House Atreides.

Duke Leto proves a trickier case. He's more virtuous than the Baron or the Emperor, though that isn't saying very much. He certainly seems more honest than his rivals, doesn't steal, and never plots to betray his friends. Leto shows courage by walking into the trap he knows the Baron has set for him on Arrakis. On the other hand, his intention to gain a politically advantageous marriage without giving up his beloved concubine Jessica is presumably an intention to commit adultery.

From our own twenty-first century perspective, it's hard to think of Duke Leto as being just. After all, he's a dictator, taking whole

planets for his fiefs whether the locals like it or not. Socrates, however, despised democracy, recommending rule by the wisest—a
description that Leto arguably fits. More damning in Socrates's eyes
would be the fact that Leto breaks rules in order to further his goals.
He orders Thufir Hawat, for example, to forge certificates of allegiance over the signatures of Harkonnen agents in order to allow
him to confiscate their property and "turn out their families" (*Dune*).
Socrates, on the other hand, refused to break the law of Athens, even
while awaiting the death sentence after a wrongful conviction. His
friends bribed the jailer to let Socrates escape, but he refused to run.

Leto certainly has a reputation for justice, to the point that other
nobles commonly address him as "Leto the Just" (*Dune*). Perhaps
those who call him "Leto the Just" do so to flatter him or in
response to his propaganda department, which he admits is "one
of the finest" (*Dune*). More likely, given what we see of his behavior, Leto has won his reputation through genuinely being a model
of justice compared to his rivals. Whether meeting that standard is
sufficient for truly being "just" you will have to decide for yourself,
but I doubt that Socrates would be satisfied.

Paul Atreides is an even more complicated case than his father.
Paul may not break promises, but he is extremely misleading. He
manipulates the Fremen into thinking he is introducing them to a
golden age, when he knows that the future he leads them to is no
such thing. Nor does he clue in the rest of humanity. By his own
admission, he relies on "myth-making" and "pretensions" to
deceive his subjects with religious propaganda (*Dune*). (Plato,
using Socrates as his mouthpiece in *The Republic*, is sympathetic to
the idea of using myth to control people, but that's a different ket-
tle of sandtrout).

Whether Paul betrays his friends or not is debatable, but he isn't
above using those close to him for the greater good. Even his
mother, Jessica, and friend, Stilgar, become political tools. More
dramatically, Paul apparently sells out his own sister, Alia, using her
to confront the Emperor on his behalf when she is only a child,
then abandoning her to confusion and loneliness as an adult, even
as he cedes her the throne. He's happy to periodically appear out
of the desert to stir up trouble against her, but never offers her a
brother's friendship or any practical advice. As for adultery, Paul
must be judged the same as his father—though he marries the
emperor's daughter Irulan, he continues to sleep with his beloved
Fremen concubine, Chani.

I think that Socrates would judge Paul to be unjust, even though the injustices he commits are intended to help humanity in the long run. Between *Dune* and *Dune Messiah,* Paul imposes his religion on humanity by force, waging a war of conquest and suppressing all dissent. By *Children of Dune*, Duncan Idaho complains that "Muad'Dib's teachings have become the playground of scholastics, of the superstitious and the corrupt" and Stilgar observes that "Muad'Dib's Golden Elixir of Life had created a bureaucratic monster which sat astride human affairs. Government and religion united, and breaking a law became sin. A smell of blasphemy arose like smoke around any questioning of governmental edicts."

Moving on, Paul exemplifies temperance in his personal life, preferring the Spartan existence of a desert Fremen to the opulence of an imperial court. He even refrains from participating in the Fremen tau orgy (although it's possible that the presence of his mother in the room has something to do with that). Paul is extremely courageous, to the point that eventually, like Socrates, he ceases to fear death.

So, did Paul live the good life or not? Taking everything into consideration, Socrates would probably say not. Paul himself certainly didn't think that he was living the good life. Everyone around him might have been lusting after the imperial throne, but Paul finds his destiny a burden and wishes that he could escape it.

Socrates Considers the Human Race

Everywhere I look, I see people kept in ignorance by the unjust rule of the tyrant Leto II.

—SOCRATES as quoted in *The Fish Speakers' Funniest Death-Cell Interviews*

So much for the great nobility. What about the ordinary people who make up almost all of the population? Do they get to live a life of virtue, the sort of life that Socrates might call the good life? We don't get a close enough look at life in the Imperium to make many sure judgments about its justice, temperance, courage and wisdom or about how much stealing, promise breaking, betrayal of friends and committing of adultery goes on.

The common people we get the closest look at are the Fremen, and Socrates would find a lot to admire in their way of life, just as he found much to admire in the harsh existence of the ancient Spartans. The extreme nature of the Fremen's environment forces them to be temperate, getting by with little water and not much of anything else. As Muad'Dib says, *"The Fremen were supreme in the self-imposed delay between desire for a thing and the act of reaching out to grasp that thing"* (*Dune*). (Of course, the Fremen do like the occasional tau orgy too, complete with drugs, dancing and sex, and it's hard to see Socrates approving of that.) The Fremen are famous for their courage, being even braver than Shaddam IV's feared Sardaukar. Fremen are bound by the Ichwan Bedwine to view all other Fremen as brothers and take their promises and friendships seriously. On the other hand, they are adulterous by ancient Greek standards, since the men sometimes take multiple wives, as Stilgar does.

In the wake of Paul's victory at the end of *Dune*, these old ways break down. Ambition and avarice replace Fremen unity as a vast Fremen empire based on injustice replaces the Fremen sietch. Could it be that rather than bringing the good life, Fremen prosperity and power made their lives worse by making them morally worse? That might explain why Paul increasingly turns to the life and traditions of the desert, turning his back on ways of the new imperial Arrakis.

Socrates would criticize the Fremen of all periods for being too sure of themselves. The Fremen tend not to question traditional wisdom. Their religion, carefully nurtured by the Bene Gesserit's Missionaria Protectiva, tells them the way that things are and the way that they will be in the future. The Fremen take these things on faith, and it is only by manipulating the unshakeable religious convictions of the Fremen that Paul makes himself emperor in the first place, and only by invoking this religion to silence all dissent do Paul, Alia, and Leto II hold on to power.

Socrates, on the other hand, thought that people should question everything they could, since it's better to know that you are ignorant than to think you know something that you don't. The person who knows she's ignorant sits in a position to look for the truth and so gain wisdom. If only the Fremen had felt the same way, they might have been wise enough not have been taken for a ride so easily.

Neither Paul, Alia, nor Leto II makes it a goal to bring greater wisdom to the people of Arrakis; nor, for that matter, to the rest of the human race. As a revolutionary in *Dune* and dictator in *Dune*

Messiah, Paul keeps his revelations and plans secret from the public, even though he is plotting the history of humanity. He doesn't even tell the Fremen as he leads them into holy war. By *Children of Dune*, he becomes so secretive that he devotes his life to wandering around in disguise as a prophet from the desert, making cryptic comments to influence political events. Nor do the dictators Alia or Leto II cultivate wisdom in the ruled masses. They hide the true nature of society and history, preferring the cynical manipulation of religion to spreading understanding. Socrates couldn't approve of the ignorant lives of their deluded subjects and would judge that the ordinary people of the Atreides empire are not living the good life.

Fulfill Your Human Potential: Be a Mentat.

Aristotle? Athens was going to execute him just like Socrates but he ran away into exile too fast. Why would anyone want to take advice on how to live from a man that spectacularly unsuccessful in dealing with other people? Deny his visa. Also, kill him.

—From *Collected Rants* by BARON VLADIMIR HARKONNEN.

Aristotle was a student of Plato, who was a student of Socrates. Like Socrates and Plato, Aristotle thought that one could not live the good life without living a life of virtue. He differed, however, because he believed that living a life of virtue isn't enough.

Aristotle states in his *Nicomachean Ethics* that the best existence for anything is an existence in which it functions well. For instance, the best existence for a knife is being used to cut, and cutting well. Aristotle would thus say that a Fremen crysknife has a good existence for a knife because it is so hard and sharp and, thus, performs the function of a knife extremely well. Just as the best existence for a crysknife is one in which it performs its function as a crysknife well, the best life for a human being consists in performing one's function as a human being well.

Aristotle said that to determine the function of something, we must consider what it does best. A crysknife cuts things better than anything else, so we can tell that the function of a crysknife is to cut. A Shai-Hulud is better than anything else at producing spice, so that would be the function of a Shai-Hulud. Aristotle said that what a human does better than anything else is to reason, so reasoning well is the function of a human being. In other words, a life of reasoning well comprises the good life for a human. Of the various fields in which one might have the ability to reason well, the very best is politics, since politics governs the use of all other abilities. The Fremen may reason well about irrigation, but Paul, who understands politics, controls them.

However, Aristotle didn't think that reasoning well is all that matters in life. He thought it was important to be virtuous, to be skillful, to have friends, and to be honored, and that pleasure is worth pursuing for its own sake. Even wealth is an important component of living well, most importantly because it gives us more time to hone our intellect and more opportunities to perform virtuous acts. To take an example from *Dune*, Duke Leto shows generosity to the Fremen by giving out a full cup of water to every beggar who calls to the door during his feast. However, it's only because he's rich enough to be able to spare enough water "to keep a poor Arrakeen family for more than a year" (*Dune*) that he has such an opportunity for virtuous action.

Still, virtues take the center stage in living a good life. Aristotle believed that we could work out which characteristics comprised the virtues because virtue always lies in the moderate state between an excess and a deficiency. For instance, if we are too confident, we are rash, while if we aren't confident enough, we are cowardly. The moderate state between these two extremes is courage, so courage must be a virtue. For example, consider the first time that Paul rides the Shai-Hulud. If he had been so confident that he hadn't bothered to learn the Fremen techniques for worm-riding, but instead simply charged the animal with the intent of wrestling it into submission, he would have been acting, not out of courage, but from rashness. If he had been so lacking in confidence that instead of approaching the worm, he ran all the way back to Sietch Tabr and hid, he would have been acting, not out of courage, but from cowardice. However, because he took a path between these extremes, carefully learning the ways of the Fremen worm-steerman and approaching the Shai-Hulud cautiously but resolutely, we may say that he was acting out of courage.

For Aristotle, then, the good life is a life of intellectual activity. It's a life that boasts not only a morally healthy soul, but also less-romantic assets such as wealth, friends and pleasure. The good life is a life in which each characteristic of the personality is possessed in moderation, since it is in moderation, between excess and deficiency, that human virtues lie.

Aristotle Tours the Duniverse

My main recommendation is that everyone calm down. Political involvement is a good thing, but people have become fanatical. Religious hysteria is clouding reason throughout the empire.

—From *Letters from an Arrakeen Jail* by ARISTOTLE

Aristotle would find much to like in the Duniverse, believing, as he does, that the good life lies in reasoning well. If there's one thing the main characters of the *Dune Chronicles* can do, it's think problems through. The political calculations undertaken by the likes of Duke Leto, Lady Jessica, Shaddam IV, and Alia prove amazingly insightful and skillful. Even Baron Harkonnen, symbol of all that is evil in *Dune*, shines in this one regard. However vile and cruel he might be, he is a brilliant strategist.

The complex plans of the Houses pale in comparison to the complex plans of organizations like the Bene Gesserit and the Spacing Guild, which unfold over thousands of years. Not every Reverend Mother or Guild navigator may be a genius, but reasoning well is clearly a common trait. Mentats like Thufir Hawat and Piter de Vries are specifically trained to be brilliant thinking machines, a human replacement for the forbidden technology of computers. As if that weren't enough to make Aristotle salivate, the superhuman intelligence achieved by Paul Atreides and godlike intelligence achieved by his son, Leto II, would mark lives that approach Aristotelian perfection. Paul and Leto may come to regard their own existences with feelings of angst and woe, but I'm sure that Aristotle would have given anything to change places with either of them.

What about virtue? No life can be good without that. Would the characters of the *Dune Chronicles* be virtuous in Aristotle's eyes? Aristotle never gave us a complete list of what he thought the virtues are, but fortunately, he gave us a method to work out which characteristics are virtues by finding the point of moderation between extremes. We've already looked at the virtues of justice, courage and temperance (all of which Aristotle thought were very important) so let's use his method to identify other virtues that the characters have or haven't got.

Here's how I think it plays out. The Baron's treatment of the people of Arrakis shows that he lacks compassion (the mean between callousness and naivety) while his endless lies demonstrate that he lacks honesty (the mean between deceitfulness and tactlessness). On the other hand, the subtlety of his plans shows that he does have patience (between the deficiency of inactivity and the excess of rashness). Also, Aristotle thinks that political skill is a virtue, and the Baron certainly has that. After all, if it hadn't been for the coming of the Kwisatz Haderach, he might have made himself second in power only to the emperor. Still, when we weigh moderation and justice into the bargain, I don't think that the Baron has a chance of being judged virtuous by Aristotle. Since the Baron isn't virtuous, he isn't living the good life.

Duke Leto and Lady Jessica have a better shot at impressing Aristotle. Not only are they courageous, moderate in their personal habits and (perhaps) just, they are also kind (between callousness and naivety) and disciplined (between laxness and rigidity). Their plots involving Arrakis may indicate that they are deceitful (a deficiency of openness) and gullible (a deficiency of suspicion). Moreover, there's nothing moderate about Leto's ambitions. Thufir Hawat notes that the Duke "couldn't turn down the richest planetary source of income in our universe" despite the danger, while Jessica observes that Leto's ambitions can make him "cold, callous, demanding, selfish—as harsh and cruel as a winter wind" (*Dune*). It is true, Aristotle raised no objections when his own student, Alexander the Great, conquered what was then the known world, but I suspect that like Stilgar, Siona and so many other dissidents in the *Dune Chronicles*, Aristotle was just keeping his mouth shut to avoid execution.

Paul and Leto II are both problem cases, because the virtues that we most want to ascribe to them seem to have no place under Aristotle's system. Their most impressive feature is their selflessness. Paul devotes his life to bringing about the best possible future for humanity, sacrificing his happiness, his wealth and his sight to that end. Leto II devotes millennia to ensuring that humanity survives and even sacrifices his own humanity. We might want to call selflessness a virtue, but for Aristotle, a virtue must lie at the point of moderation between a deficiency and an excess. A deficiency of selflessness might be selfishness, but what could an excess of selflessness be? The selfless person is already at an extreme and is already giving all that they can give, so it seems impossible to find an excess for which selflessness is the moderate alternative. The extreme protagonists of the *Dune Chronicles* simply don't fit the Aristotelian model of a virtuous person. Without a virtuous character, they cannot be living the good life.

As for pleasure, that doesn't seem to be something that the main characters in *Dune* get much of. Baron Harkonnen and his inner circle seem to have a pretty good time, what with the feasts and the gladiatorial shows and the drugs and the orgies. Duke Leto and Lady Jessica also probably had it pretty good as rich nobility. Alia, on the other hand, spends most of her time being lonely, worried, and depressed. Paul and Leto II are both very unhappy people, weighed down by their terrible responsibilities—for thousands of years in Leto's case. Despite the fact that they are emperor-Mentats, they fail to live a good life. You might think it would be difficult not to get at least a little fun out of riding giant worms and being galactic emperor, but they manage it.

Aristotle Considers the Human Race

The victory of Paul Atreides over Shaddam IV was a terrible tragedy. The Atreideses built an empire of wasted human potential. Instead of helping their subjects to flourish, the Atreideses deliberately stunted their intellectual and political growth.

—From *Politics II: Melange and Mentats* by ARISTOTLE.

So much for the lives of the nobility. Do ordinary people get to live the good life? Certainly, the traditional desert Fremen met by Paul Atreides in *Dune* certainly don't think their life is a good one, and Aristotle would agree. Aristotle would begin by asking whether the Fremen are living lives of the intellect—existences devoted to reasoning—and would have to conclude that they aren't. Fremen live lives devoted to the brutal task of survival, a task made bearable only by their mystical religion. Naibs like Stilgar don't lack for intelligence and are perfectly capable of carrying out complex, long-term plans, but the average Fremen has little time to devote to the life of the mind and little education for the mind to work with. In particular, there's very little opportunity for the Fremen to develop or practice skill in politics, being mere chattels of House Harkonnen.

It may be hoped that life for the common folk elsewhere in the Imperium is, if not freer, at least a little less miserable, but there isn't much information to go on. We know that conditions on the military planet Salusa Secundus are not much better than life on

Arrakis, but on the other hand, we also know that the people of Giedi Prime get to watch gladiatorial shows and that Gamont is "noted for its hedonistic culture and exotic sexual practices" (*Dune*). Still, we have little idea of what life is like for the average person on Caladan, or Giedi Prime, or Corrin or any of the hundreds of other worlds of the Imperium. I'm guessing that Caladan was a pretty good place to live and Giedi Prime a pretty bad one, but for all I know, the peasants felt exactly the opposite.

What of virtue? We have already noted that the Fremen of *Dune* are courageous and temperate. Furthermore, their secret world-irrigation project demonstrates that they are patient (between inactive and rash) and hard working (between slothful and slavish). They are also a skillful people. Their achievements include an ability to survive in conditions that would quickly kill anyone else, being advanced terraformers, having a rich and poetic culture, and being the best soldiers in the Imperium. On the other hand, while Fremen tenacity may avoid the deficit of dedication that indicates spinelessness, their dedication goes far beyond any moderate position and reaches the excess of being obstinate. After all, they support the projects of their messiah and his heirs long after it should have been clear that they brought oppression. Many virtues are beyond the grasp of the Fremen of *Dune* purely because of their condition. They can't be very generous, because they have little to give, they can't be very hospitable because they must live in secret communities, and they can't be politically active because they have no say in their own government.

Did life get any better after Paul's victory? Paul's twelve year holy war must have been a horror to live through, but it's followed by thousands of years of peace and even the poor Fremen eventually get plenty of water to drink. Even so, I can't see Aristotle approving of the new empire. Life on Arrakis may grow more prosperous, and peace may come to billions, but free thought is crushed throughout the Imperium by the theocratic government. It must be conceded, many of the Fremen achieve positions of power that allow them to make use of political skills. However, the citizens of the empire are told what to believe by the government and, as in Socrates and Aristotle's day, dissenting is liable to get you killed. The Fremen of the new Arrakis become known for greed, ferocity, and injustice. Furthermore, their political activity is limited to propping up a corrupt regime. Aristotle would be horrified at what has become of humanity and would certainly not think that the people of Paul and Leto's empire live the good life.

Alone into the Desert

Ah-h-h, Aristotle has eluded us, Piter. Our little philosopher fled the Imperium for Tupile one step ahead of a hunter-seeker. Now I suppose people will just have to think for themselves. Ha ha ha ha!

—From *Collected Rants* by BARON VLADIMIR HARKONNEN.

So who's right about the good life for a human being: Socrates, Aristotle, or neither? Is the good life for a human being a life of wealth and power? A life of indifference to worldly things? A life of intellectual contemplation? Or something else entirely?

Socrates was dead right to reject the popular conception of the good life. Surely someone can be rich and "successful" in a material sense while being an utter failure as a human being. Wealthy but despicable individuals like Baron Harkonnen, Feyd-Rautha, and Piter de Vries live badly, even while living it up. On the other hand, I can't accept Socrates's notion that moral virtue is sufficient for living the good life and that the only harm that can come to you is moral harm. If Socrates were right, then Duke Leto and Jessica were not harmed when Yueh betrayed them, Baron Harkonnen was not harmed when he was poisoned to death by Alia's Gom Jabbar, and no harm was done to any of the vast number of ordinary people who took a crysknife to the belly or a lasgun blast to the face in Paul's twelve-year holy war.

I don't buy it, and I think the Fremen of *Dune* would agree with me, since they devote too much of their time and energy to surviving on Arrakis to dismiss survival so lightly. If the only harm you can suffer is acting unjustly, why do up your stillsuit in the morning? I can't see the nobles of the Duniverse siding with Socrates either. Their world is an opulent one but a dangerous one, and those who don't take great care will soon fall prey to a hunter-seeker, or a poison-gas tooth, or a slow knife through the shield.

Moreover, survival alone isn't enough. People must have a certain level of material comfort to be living well. Socrates was right to value temperance, but people must have access to adequate food and water, medicine and basic social services. Humans who are suffering from privation and poverty aren't living well, even if they are virtuous. I think that this becomes very clear when we

consider the lives of the desert Fremen. Though their existence cul-
tivates many virtues, they cannot be living the good life simply
because their lives are so hellish. Their quest to irrigate Arrakis is
important precisely because doing so will improve their thirsty lives
so much.

Aristotle shows a much better appreciation of the dependence of
the good life on factors other than moral virtue. His account of the
good life gets closer to the truth than either the popular view or
Socrates's account. He's right to recognize the importance of external factors such as money and friends in living well. As the Fremen
well understand, privation brings suffering. Unlike Aristotle, I don't
think that humanity has a "function." I can't accept his claim that
humanity's function is to reason well. However, I think he's right
that reasoning well is part of living well, since someone who can
reason well is in the best position to make judgments about how to
live. A Mentat like Thufir Hawat is going to be able to organize his
life and weigh long-term consequences against short-term gains in
a way that an ordinary person could never manage.

Aristotle, like Socrates, is perfectly right to stress the importance
of moral virtue in any life worthy to be called "the good life."
However, I don't buy his claim that virtue must always lie at a point
of moderation, and I think the *Dune Chronicles* demonstrates why
you shouldn't buy it either. Sometimes, an extreme characteristic is
better than a moderate one. Paul and Leto II are both extreme in
their selfless service of humanity, and save humanity by being that
way. There's nothing moderate about the single-mindedness they
show or the sacrifices they make, in Leto II's case for thousands of
years. By acting as they do, Paul and Leto are doing the morally
right thing given their circumstances. They clearly aren't living the
best lives possible because they have to bear so much suffering and
find their responsibilities such a burden; but they save the entire
human race, which must surely be a consequence that justifies their
actions.

Similarly, in the real world, it can be the people with the most
extreme personalities who live the most exemplary lives. Not many
people get to save the human race, but some devote themselves
selflessly to fighting world hunger, or abolishing torture, or any one
of a number of worthwhile causes. I can't accuse such giving individuals of lacking virtue, though there's nothing moderate about
their character. I think that individuals like that are living the best
lives of all.

Lastly, I disagree with both Socrates and Aristotle that a person can only be living the good life if they are just. I think that sometimes it's better not to act with justice, and again, I think the *Dune Chronicles* demonstrates why. Paul and Leto II are both oppressive rulers who prop up corrupt empires. What they do benefits humanity in the long run, but they do it at the expense of innocent people who must endure their repressive theocratic dictatorships. I think that there's no way to call these two just, and yet I think they're taking the best path open to them, doing what's morally right even though they aren't doing what is just. Being just wouldn't take them closer to the good life, but further away.

In real life, the just thing to do is almost always the right thing to do, but there's no reason in principle why it must always be. It's possible for a situation to arise in which, as in the case of Paul and Leto II's rule, the benefits of being unjust outweigh the need for justice. For example, during a sufficiently terrible epidemic, a desperate community might rightly turn away innocent strangers who need help, even if they don't know for sure that the strangers are infected. That doesn't strike me as a just way to treat innocent people, but if the danger is great enough, it may be the right thing to do all the same.

So how should we pursue the good life? Personally, I think human happiness is what truly matters in life and that a person living the life they should will be as concerned about the happiness of others as they are about their own. I think that human happiness is best served by kindness, justice, democracy, skepticism, and freedom of thought and speech. That doesn't sound much like life under Muad'Dib or Leto II, but then, they had prescience and could see that they were making the best choices available to them.

You'll have to make up your own mind as to the best sort of life for a human being. As a fan of the *Dune Chronicles*, you know only too well what happens when people allow someone else to do their thinking for them. Bi-la kaifa!

As submitted by:
GREG LITTMANN

From: *The Myth of Dune*
Date: 13000 A.G.

Good and Evil in David Lynch's *Dune*

The theme of good versus evil recurs throughout the cinematic and television work of director David Lynch. From the demonic character of BOB and the rational and conscientious Special Agent Dale Cooper in *Twin Peaks* to the mysterious force that is Mr. Roque and the good Betty Elms in *Mulholland Drive*, Lynch has frequently dealt thematically in evil and its consequences, using imagery and symbolism that suggest sinister, and often supernatural, forces.

Lynch has often conceived of the existence of evil in quite a localized way. Both in his earlier work, uncovering the dark secrets of small-town, picket-fenced America, perhaps most prominently in *Twin Peaks* and *Blue Velvet*, and then in later work drawing attention to the menacing underpinnings of the affluent regions of Los Angeles, in *Lost Highway*, *Mulholland Drive*, and *Inland Empire*, the effects of evil forces tend to be localized to a particular figure and to a specific, often fairly isolated, community.

Yet this distinctively Lynchian theme takes on an altogether more expansive dimension as depicted in his epic film adaptation of Frank Herbert's novel *Dune*. In *Dune*, Baron Harkonnen and the Emperor represent the forces of evil, and the mysterious population known as the Fremen, who are eventually led to freedom by the prophesied messianic 'one' Paul Atreides, stand for the forces for good. Whereas other Lynchian characters who personify evil, such as *Blue Velvet*'s Frank Booth, *Lost Highway*'s Mystery Man, and *Twin Peaks*' BOB, inflict their evil in quite a localized way, on particular individuals or on the inhabitants of one specific place, the evil—as it takes effect in *Dune*—resonates throughout an entire universe. In this context, the evil possesses an inter-planetary dimension. The universe of *Dune* experiences huge wars, political disputes between kingdoms, and whole populations who endure suffering, all caused by and directly connected with the impact of evil forces.

One of the most memorable aspects of Lynch's adaptation of *Dune* is the characteristic way he manages to *convey* this universally felt conception of evil through his depiction of the character of Baron Harkonnen. Although the Emperor also represents the evil forces at work in the universe of *Dune*, Baron Harkonnen really takes on the role of the Satanic figure, who is seen to be evil *personified*. This presentation of evil has both mental and physical aspects. Baron Harkonnen is evidently unhinged. The derangement and sexual deviance that manifests itself when he kills his victims gives his evil a deeply unsettling quality. And, at least superficially, his physical disgustingness—his grotesquely overweight body and his seeping boils—supplements his evil.

The Messiah and His Dreams

Cast against this background of a universe under threat from evil forces is Paul Atreides, son of Duke Leto Atreides and Lady Jessica and heir to the Dukedom of the House of Atreides on the planet Caladan. A fine student, both in his physical and intellectual training, Paul evokes much pride in his father.

Throughout the story of *Dune*, Paul has what we might call dreams or waking visions. Religious imagery saturates these experiences, serving to provide him with some warning of future evils. Ultimately, they attempt to reveal to him his true purpose as the individual who can overcome these evils. In an attempt to understand the meaning of these dreams and their role in the Duniverse, we might recall some of the stories in the Old Testament, those in which God speaks to particular individuals—and reveals Himself to them—through their dreams. Many individuals in the Bible, such as Joseph, Jacob, Moses, Abraham, Mary, and Mary's sister Elizabeth (the mother of John the Baptist), underwent such prophetic experiences.

Applied in the case of a messianic figure such as Paul Atreides, we might think of this experience as reminiscent of a case in which God the father figure reveals himself to God the son, warning him—through prophetic visions—of the evil that he must conquer.

The biblical idea present here is that these dreams can be said to reveal the *will* of God, or God's nature, and, as such, they function as a revelation for religious believers. In *Dune* these dreams are represented as a kind of spiritual awakening. This fact is perhaps most obviously revealed by the dictum repeated throughout the film that *the sleeper must awaken*. In this regard, this idea of God the father speaking to God the son is given some figurative expression in an early scene, when Duke Leto Atreides—in a deeply personal and fatherly moment—says to his son Paul that "A person needs new experiences. . . . Without change something sleeps inside us. . . . The sleeper must awaken." The idea implicit in the Duke's message—as it has been throughout Paul's dreams—is that one must awaken from such dreams profoundly changed and spiritually stronger.

As the film makes clear, a messiah had long been prophesized for the Duniverse. As Princess Irulan says in her opening monologue: "the Fremen have long held a prophecy, that a man would come, a messiah, who would lead them to true freedom." These waking vision scenes provide us with a precursor to the messianic qualities that Paul later exhibits as the man who leads the Fremen to freedom.

The Problem of Evil

The spiritual and religious content exhibited in *Dune* isn't limited to that presented in Paul's dreams. From the outset of the film, again in the opening monologue by Princess Irulan, we learn that "the spice extends life, the spice expands consciousness." Throughout the film the main characters exhibit a belief in God and acknowledge God's presence. Consider, for instance, the religious faith exhibited in the exchange between Duncan and Paul. Duncan says, "May the hand of God be with you;" Paul replies, "May the hand of God be with us all, Duncan."

Such elements of religious belief, when coupled with the universality of evil depicted in the Duniverse, raise the philosophical topic of "the problem of evil," which philosophers of religion have discussed for thousands of years. The philosophical problem of evil brings into doubt belief in the existence of God.

In the Judeo-Christian tradition, God has three defining characteristics. First, He is held to be *omnipotent*. In other words, he has unlimited power to do whatever He wishes. If we consider how this manifests itself in the case of dreams, for instance, then we see how God is able to ensure that individuals such as Paul do dream and are spiritually awoken as a result of these dreams. The second characteristic is that God is *omniscient*, which means that He is all knowing. In this sense, He will have knowledge of everything, which includes knowledge of the future and so He will be able to provide individuals with prophetic messages through their dreams. The third characteristic is that He is *omnibenevolent*. Since He is *all good*, He therefore performs no evil deeds.

And yet evil exists in the world. Harkonnens kill people for their own purposes; Fremen live harsh lives in an unforgiving desert that worms and sandstorms destroy. If God is all powerful, all knowing, and wholly good, then why do things like evil, pain, and suffering exist in the world? Why does God allow them to exist?

Some philosophers think that the problem of evil casts serious doubt on, or even refutes, the existence of God. They claim that the idea of a supposedly wholly good God, who nevertheless permits evil in the world, despite being all powerful and therefore able to prevent it, proves an incoherent idea. We might regard this as the *logical* problem of the problem of evil. The logical problem is that the Judeo-Christian idea of God is simply incompatible with evil and suffering. Since evil and suffering undeniably exist in the world, the logical problem might be thought to simply refute the idea that there is a God.

Some, however, use human freedom as a way of defending religious belief in the existence of God. As we shall see, the subject of freedom as it relates to the problem of evil raises some interesting questions with regard to the evil forces at work in the Duniverse. Perhaps the most common amongst these defenses against the problem of evil is one that is known as "the free will defense." The *Dune* saga, however, presents an alternative freedom-based response to the problem of evil, one where goodness appears to emerge from evil and be defined by contrast with it.

The Free Will Defense

Philosophical arguments trying to resolve the problem of evil are known as *theodicies*. The "free will defense" against the problem of evil is the most popular of these theodicies. Broadly characterized, this defense claims that God created human beings as free agents, presumably because He thought it was more advantageous for human beings to be free agents than for them to be limited by not being free (and perhaps even as a test of man's faith). As a consequence of this fact, human beings bring about the evil in the world through their free actions. According to this view, God is effectively innocent of the evil in the world—it's blamed instead on the world's population, and thus religious believers argue that the problem of evil doesn't provide a good challenge to the existence of God. So when Baron Harkonnen exercises his free will to kill Duke Leto, seduce young boys, and squeeze Arrakis to get his stock of spice, God cannot be blamed for Baron Harkonnen's actions.

Despite the initial plausibility of such a view, many philosophers have argued that certain problems plague this kind of defense. For instance, we might ask if there is any good reason to think that God couldn't create human beings in such a way that they're both free *and* always perform good acts. The Judeo-Christian God is supposedly all-powerful, after all, so why should it be impossible for Him to make it the case that humans always freely do good? Why can't He create a world of Duke Letos and Paul Atreideses and not Baron Harkonnens and Feyd-Rauthas?

Perhaps one might argue that this wouldn't be true free choice, but it still seems possible to argue that humans could still be able to choose freely between a range of good acts. As the Australian philosopher John Mackie writes:

> If there is no logical impossibility in a man's freely choosing the good on one, or on several occasions, there cannot be a logical impossibility in his freely choosing the good on every occasion. God was not, then, faced with a choice between making innocent automata and making beings who in acting freely, would sometimes go wrong: there was open to him the obvious better possibility of making beings who would act freely but always go right. Clearly his failure to avail himself of this possibility is inconsistent with his being both omnipotent and wholly good. (p. 231)

Perhaps a more significant objection to the free will defense can be made apparent if we distinguish between two kinds of evil that exist in the world: *moral evil*, on the one hand, and *natural evil*, on the other. Moral evil, we might say, is evil brought about by human beings or other moral agents. Feyd-Rautha poisons his blade and kills the Atreides gladiator. By contrast, natural evil results from the forces of nature. A worm hears a spice crawler and attacks it, taking spice, men, women, and machine with it.

This distinction raises an objection to the free-will defense. Take the example of the sandworm destroying the spice crawler. If we adhere to this distinction between moral evil and natural evil, we might say that this evil was caused, not by any particular human being, but by the forces of nature. It seems difficult to imagine how the free will of any particular individual or by a range of individuals caused this evil. It seems that God must cause at least *some* of the evil in the world.

Religiously motivated philosophers have been keen to respond to this objection. Some have invoked the existence of "fallen angels" in order to explain natural evil. So although we might argue that the natural evil cannot be attributed to the free will of humans, it might be attributed to the free will of such fallen angels. However, one problem here is that, in order to argue for their desired conclusion—that there is a God, these religiously motivated philosophers are relying on the existence of another, equally unexplained form of supernatural entity.

Other philosophers on the side of the free-will defense have provided a potentially more plausible response. They have argued that natural evil *is* ultimately brought about as a result of human free will because, with their free will, human beings have corrupted the natural order of things with their continual sinning. They have in mind examples such as global warming. Such an argument claims that human beings aren't good stewards of the environment, and this explains why there's natural evil.

Lynch's *Dune* provides a different response. It appears to offer figurative expression to something like the converse of the role human freedom plays in the free-will defense. In *Dune*, freedom arises against the background of evil. We see a population enslaved by evil and who are subsequently freed from evil. We might view this evil as a way of defining goodness.

The Emergence of Good from Evil

One way to think about the existence of evil in the world, and to reconcile it with religious belief and the existence of God, would be to think that the existence of evil and suffering provides a necessary condition for the existence of good. Although *sympathy* and *compassion* as moral virtues, for instance, rest their existence on preceding suffering, there's also a more general point here about the relation between good and evil.

Lynch's *Dune* gives figurative expression to this idea. One might argue that the Fremen comprise an essentially dormant race whose "goodness" is only awoken in them by the battle against evil forces. Here, *goodness* is a sleeper that must awaken. One of the most important themes in *Dune* is the idea of a liberation of a people. After realizing his potential and adopting the role of the messianic figure, Paul Atreides leads the Fremen to their freedom.

There's an interesting parallel here with the story of Christ. According to the Christian doctrine, human beings are sinners and Christ, who is free from sin, dies for—and so pays for—our sins, and thus human beings are set free. Though Paul doesn't die in his role as the Fremen savior, he's Christ-like insofar as he sets a population free from that which enslaved them. Evil forces first enslaved the Fremen, and then a messiah set them free. Without this evil presence, the Fremen would have nothing to fight against, and there would, therefore, be no sense in which their "goodness" could manifest itself. So we might think that the concepts of "good" and "evil" depend on one another for their definitions: one literally cannot exist without the other. According to this view, the fact that evil is necessary for the existence of good overcomes the problem of evil.

Through this idea of liberation, therefore, we can see *Dune* representing "good" and "goodness" as something that emerges from evil. So, in contrast to work like *Twin Peaks* and *Mulholland Drive,* where Lynch depicts evil as the dominant and all conquering force, *Dune* presents us with an alternative way of looking at evil, a way that is for the most part optimistic and empowering. Thus the film addresses the problem of evil in an interesting way. It takes the notion of freedom and argues, not that the free will of human beings brings about the evil in the world (as in "the free-will defense"), but that the very idea of goodness is to be defined against this background of liberation or freedom from evil. To take one example, Paul is defined as good against the background provided by Baron Harkonnen.

Conceiving of the existence of evil as a necessary condition for the existence of good seems a promising way to account for the problem of evil. However, there are problems with addressing the problem of evil in this way.

Consider a problem that we might call the evidential problem. This problem raises the question of why there is so much evil and suffering in the world. So this objection doesn't call into question the fact that some evil and suffering exist (as in the logical problem).

Rather, the evidential problem objects specifically to the quantity of the evil and suffering that exists in the world. So it asks, not why there is evil in the world, but instead why there is *so much* evil in the world. We would only need a small amount of evil in the world for good to be defined by contrast to it. So the evil in the world of *Dune*—like the evil in our world—seems far too great in terms of its quantity to render this explanation without problems.

Another problem here is that the Judeo-Christian God is supposed to be a personal God—a God who has a personal relationship with each of us. In accordance with this idea, God cannot be a utilitarian God—He cannot simply be trying to maximize the good for the greatest number, because this would appear to transgress the personal relationship God supposedly has with each of us. After all, He is supposed to care for all human beings equally. It seems unlikely that he would want to cause pain and suffering for any particular individual in order to maximize good for the greatest number.

So although Lynch's *Dune* can appear to provide some figurative expression to a response to the problem of evil that says that the existence of some evil is necessary in order to define goodness, this account faces a challenge from the evidential problem and from the fact that it views God as impersonal in His nature. Such an account does, however, seem to be in line with *Dune*'s theme of spiritual growth and struggle over adversity, a theme made very apparent throughout Paul's attempt to liberate the Fremen. On this view, there's a sense in which the evil generates good in terms of the way that an individual responds to it. As the contemporary British philosopher John Hick writes, echoing the message in Duke Leto Atreides' fatherly advice to his son:

> A world without problems, difficulties, perils, and hardships would be morally static. For moral and spiritual growth comes through response to challenges; and in a paradise there would be no challenges. (*Evil and the God of Love*, p. 372)

In the case of *Dune*, we might say then that it's precisely in the *way* that one responds to evil that reveals *how* the sleeper must awaken.[1]

Translated by:
SIMON RICHES

---

[1] Thanks to Anna Ferguson, Jill Riches, Sophie Archer, and Jeffery Nicholas for comments on earlier drafts.

Self of Muad'Dib

A Ghola of a Chance

"You know what you let get away, Daniel?" she demanded, coming up beside him. "The Master had a nullentropy tube in his chest. Full of ghola cells, too!"

"I saw it."

"That's why you let them get away!"

"Didn't let them." His pruning shears went snick-snick. "Gholas. He's welcome to them."

—Chapterhouse Dune

Duncan Idaho lies on the floor of a Harkonnen no-chamber on Gammu, twitching in agony, mind in turmoil. He remembers being raised by his sweet mother. She was tortured and killed by the Harkonnen beasts . . . and simultaneously he remembers a second childhood, also his, being reared on Gammu and trained by the Bene Gesserit witches. His memory is like double-vision, meshing and splitting. Worse still, he remembers dying. He died on Arrakis, fighting off nineteen Sardaukar so Paul and Jessica could escape. Where am I? When is this? You can hear his thought screaming from him, Who am I?

His question is our question. Is this Duncan the same Duncan Idaho we come to respect and admire in *Dune*? Does a ghola clone, its original memories reactivated, bear the same relation of personal identity to its original self as people like us do?

Gholas present us with special problems to do with their identity. And this particular ghola is very special. The Tleilaxu have printed something extra on his genes: as well as the memories of his original self, this Duncan also carries hidden inside the memories of all

131

the serial Idahos from Hayt to the last Duncan who served and betrayed the God-Emperor. The Bene Tleilax have primed these serial memories to reactivate in the Duncan when he has sex with an Honored Matre. (It works, too. Talk about a rude awakening!) When all those lives explode into his consciousness, and he successfully assimilates them, is the final Duncan, Duncan? It seems pretty far-fetched—even for great science-fiction like Frank Herbert's—that a clone alive centuries after its original and crammed with consciousness of the experiences of so many, many lifetimes is the same person he has always been. Frank Herbert treats whichever Duncan is before him in the *Dune* saga as Duncan. We believe that, despite first impressions, he has very good philosophical reason for doing so.

The Ghola in the Machine

In the *Dune* saga, a ghola is a clone created from cells that have been collected from a corpse and cultivated in an axolotl tank. More than just clones, gholas are a re-creation of a person's body after death. The mere creation of the flesh does not bring with it the relation of personal identity, however. In Herbert's Duniverse, a ghola original consciousness can be reawakened, with all its memories intact and available to the ghola, becoming a fusion of the ghola and the person he or she was created from. The reawakening occurs always through a profound, extremely painful, and usually highly personal crisis.

The Bene Tleilax, a civilization of xenophobic, religious zealots who are geniuses of genetic engineering, are the exclusive creators of gholas. The Tleilaxu's great secret is that they believe their work is ordained by God. They think of the genetic code as "the language of God." Their suspiciously homely, elfin looks aside (which may be insultingly manufactured to placate), most of the bad press they get results from the fact that they run traffic in products like slaves, organs, and genetic engineering to anybody who can meet their prices. The Tleilaxu horrify others because the bodies of sentient persons are to them merely the raw material for their genetic trade.

Careful though! The Bene Tleilax aren't mere businessmen. They traffic with the mainstream Imperium for their own ends—chiefly, a religious belief in their predestined ascendancy that reaches its climax in *Heretics of Dune*, only to fail. What then do they want with the gholas? The first ghola we're introduced to is Hayt, a genetic recreation of the Swordmaster Duncan Idaho. This ghola cannot access his memories, and the history that precedes his introduction in *Dune Messiah* indicates that the Tleilaxu have not yet managed to induce the memories of the original in gholas. Gholas are at first a minor side-project for the Tleilaxu.

The ghola Hayt is given to Emperor Paul Muad'Dib by the Tleilaxu. The gift's surface purpose is clearly a façade, but even Paul Atreides can't see that the ghola is meant to kill him at the prompt of a command implanted in him under post-hypnotic suggestion. The assassination attempt fails. But, as the Tleilaxu hoped, the stress of attempting to kill someone who was deeply loved in the ghola's previous life breaks the mental barrier between the ghola's consciousness and the life-memories of the original. The ghola who knew himself as Hayt recovers the memories of the original, resuming the identity of Duncan Idaho.

Plans within plans: the assassination attempt does not succeed, but now the Bene Tleilax have new leverage. Paul's beloved concubine Chani has just died. The Bene Tleilax can, if the grieving Paul wishes, replace her with a ghola complete with her original memories; a singular political bargaining chip!

Paul-Muad'Dib's son, the God-Emperor Leto II purchases a series of Duncan Idaho gholas with restored memories of the original Idaho. Leto II requests them over a period of 3,500 years, both for his breeding program and for their company. Only the memories of the original Duncan Idaho are reawakened and available to them, presumably because all of the gholas, of whom there are hundreds, are created from cells taken from the same physical body, the corpse of the original Duncan Idaho who died in battle in *Dune*.

Later, in *Heretics of Dune*, the Bene Gesserit become consumers of the Tleilaxu's Duncan Idaho gholas. The last of these Duncan gholas recovers his memories, but also recovers the memories of all his ghola incarnations. The capacity of gholas to recapture past lives changes the nature of the Tleilaxu Masters themselves: Masters grow gholas of themselves in axolotl tanks. Every Master is "recreated" upon his death with recovered memories, accumulating many iterations of knowledge and experience. This confirms what we and the Bene Gesserit have long suspected: the Tleilaxu really wanted a virtual immortality out of their minor side-project of making gholas.

Let's Get Physical

A clever fictional device in Herbert's Duniverse is that memory is physically stored in the genes. There are different kinds of memory: factual memory, procedural memory of techniques and how to perform tasks, and experiential memory of what it was like to sense, feel, and think at a given time and place. Memories of past lives become present to the consciousness of Bene Gesserit in the Spice Agony as Other Memory. These are memories of their ancestors, come back to haunt them—in Alia's case, when she's possessed by her evil grandfather Baron Harkonnen, literally haunted. For gholas, the situation is different. They're clones from original cells saved and regrown in the Tleilaxu axolotl tanks, not ancestors.

Our question is, Is the final Duncan the same person as Duncan Idaho?

A simple answer would be that Hayt, the first Duncan ghola, is Duncan Idaho because Hayt's body is physically continuous with the original Idaho. Hayt's body was grown from cells that were physically part of the original Idaho. Presumably also Hayt has exactly the same genetic structure as Idaho. The memories were stored in his physiology, but it is the physiology that makes Hayt the same person as Duncan Idaho. Same body, same man.

Physical criteria are practical, real-world entities and they are easily measurable and observable. They're the common-sense criteria for determining whether somebody is the same person as somebody else, (for example whether Samuel Clemens is the same person as Mark Twain). Consult the physical evidence, make a decision. In general, this suffices in the real world of today, outside the fictional Duniverse. The way to tell a clone from its original is by tracking the physical bodies though space and time. One, the original, was born of man and woman, conceived the old-fashioned way. The other, the clone, conceived in a test tube years after its original. It seems as though the two—the original and the clone—would be different persons due to the varying trajectory of their physical histories.

In the case of gholas, physical criteria might also give us a nice, neat principled distinction between the final Duncan and the universe's other contender for most senior citizen, Leto II, the God-Emperor. Relatively speaking, Leto is nearly as long-lived, but intuitively he seems a much more singular person. Same body, no breaks in time. One birth, one lifetime, one death; one particular individual. Not the Duncans' many lives, many deaths, many re-creations.

Sadly, concentrating on the physical lacks a certain nuance. In the ordinary non-fictional cases we're the same physical object over time, mostly because we perceive gradual changes in our physical bodies. Over time, our allowances for the kinds of changes we accept adapts to our technologies. Imagine the reaction of a tenth-century physician to the notion of a heart transplant. Given what people understood about the human condition, they would have thought the essential identity of a person changed because of the heart-transplant procedure. We can accept heart transplantation now. Even face transplants! But what would we make of a brain transplant?

It seems that if physical continuity isn't enough for us to establish identity in the ordinary non-fiction cases, we certainly can't rely on it for a concept as speculative as Herbert's ghola. Furthermore, tracking the physical, such as in the case of gholas the physical human cells, doesn't really speak to what seems exceptional about the final Duncan ghola. He remembers all his past serial lifetimes, which somehow makes him qualitatively different from the previous Duncans in the series. The final Duncan's personality also differs from other post-awakening Duncans because it contains so many, many more memories – and new powers such as Mentat awareness, Zensunni philosophy, and Truthsaying.

As Duncan As Far as Mind's Eye Can See

Simple answers look attractive, but their beauty is skin-deep. Since we don't know precisely how the Tleilaxu implanted the extra serial memories into the final Duncan, we can't decide whether there's any physical continuity at all between that ghola and any past Duncans except the original. And it's the final Duncan whom we feel requires the most explanation. A psychological criterion for personal identity may help us out where a physical criterion doesn't.

In 1690 in his *An Essay on Human Understanding*, John Locke explores what it is for a person to be self-same, that is to say, be one person and remain that same person over the course of time. Sameness of person is marked out by unity of consciousness. "Self is that conscious thinking thing," Locke writes, "which is sensible, or conscious of pleasure and pain, capable of happiness or misery, and so is concerned for it self as far as that consciousness extends." So, if an individual can, within their consciousness of the present, repeat the experience of a past action with the same consciousness they had of it originally, then the individual is the self-same person. In other words, can they remember it?

Locke argues that insistence on physical criteria leads to counterintuitive results. Hayt might share the same physical matter (or genetically-determined physiological structure) as the original Duncan, but it would make no sense to call Hayt the Swordmaster of the Ginaz. When Hayt is first presented to Paul Atreides as a gift to the Lion Throne, Paul asks him if he remembers anything of Duncan Idaho. Hayt replies that certain voices such as Paul's bring him pleasure, and a sword or a thopter's controls fit into his hand as though once-familiar. He believes this is nothing more than a pattern set in his genes. (As is later discovered, they are more like unconscious memories.)

Still, without proper consciousness connecting them, Locke may have to admit that Hayt, or any of Leto's Duncans, is not Duncan Idaho until the original memories are reawakened. Only when they are united in consciousness does Locke's "sameness of person" apply to Hayt, the second Idaho. This is why it makes sense that he goads Stilgar into killing him, dying for a second time out of the old loyalty to House Atreides. It's as much Hayt's loyalty as it was his original's loyalty, now that he is conscious of it again.

Locke kick-starts modern philosophical discussion about personal identity—a discussion that's still ongoing. Personal identity is a complicated affair, and memory is at the center of it, as you will see also in Adam Ferner's chapter "Memories Are Made of Spice" where Locke pops up in regards to the Bene Gesserit and their Other Memory. However, unlike the Bene Gesserit Sisters, gholas supposedly recover their own original self's former memories, not those of their ancestors. Gholas, being clones, somehow or other share the physical matter, biology, or genetic structure of their original selves. And unlike the Sisters, gholas appear to merge consciousness with their recovered original selves. To understand personal identity for especially complicated beings like gholas, we need to go beyond Locke. We need to go neo-Lockean.

I Survived My Past Self and All I Got Was This T-shirt

Derek Parfit is a Fellow at Oxford's All Souls College with a special interest in personal identity and a neo-Lockean spirit. In his 1984 book *Reasons and Persons*, Parfit took Locke's theory to its logical extreme.

Parfit argues that by 'consciousness', Locke cannot only mean memory. For one thing, consciousness and memory are different faculties with different objects. Consciousness is the immediate knowledge of your present, memory is the immediate knowledge of your past. And then there's intention, your immediate knowledge of how you will act in the future. Intention is, when combined with a desire, the thing that determines your actions.

Parfit considers all of these and other, unspecified but relevant psychological connections as alike. You have psychological connectedness with a past self whenever there's a particular direct psychological connection between the two selves. When you have enough direct psychological connections between your present self and a past self, you and they are strongly connected. Psychological continuity is the holding of overlapping chains of strong connectedness. Connectedness helps us understand how Leto is still Leto despite having changed, as all creatures in time do, and having presumably forgotten some things in his boyhood three millennia ago. Leto has always had enough direct psychological connections from week to week, year to year, with enough overlap, so that even though he has lost some connections, the overlapping chains make him the same person.

Parfit slips by us an argument for a new language of identity. Strictly speaking identity is formally a relation that does not admit of degrees: Mark Twain and Samuel Clemens are either utterly identical with each other, or else they are completely different persons. Holding enough direct psychological connections is equivalent to retaining every single psychological connection—and not even Leto does that! A few memories and intentions are lost here and there, many others gained, as you move through time. The God-Emperor is the same person as the young Leto only in the sense that he has survived his past, younger self to a degree. All the word 'identity' signals is that somebody has the usual close relations of survival. Normally, particular, usual and close relations hold between yourself and your past and future selves. Normally—but not necessarily. In other words, Parfit argues, don't assume that what matters is the concept of identity, with its particular formal properties. Really, what matters is survival. But that's okay, because all people ever have is a relation of survival.

All the relations that are significant to psychological continuity get redescribed in the new language of survival. Memory becomes quasi-memory. You appear to remember an experience; that you appear to remember having that experience is dependent on the fact that somebody did have the experience; the apparent memory is dependent on the experience as would be a memory. No presupposition of personal identity, no circularity there. Intention becomes quasi-intention and so forth. Survival itself is like a quasi-identity.

Conversation with Mother Superior

The most crucial scene in answering our question as to whether it's right to treat the final Duncan as the same person as Duncan Idaho occurs in the no-ship grounded on Chapterhouse, the Bene Gesserit home planet. The Duncan isn't allowed out of the no-ship, because that would reveal him to the Honored Matres' prescient watchers; he does not bear Siona's genetic marker which would hide him from oracles.

Duncan is standing in the ship's Great Hold when Reverend Mother Superior Darwi Odrade confronts him. The Sisterhood suspects that Idaho remembers more than one ghola lifetime. Recognizing that Odrade wants the subterfuge to end because there's no time to waste, he confesses.

"Tell me about your serial memories," she orders him.

Duncan tells her, "I know those . . . lives. It's like one lifetime" (*Chapterhouse Dune*).

Our questions stand, however. We're happy to allow that Leto II is as psychologically continuous as any mere mortal. Duncan's many deaths and rebirths seem strikingly different from Leto and everyone else. Are any of the Duncans as psychologically continuous as Leto is? Could somebody be strongly connected and psychologically continuous if they die and have been reborn? As many times as Duncan has? Even once?

Parfit suggests three versions of the relation to meet a psychological criterion of personal identity over time. On the narrow version, the right cause must be and is only the normal cause. On the wide version, the right cause must be any reliable cause. On the widest version, the right cause may be any cause.

The widest version plays fast and loose, and the Duncan surely meets that. The Duncan also meets the wide version. We know the reactivation of serial memories works reliably because we have observed it in other Duncan gholas as well as in, we discover, the Tleilaxu Masters, who have probably been using serial ghola technology to achieve virtual immortality since Muad'Dib's time.

On the narrow version, well, nothing beats normal people's strong psychological connectedness. However, "normal," to use the word in its ordinary sense, depends on social and historical context. In a universe where there are gholas, what counts as normal has already shifted. With gholas that remember the past lives of their original selves, normal has shifted even more. Importantly, this isn't just because as readers we suspend disbelief. The Tleilaxu have made the practice commonplace, and the Bene Gesserit's swift accommodation of the revelation that their Duncan is effectively a five-thousand-year-old man normalizes it all the more.

It's a compelling and familiar attitude that times change, technologies change, and so too does the status quo. Yet we ought to be suspicious. Normality does not always make a good norm of judgment. The Bene Tleilax and the Bene Gesserit treat serial gholas as having something like the normal relationship of personal identity normal people do. Fine . . . but should they? Is there a good reason to?

Memory is the key. Why should any of the Duncans treat the apparent memories that come rushing back to them at awakening as genuinely his? After all, the gholas did not live those lives, did not learn how to fly an ornithopter or handle a sword. All of that happened to and rightly belongs to somebody else long dead. Worse than some hi-falutin' sophistical parse like quasi-memory, these might just as well be treated as pseudo-memories. Why doesn't the Duncan treat them as, say, veridical hallucinations? Hallucinatory because much as they resemble having an ordinary memory, they aren't his memories but some other man's. Veridical because it must be admitted that each reawakened memory is an historical datum that something happened just like that to the original when they were alive.

Given the challenges facing Locke's theory of personal identity, maybe the reading was wrong from the start.

Schism of the Neo-Lockeans

In the last twenty years a rival theory has developed: narrative theory. Narrative theorists style themselves like Parfit as neo-Lockeans but break with the traditional reading of Locke. Marya Schechtman, one of narrative theory's leading lights, wonders whether perhaps Locke believed there is a subtle, sophisticated relationship between consciousness and memory, a relationship of feedback and interpretation.

In her ground-breaking book *The Constitution of Selves*, she argues that self is the persisting subject of experience but no passive or reactive detached perceiver. Selves are actively self-concerned. Selves display engaged self-interest. We constantly monitor ourselves in an effort to control the character of our experience. Schechtman argues that the activity of self-monitoring "gives us our sense of continuation and coherence as a self, and so provides the kind of self-conception and relation to a particular past that constitutes personal identity" (Schechtman 2005, p.18). Self-monitoring is not just a double-check: it means checking, balancing and counter-balancing. Selfhood is not just being there, but doing it: dynamic, responsive, selective, partial. We see this type of behavior in many of the heroes in the *Dune* saga: the Bene Gesserit and Mentats, but Paul and Leto as well. As readers we identify with them (that word again!) because they do what we recognize in ourselves as doing.

Schechtman views Locke as seeing personal identity to be a robust, psychologically rich, and forensic definition. We selves are driven towards a unity of coherence and intelligibility so that our lives have trajectory and its episodes fit together; human beings are compelled to seek out meaningful order, or, if you prefer, narrative. Narrative theory draws on new research in philosophy and psychology into human mental development and the role of language and social environment to arrive at a startling new definition of self: to be a self is for you to be as though you were the main character in a first-person story that you are telling.

Narrative theory is a theory of self-constitution. Selfhood relies on our past and present experience being organized, partly consciously, partly unconsciously, by a set of ordering principles. The organizing scheme filters, as though a sieve or a lens, raw experiences into the unique experiential perspective. To be a self is to be such that there is a coherent and intelligible, ergo, somehow organized, "story of your life," potentially available for access, if not by you, then by members of your community. As a subject of experience, your perspective really shapes your experiences.

The form of narrativity itself is not necessarily drawn from any particular literary genre, although many narrative theorists wouldn't be surprised if humans understood and expressed their self-experience through the familiar constituents of narrative: character, story, plot, device, motif, theme, character arc and story arc. Storytelling is a universal human practice and a powerful vehicle for ordered significance and meaning, and narrative and narrative explanation is a way of our making sense of our experience as creatures of being in time.

Narrative theory also means a new meaning of memory. Remembering an event or action or experience is not a flat, emotionally impoverished cognitive access. When the Duncan remembers his mother's torture or the head wound that kills him, it is a memory thoroughly infused with feelings. Importantly, often the same feelings as were experienced at the time recur again fresh and vital, not cold and distant as a filmbook playing out before the mind's eye. The affect of the original Duncan's colorful past life is now with the ghola, coloring his present and probably explaining the different demeanor and outlook he immediately manifests after his awakening. He is integrating, as much unconsciously as consciously, a new set of procedural and experiential memories with the set collected in his pre-awakening life.

Narrative theory explains why the final Duncan on Chapterhouse treats his original's memories as his own: all of those lives have been integrated into his present consciousness. They have returned to him, all those lives, all those births, deaths, careers, friends, wives, children, across three and a half thousand years of lived existence, as much him as the memories of his one present ghola is.

My Own Duncan Idaho

J. David Velleman is Professor of Philosophy at New York University who, if you hold him up to the light at a certain angle, looks like a narrative theorist. He notices that the first-person singular pronoun "I" is a fickle fellow. On the one hand, a past self of mine might be one and the same person as me, identified at some time in the past; so, a metaphysical relation across time. Metaphysical here just means something beyond or supporting the physical. For example: I died on Arrakis and they stole my cells to clone me. On the other hand, a past self might be someone in the past whom I can think of reflexively, in the first-person: A Sardaukar got past my knives and killed me. That's a psychological relationship myself and I have because we are subjects who are on first-person terms. Our autobiographies or, better, narratives are fictions yet true. "We invent ourselves . . . but we really are the characters whom we invent" (Velleman 2006a, p. 206). The old chestnut about life being a work in progress? On narrative theory, it turns out so is the person living it: a work of art.

Why has the final Duncan's integration of his many previous serials gone so well, so apparently smoothly? Well, firstly, he now has all the reawakened powers of a Mentat, a Zensunni philosopher, and a Truthsayer at his command to aid him. Secondly, the ghola has had reawakened in him a man very much like himself. He does not have to fight these past selves off as they swarm into his consciousness as a Bene Gesserit does with her Other Memory. The Duncans are all of extremely similar personality, and even each of their pre-awakening ghola selves are unconsciously very much like their post-awakening, integrated selves.

Thirdly, and we think far and away most importantly, the final Duncan is a human self. Velleman points out that human selves have a powerful impulse to self-consistency, and in the face of an onslaught of immediate, vivid, unavoidably subjectively present experiences that are recognizably memories as though held by a man extremely similar to himself, he does what selves do. He integrates. Whether he knowingly prosecutes the integration or it just happens reflexively the way humans normally do it, does not matter. Truth and falsity are not the real issue. The final Duncan is a psychologically continuous fusion of all the past Duncans' consciousnesses and his own, present consciousness.

Selfworms of Dune

Frank Herbert seems to take this approach: persons in the fictional Duniverse vary in their shape, size, and number. There are collections of one, such as Leto II, and others whose criteria for personal identity differ radically from others. Face Dancers are both themselves and somebody else (unless they mimic too well for too long, in which case they "forget" who they were and "remember" only the mimicked individual). Reverend Mothers have within them Other Memory that is a form of consciousness they can become dangerously united with if they immerse too deeply.

Can the strange boundaries of gholas' identities help us to understand personal identity as a whole? We have to take account of these three facts

1. **The pre-awakened ghola is not the original person;**

2. **There is some distinction to be made between the naturally-occurring original and the gholas by those who inhabit the mainstream Imperium;**

3. **This distinction does not appear so clear-cut in the case of the Tleilaxu themselves and the final Duncan ghola.**

Duncan's past ghola lives become one with his own present lived consciousness when he becomes aware of them all. Integrative self-consciousness that spans and unites—properly, reunites—separate consciousnesses makes sense of the attitude that the final Duncan strikes towards his past lives, that they are one lifetime, but that's a first-personal psychological relation. It's still not "one lifetime" he led, but separate lifetimes all of the separate predecessor Duncans led. Can we revise our conception of the metaphysics of personal identity to back up his attitude?

Given that ghola technology boils down to physical re-incarnation of dead cells as living tissue grown into new human bodies, Herbert could be called a reductionist—in that he believes that being a person is not a property in its own right, that it can be reduced to some other property or set of properties. It's Duncan if it shares the same cells and the same genetic structure—a structure on which psychological states such as original memories are somehow impressed or otherwise supervene, dormant or reawakened. We think, in the example of serial gholas like the final Duncan and the Tleilaxu Masters, Herbert instead shows us that when it comes to questions of personal identity, you have to take the long view. The really long-view.

Let us consider a possible version of reductionism according to which identity still matters: four-dimensionalism. Everything that exists in the universe exists in space but also in and across time. Creatures like persons have both spatial and temporal parts. A person could be thought of, on this view as the perduring object that snakes through the fabric of space and time. This approach allows us to think of the temporal history of a person as a part of the whole person. You are more than just your physical and psychological continuity; you are your entire spatio-temporal history.

Life in 4-D

Like a sandworm: you can't have the worm without the segments or the segments without there being a worm they belong to. Persons can be thought of as the entirety of their space-time slices, their worm's length. The parts stretched across time, like slices of time, are what survive each other. The person is the sum of the whole of them, the continuant thing made up of all those slices lined up in sequences next to each other across time. Gurney Halleck steps forward as a good example. Gurney is a space-time worm who snakes in space across Giedi Prime, Caladan, Arrakis and other planets and snakes in time across the length of his normal human lifespan. The Duncans together describe a much longer selfworm that has gaps where the latest in the series of Duncan has died and only the original's cells perdure.

It's difficult to imagine how identity matters in one's relation to a distant-future person-stage. Consider Leto II who lives for three and half thousand years. On the four-dimensionalist account, at any moment he is unified with—he's part of—the same space-time continuant as his 3,500-year-old self. For you and us, though, it is extraordinarily difficult, if not psychologically impossible, to project so far into the future. We would be tempted to worry about what is temporally local to us, and let that other person (our future self) worry about things a thousand years hence. Leto II could have had exactly this reaction, for when he was a boy he was entirely human, and as he aged he transformed into a giant sandworm-human hybrid.

We would usually expect our distant-future selves to be radically different. It seems that our future selves would be different enough so that the identity relation might seem to be strained. For it would seem that virtually nothing of what actually matters in ordinary survival is present in that future person, despite the spatio-temporal identity.

Herbert's careful construction of Leto's psychological character proves instructive. The idea of time, continuance, and future is so different, because his time span reaches forward, but also because it reaches much further backwards—as he has all the memories and identities of all of his ancestors within him. Now, it might appear that some strong degree of psychological connectedness provides the unity relation between the various temporal stages of Leto II. If so, it seems to follow that the relation preserving "what matters" to Leto as self-same as himself is, as Parfit would have it, just psychological continuity.

Herbert shows us how the concept of personal identity can change, depending on our physical and psychological circumstances. Leto exists in—indeed, creates for himself—rather extraordinary physical and psychological circumstances: a human body physically fused with insensate, physically near-indestructible sandtrout in which is housed a mind with access to all his ancestor's memories and a prescient vision that sees the distant future. In full knowledge of the long-view, Leto fashions an identity that can sustain itself for a life long enough to achieve his goal: the Golden Path. At the end, he will be the same person who set these events in motion. Same man-worm, same person. The God Emperor is as much a single, continuous space-time worm as is Gurney—just one three and a half thousand years longer.

The final Duncan Idaho, who persists into the two Herbert and Anderson sequels *Hunters of Dune* and *Sandworms of Dune*, also changes our concept of personal identity. When he becomes aware of the memories from all his past ghola lives in addition to the memories of the original Duncan, he is psychologically continuous with all of those—now his—previous lives. If the Bene Tleilax have physically fused his original cells with the cellular memory traces of his serial ghola lives lived in the service of the God Emperor, then the final Duncan is at least minimally physically continuous with all of his previous lives. (The technique is not revealed. No matter. Remember that insofar as the method they use is reliable, that only serves to normalize it.)

However, unlike Leto II, Duncan's space-time worm leaves some very broken tracks across the fourth dimension, time. There are long gaps when there is no human being alive who is physically continuous with the original, only cells in storage in the Tleilaxu labs. Sometimes the original cells are both in storage and incarnated in a living Duncan. And if the final Duncan is a physical fusion of the original Duncan Idaho's cells and select cells extracted from every single one of the serial gholas too, then at least at one time the final Duncan is a partial physical and psychological survivor of all of the serial gholas put together. He is a space-time worm with segments dotted across the past five thousand years. Quite unlike the Tleilaxu

Masters, too, he has led his many different lives isolated from the other. The final Duncan's personality is a corporate entity of very similar men. All of them consciously or unconsciously influenced by the original Duncan Idaho. He is a collective consciousness, a very psychologically-tight collective.

Long-Term Identity

The overarching storyline of the *Dune* novels requires certain people to be the same person as certain other people, so the concept of personal identity really must matter in Herbert's mind. He might be making an allowance for the idea that one's identity may not be in one's control, and also is in part created by what those around us believe.

Herbert gives us a multifarious theory of identity, whose end result is that the idea really does matter, and that we care about it a great deal. Herbert also shows us that the relative state of our physical incarnation lays down the basic boundaries of persons. Further, the idea is constantly shifting, in part due to the way societies recognize, and so in their shared interpretation create new, more open definitions of person. By pushing the physiological and technological limits, we can also set new temporal limits and relationships. Herbert tells us that if we can transform ourselves into anything we would like, then we have the same dominion of the concept of identity. Depending on our technology, we can collectively fashion it into anything we like.

Herbert gives us several approaches to long-term personhood. On the ordinary understanding of identity, we assume that if there is a connection between our identities and our practical concerns, it must be one of parity. On the naive view, we expect a single thread—running from a single, accurate conception of personal identity—between our individual practical concerns and our future well-being. And the normal-lifetime practical concerns function perfectly well with our naïve sense of identity. But must this be the case? Herbert shows us that practical concerns on a large scale, for Leto, the Tleilaxu Masters and the Duncans, might bear a relation to criteria of identity that outstrip what we think of now as a normal lifetime. If Herbert's intuitions are correct— and they are—the correct criteria of identity can change depending upon the particular aspects of the mental and physical aspects of our existence.

The particular example of gholas in the Duniverse is just one way in which Herbert shows this to be true. The final Duncan becomes aware of his past ghola selves and he identifies with them as a single individual, united by the genetic and social identity makers. If we were able to be aware of past selves, we could potentially weave them into our current selves, as in the case of Bene Gesserit Reverend Mothers, and the pre-born, such as Alia, Ghanima and Leto II. Likewise, we can project our selfhood into the future if we can imaginatively anticipate survival, no matter how distant the future continuant might be. All we need is the live possibility of a distant future continuant, and we can think of that future self as one with our present self.

This kind of long-term anticipation of survival is rational, if the identity relation depends on the psychological criterion, since gholas allow the possibility of long periods of being unaware of one's identity. The final Duncan comes to understand his true identity through the capture of his past ghola memories. It's the same thing that a person with amnesia does when she regains her memories—just on a larger scale. The ghola also allows Herbert's characters to plan for their future selves—as the Tleilaxu Masters do. Master Scytale is one of a long chain of gholas of himself. Each ghola has the memories of the prior, since the cells are taken and cultivated before his death. In this case, the biological criterion of personal identity may apply, since it is possible to imagine multiple gholas of the same person (as Brian Herbert and Kevin J. Anderson do in the sequels with the Tleilaxu Master Waff). The possibility of immortality only makes sense if the genetic copies hold the same moral significance as the original. The facts about the life and body of a person can change the way in which it is understood, and its scope.

On the floor of the Harkonnen no-chamber, as the final Duncan has his original's memories wake inside him, and he accepts them as his, painful and traumatic though it is, nothing very out of the ordinary is happening in the Duniverse. Nothing extraordinary as a question of personal identity, that is. We've seen it all before, we're accustomed to it. However, making love to the Honored Matre Murbella, the memories of his every previous Duncan ghola primed to be activated by just such a scenario and bursting upon his consciousness in wave after wave, a new kind of person emerges and a new concept of what it is to be the same person over time emerges with it. A concept of identity that is comfortable with centuries-long breaks in the same person's history—or should we say the same persons' history? Same Duncans, same person.

Discoverers:
SAM GATES-SCOVELLE
STEPHANIE SEMLER

Wiping Finite Answers from an Infinite Universe

> This is the fallacy of power: ultimately it is effective only in an absolute, a limited universe. But the basic lesson of our relativistic universe is that things change. Any power must always meet a greater power. Paul Muad'Dib taught this lesson to the Sardaukar on the Plains of Arrakeen. His descendants have yet to learn the lesson for themselves.
>
> —The Preacher at Arrakeen (*Children of Dune*)

Dune, despite being galaxy-spanning space opera, is entirely about humanity. There are no aliens, no gods, and no natural disasters to guide or threaten us—only ourselves. Arguably, this focus on humanity is what makes the *Dune* saga literature. I do not doubt for a second that it is, but I would argue that the depth of Frank Herbert's analysis of humanity and its problems also makes *Dune* a work of ethical and political philosophy.

Dune doesn't just employ (in masterly fashion) the hero-myth, but inverts it, comments on it and tells us something important about heroes. And it does not just have a (brilliantly intricate) plot about intrigue, politics, and power—it teaches a whole political philosophy. Frank Herbert's true stroke of genius consisted, not in making an ecological science-fiction setting and story, but in inviting a way of thinking about humanity, history, religion, and politics as complex and interdependent—as ecosystems themselves.

One can trace this "ecological" approach through the entirety of *Dune* and most of Herbert's writing—a political philosophy which insists that technology, science, and singular courses of action for every problem are abhorrent and self-defeating. Or, in the words of the planetologist who set the many transformations of Arrakis in motion: "No more terrible disaster could befall your people than for them to fall into the hands of a Hero."

By looking at these philosophical themes, and the schools of thought common in Herbert's writing, we can gain a fuller understanding of the Butlerian Jihad and its role in the *Dune* saga. It too, was about an ethical and political choice to reject a static answer to the problems of humanity. In *God Emperor of Dune*, Leto II tells us the motivation behind it: "Humans had set those machines to usurp our sense of beauty, our necessary selfdom out of which we make living judgments. Naturally, the machines were destroyed." Leto II isn't the simplest character to grace literature, and Frank Herbert is, once again, making us work to understand exactly what happened, and what's at stake here. But what is clear, is that humanity "set up" the machines in our society and were somehow affected on a deep and important level. Because of this change in ourselves, they were eventually destroyed and banned. Another simple, neat, and wrong solution is rejected.

The Duniverse, and Herbert's writing in general, is rife with examples of such failing absolutes. Sure-fire solutions are exactly the wrong thing, no matter what the Haigh Company Employees Handbook may say. Bureaucracies become tyrannies, unless disrupted properly. Only those who accept their conditions and adapt, instead of clinging to Earth standards on new worlds, stand a chance of surviving a constantly changing universe.

But simple solutions, be they heroes, technologies, or easy answers, are so alluring. Humanity has shown a very clear historical preference for charismatic leaders who can point to some paradise over the horizon. We quickly adopt a new technology as long as it's convenient, and just as quickly forget all misgivings and drawbacks. We accept "scientific truths" as comforting blankets, when the very concept of science is to test assumptions, to be open to faults in our dearest theories and to make new, bold guesses.

Herbert is teaching the science of ecology: to accept the forces around us, work with them, and accept that the world changes us in turn. Enough power, or one perfect tool, cannot solve everything—and certainly not when that tool is static machine thinking: "The real universe is always one step beyond logic" (*Dune*).

Butler and Heidegger

One inspiration for the Butlerian Jihad is easily identified by its very name. In the nineteenth century, Samuel Butler published *Erewhon*, a book about a fictional country whose inhabitants have made a "clean sweep" of all machines. Though the purges are done for different reasons, the allusion to a human decision to get rid of certain life-altering technologies is clear.

But Herbert is not borrowing the motivation and thoughts of Samuel Butler, merely his name. And neither is the Jihad just a literary device which absolves a lazy writer from having to handle the unknown computer advances of the far future. It does set the strange stage of an almost medieval future and that Camelot feel which permeates the loyal household of Castle Caladan—but it does so much more. The Butlerian Jihad foreshadows the philosophical themes of *Dune*. It's a prophetic anticipation of certain topics with which the entire series will deal. Just like the chapter headings of the book, and Paul's earliest dreams, it hints at what will befall Paul and what threatens all of humanity.

During Paul's first trial of the Gom Jabbar, he must prove to the Reverend Mother Gaius Helen Mohiam that he is truly human. Along with the reader, he receives insights from the Bene Gesserit's vast political and historical expertise. The Reverend Mother speaks of letting the machines think for us, and how doing away with this crutch forced humanity to improve and adapt. Characteristically, Herbert goes straight for the point and skips over the cold hard facts—we're given no historical lesson on the Jihad, save that it was a societal upheaval, a religious revolt, and a change in humanity's overall course. We are told of no singular reason, fault in the system, or calamity, and, rather than assume Herbert was being forgetful or sloppy, we should conclude that no one thing started the Jihad. It was a reaction to technology that thinks for us, and addressed a problem with that technology in itself. To understand the Jihad at all, we must look at the broader issues behind it and the themes Herbert examines with it: humanity and its use of such technology.

A clear source of inspiration for Frank Herbert was German philosopher Martin Heidegger. In Herbert's small gem, *The Santaroga Barrier*, the protagonist is even named after one of Heidegger's key terms, "Dasein." In his views on machines and humanity, Herbert's work reflects the phenomenological approach to technology, which Heidegger pioneered. Heidegger famously insisted that to understand something, we should look, not to its constituent parts or inherent attributes, but at what it is to us.

Take the maker hooks of Fremen culture. When a Fremen embarking on the Hajj is hefting one, as he readies for the passing of a worm, he isn't thinking about how many standard kilos it weighs, its color, or constituent parts. He feels its weight as an extension of himself, and knows the curvature and length as intuitively as he knows the reach of his arm. At that moment, it isn't an object to him, but a part of the social and physical activity he's immersed in. There's no Fremen with a maker hook, but just the hookman. These individual relations, of extending the body and being part of a sacred cultural practice, are infinitely more interesting, authentic, and important than what metal it's made of.

Heidegger applied this realization, that the scientific and materialistic way of perceiving the world is only one perspective, to more abstract terms. Technology is not whatever tools we happen to be using or some specific level of sophistication of those tools. Rather, it's our way of using the tools and the world with them - and it's the way this use of tools and the resulting worldview changes us.

To Heidegger, the interesting feature of a windtrap is that it results from a way we have of seeing the world; as an unrefined reserve of energy, water, and other resources to be harnessed for easier use. The important thing is not the windtrap as a device, but the way of thinking about the world which leads us to built windtraps. Of course, we're not completely wrong in saying that the world consists of useful resources. But thinking of the world solely in these terms obscures what it also is. Heidegger was very critical of this way of "enframing" the world as just a number of useful assets - because it is a poor and soulless way of thinking about our universe and our fellow humans.

The Harkonnens and the empire saw the Fremen only as riffraff and sand pirates, wasting resources and making enemies by trying to subdue them. The Baron even thinks of his own soldiers as working bees; just drones to do his bidding. Duke Leto respects the unknown Fremen as a separate culture and sends Duncan Idaho to live among them, to eventually become part Fremen himself. The knowledge and friendship gained becomes the "desert power" which Paul will eventually make full use of.

If one follows Heidegger and Herbert's reading of him, the Jihad becomes a moral warning in the tradition of ancient prophecies, like the preacher from the desert who admonishes his culture, not with a specific prediction, but a warning about the current path. The Jihad speaks to us about the dangers of relying on a tool and a specific way of thinking. What the world-as-asset mindset does to you is exemplified and known beforehand. In *Dune* and beyond, Herbert shows us both the inherent fault and folly of relying on a static solution in a dynamic universe, and also the personal and moral implications such a calculating stance towards the world will impart on you.

Sardaukar Brute Force or Fremen Adaptivity?

An incisive critique of cold pragmatism runs through *Dune* and targets, not only reliance on "computer brains," but the technological worldview in which the world is a reserve of things to be harnessed for our own consumption and use. The clearest example may lie in the different ways in which the respective groups think of and treat Arrakis.

To the Harkonnen's pragmatic worldview, Arrakis is a treasure trove. When we first meet the Baron, he is exulting in his prize and his plan. He presents Arrakis to Feyd-Rautha as a precious model, likened to caramel and made of riches and diamonds. He ultimately treasures it for its function: as the trap that will defeat Duke Leto. This is the technological worldview Heidegger warned about, in a nutshell; to the Harkonnens, Dune is what it can do for them.

The Fremen outlook, which Paul acquires over time, contrasts sharply with the Harkonnen view. Dune is their home, and it dictates every detail of their lives, from the most trivial daily chores to the very goal of their culture. Though they seek to change the planet, it's not a change for personal or even collective benefit only. It's a religious dream, a part of the planet's holy role as their home. While they employ science and technology to effect this change, their approach is ecological and holistic. They have no simple, brute force plan involving imported water, which they understand would not even work in itself, but seek to gradually change the entire ecosystem to involve running water on the surface. The Fremen understand that they themselves are being formed by the planet, even as they form it.

Not so for Baron Harkonnen, who sees Arrakis as a business opportunity. Given such and such expenditures, some amount of wear and tear on equipment, and accepting certain risks, mining spice is extremely lucrative. Being true pragmatists, should this transaction became unprofitable, House Harkonnen would go back to working the whale fur market. The planet itself, and the people extracting the spice, are truly just reserves for the Empire's elite. This onesided view, which Heidegger warned against, makes both the Harkonnens and the Emperor blind to the fact that their own fate is intricately woven into that of Arrakis.

Paul's victory is cemented by understanding and exploiting these blind spots. After the Sardaukar have learned their lesson about power, he threatens to end the spice flow. In such examples, we are shown the dangers of tools and the pragmatic worldview they engender. The power structures of the universe—the Houses of the Landsraad, the Guild, the Bene Gesserit—cannot function without spice, but fail to see this almost symbiotic interdependence. When Paul threatens to destroy it forever, all their power is for nothing. When you rely on a tool completely, those that control that tool also control you—Arrakis is truly "at the hub of the universe."

The Jihad should have taught the schemers of the old Empire this: "Once men turned their thinking over to machines in the hope that this would set them free. But that only permitted other men with machines to enslave them" (*Dune*). If an entire culture relies on one thing, be it machines or spice, power structures (and the corruptible) will gather around it and eventually control that culture. Paul only made these controls blatantly obvious.

Hours before, the Sardaukar were disabused of their illusions about power. They thought themselves the strongest fighting force in the known universe; but of course technological or human development is eventually going to counter, disable, or simply defeat your vaunted power. The basis for hand-to-hand combat in the known universe, the Holtzman shield, is useless in the Arrakis desert; and someone might just master the Voice sufficiently to silence even the most adept Bene Gesserit. House Corrino bet their Empire on superior shock troops, and consequently lacked a way of dealing with the overlooked Fremen rabble on the Plains of Arrakeen. The better a tool works, the more you will trust it and the more you will depend on it—all the while setting yourself up for a bigger and bigger catastrophe. Some surprise will always come, sooner or later, and at that moment it's those who can improvise and ride the storm who will succeed.

Trusting in tools, devices, a certain amount of amassed power or wealth, or some master plan based on even the most precise of models will all blind us to the need for improvisation. It's so tempting to delude yourself that you're safe, that the road ahead is now known and chartered, and that nothing can catch you off-guard. You tend to forget the most human of strengths and advantages— that we're not just another resource, not mere machines, and not a reservoir of intellectual power. We can make new choices and adapt to the circumstances.

When Paul and Jessica are helpless in the desert, their equipment buried in a slope of sand, it's thinking outside the box that saves them. There's nothing in the paracompass manual about its acidic power base and how it can react with melange to create foam, which will stabilize a small life-or-death digging operation. A rigid thinker, or a machine, would never consider the inner workings and possibilities of the landscape; it is a flexible and open mindset which saves Paul and Jessica.

As Leto II summarizes it, the problem which the Jihad resolved was one of "a machine-attitude as much as the machines" (*God Emperor of Dune*). When everything, including people, are seen as mere tools and mechanical pieces that can be twisted to your advantage, you will inevitably overlook some aspects of the thing in question. The relationships to the computer-substitutes, Mentats, show just how closely the spirit behind the Jihad's proscriptions is honored among the various factions. House Atreides have trusted friends and allies, who are also Mentats. The Baron Harkonnen considers his Mentat as simply an instrument, another drone to be exchanged when he grows dangerous or useless, and he intensely dislikes it whenever Piter does not stick to his current assignment.

It is not surprising, therefore, that when the Baron has possessed Alia in *Children of Dune*, she begins to think in the same way. When Idaho is tasked with figuring out whether Irulan is a traitor, his curiosity and loyalty, not just to Alia but to House Atreides, lead him to question increasingly larger issues. Alia, like the Baron, becomes annoyed at this loss of focus: "But Alia longed now for a compliant machine. They could not have suffered from Idaho's limitations. You could never distrust a machine." Alia is right, of course, that the machine would do whatever asked of it, but what she calls limitations is really her husband's humanity: his curiosity and personal morals.

The true strength of the Mentat lies in the very fact that their power of computation is always a part of a human being, and never just a tool—a Mentat knows his own limitations, and won't be lured into thinking he has a path to the ultimate truth, nor all the answers. Humans may be difficult to work with at times, but co-operating and working with someone has advantages over employing a mere resource and tool. A fellow human can help you improvize, tell you when your assumptions are the real problem, and stop you from following the wrong course, when you cannot see which way you are heading yourself. Idaho continues to serve House Atreides, even when Alia is serving only herself. He can choose to direct his attention where needed and not just where it is pointed by others. This is not a weakness, but a strength.

When Total Adaption Becomes a Trap

The machine-attitude Leto II warns about is also dangerous in more than the immediate sense of easily leading you astray or failing to show you certain assumptions and innovative solutions. It's corroding to our morality and self-determination—both as individuals and as a species. Again, the problem lies in the entire way of thinking which the use of and reliance on tools invite. When you're used to dealing with machines with a determined behavior and no moral relevance, it becomes easy to see allies, political opponents, and power structures as pieces to be manipulated in some giant game. The Baron Harkonnen seems to revel in it as does Alia under his influence. When she wishes for a machine instead of human advice, she is wishing for the pure power of computation. She wants clear answers without human interference and emotions—calculation and advice reduced to another tool. She wishes, in effect, to reduce intelligence to a resource.

Here we see the moral implications of Heidegger's warning. Technology invites you to think of humans as less than they really are. Not only will their worth be counted only as worth to you, but their inner life of thoughts and emotions are reduced to what their logic can do for you and seen as another instance of mechanics—given the right input, the Mentat will provide useful answers, just like the ancient machines.

In *Without Me, You're Nothing*, a non-fiction book on the actual computer revolution going on around him, Herbert was himself unconvinced of the assumption that "your brain's functions can be reduced to mechanical rules" (p. 33). Others, such as philosopher Hubert Dreyfus, have been inspired by Heidegger to argue that computers and other formal systems depending on symbols can never imitate our way of thinking and reasoning. No amount of symbolic manipulation, they argue, can make up the experience of being alive—only provide an answer that may imitate human thinking. And even if such mimicry exceeded our own capacities, would we want them to take over all our thinking? Even the most perfectly calculated move can be wrong, as *Dune* shows and the Butlerian Jihad foreshadows.

Irulan is the one to first confront Alia with this danger of moral decay: "We fall upon decisions these days the way we fall upon an enemy—or wait and wait, which is a form of giving up, and we allow the decisions of others to move us. Have we forgotten that we were the ones who set this current flowing?" (*Children of Dune*). Alia dismisses this, she wants only to hold on to power and will do whatever it takes to achieve that end. But Irulan's critique is incisive; in choosing to only play the great game of politics, Alia is never making any real choices. Her personal motives and beliefs, if they exist, are ignored as impractical. She is so controlled by political necessities that one has to ask, What did Alia, as a person, really choose to do? Was any action truly her own, and not dictated by circumstances?

This is the same dilemma which the Jihad answered so forcefully, on the level of the species. Even if computers always found the correct answer, what would we be if we let them control our lives? When every answer is given, life runs on autopilot—as does Paul's in *Dune Messiah*. The warning of the Great Revolt, about giving up our "selfdom," is played out in full after the action ride and heroics of *Dune*. When the theatrics slow to a halt and the throne is won, we're forced to face facts: Paul's Jihad is a bloody conquest, the Fremen are being corrupted from within, and Paul was a flawed hero at best. His use of the Fremen has debased them, reduced them to a tool and eventually takes their pride. Even his sietch brother Stilgar becomes a zealot: "It was a lessening of the man," Paul reflects already in the last chapter of *Dune*. "I have seen a friend become a worshiper."

Perhaps most importantly, we learn that Paul's greatest "weapon," prescience, is a trap and a curse.

Having visions of the future is obviously rather practical when you have a war to win and political opponents to outmaneuver. So Paul chooses the best move by looking at what the outcome will be. Perfect advice, perfect action, every time. It seems Paul has beaten the system and truly found a "technological tool" which allows him to win every time and ensures there won't be any nasty surprises.

But obviously he will have to "stay on the path." Once he's found the route to the best outcome, he will have to keep following it. Considering how a choice of words or small deviation in action can have huge effects further down the path, Paul can only be safe while he keeps strictly to the vision. And as he becomes increasingly addicted and resistant to the spice itself, he needs increasing accuracy from his visions in order to stay on the path. He is becoming addicted to the same tool which he leveraged in order to tumble the previous dynasty. Again, the illusion of the neutral tool that can be wielded as an unproblematic asset is exposed.

The technological way of thinking and acting has costs, which that very same worldview will hide from you. Paul's prescience did achieve his political goals, but according to Bronso of Ix, it was the tool of prophecy which killed him: "There can be only one answer, that completely accurate and total prediction is lethal" (*Dune Messiah*).

That same historian was killed by the Qizarate for suggesting Paul had lost his humanity, yet it's clear that his vision was costing him just that: He hardly notices going blind—he has seen everything around him before. He grows distant and morose, as life becomes a rerun of a dream. And he walks with heavy steps to see his daughter, as he knows what news the doctors have of Chani. Leto II will eventually name this "holy boredom." What good is a life with no surprises and no "living judgments" to make?

Paul is trapped on autopilot in the same manner one can imagine those living at the time of the Jihad were. Even if the ancient machines were perfect, logical advisors, they did not allow any true respect for human freedom, just like Paul's prescience doesn't.

In a way, this is a problem of perfect adaptation. Paul is completely tuned into the entire universe, able to do exactly what is needed to help himself best at any given turn. He reacts perfectly to the circumstances—but, in doing so, he is also perfectly controlled by them. Perfect advice leaves you with no real options. In the Jihad, humanity decided that self-determination and settling their own destiny and values were more important than leisurely living.

The Test of Humanity

The lure that some future technology will save us, of a messiah to lead us to paradise, or a perfect tool that will make our lives easy is undeniably strong—the first thing Alia begins to wish for, as she spirals into madness, is indeed the same all-powerful prescience which claimed her brother. But when properly thought through, or showcased as it is in *Dune*, the implication of a "tool" which can guide your very life are horrifying: Imagine your mobile phone advising you, at all times and without error, how best to do anything. Which job to take, which boy or girl to ask out or marry, and when to cross the street—without knowing why this or that choice is right or practical. When lying on your deathbed, having followed every advice, no decision your own—that hand reaching out to smash the "computer brain" which lived your life for you is an inner Butlerian Jihad.

Paul's long years as emperor, where every second was known before it happened, held a similar horror. His son eventually wrests mankind free from all prescience by breeding humans who are hidden, even from himself. Not surprisingly, this similarity between walking one prescience-laid path, or a computer-generated one, is seen most clearly by Leto II through his Other Memory: "Humans must set their own guidelines. This is not something machines can do." He aims to free humanity, from any centralization and especially from the tool of prescience, which is powerful enough to tie humanity together to share one fate, just like the dependency on spice tied the old empire together in the hub of Arrakis.

All this is done in order to ensure our survival, and the self-determination without which we're not truly human - not as individuals and not as a species. Once again, Herbert turns the myth of the hero upside down. The great Tyrant, in the form of a monstrous worm, is the true savior of humanity. When the story of the Atreides ascendancy begins, Paul is tested for being truly human, and in the end, Leto II is the one to prove himself willing to suffer for all humanity. He stays in the trap of prescience, so he may destroy that terrible tool itself, removing a threat to his kind. In the same move, Frank Herbert also deftly reverses the science fiction cliché of the "cool McGuffin" which drives the plot and saves the day—the tool's existence itself becomes the danger!

The Butlerian Jihad, then, is a warning. In the tradition of Greek tragedies, it's a warning the characters in *Dune* do not heed, and must learn again with prescience playing the part of the dangerous tool. Herbert's political warning is not just against solutions that are too simple, but against all singular solutions—any one-track plan is potentially monstrous. This need not be a Luddite call to arms, that we should rid ourselves of all these thinking machines before they lure our grandchildren into unthinking ennui and stagnation. Nor is it a claim that we should never think ahead and plan for tomorrow.

In *Without Me, You're Nothing*, Herbert does not rail against computers: "it is not our tools that are at fault, it's how we use those tools and the beliefs we invest in them" (p. 73). The book tries instead to raise awareness about computers, cautions us on what we chose to use them for, and insists that they should be controlled by individuals and not some power elite who hold the understanding, power and kill switch to our computers and content. *Dune* urges us to consider the stock we put in any technological solution, and to ask when something like a computer begins living our lives for us: When they send our mail? Solve algebra? Plan our schedules? Tell us which acquaintance is close enough to grab a beer with, or who it is time you reconnect with?

The moral peril of thinking machines is the possibility that we let them take over our human reasoning: both in our own lives, and as a culture and species. Even if the advice was exactly right, there's a nobility to making our own judgments, which we should not dismiss - human life is "not a problem to be solved, but a reality to be experienced" (*Children of Dune*).

Phenomenological philosophy agrees, and stresses that our human way of being and thinking is something radically other than any machine mimicry—we cannot exchange one for the other without losing, in the process, some of that which makes us human. Blindly using an economic formula, a computer expert system or having a guru you trust implicitly, means you have delegated certain mental tasks outside yourself. Assign enough thinking to someone or something else, and you have hollowed yourself out. No matter the freedom of their political system, any culture which unquestioningly follows a leader, or any planning tool, science or technology, has given up some part of our essential human self-determination.

From: Dar-es-Balat II
Occasion and date: unknown.

Memories Are Made of Spice

> Someone eased her to a sitting position. She saw the old Reverend Mother Ramallo being brought to sit beside her on the carpeted ledge. A dry hand touched her neck.
>
> And there was another psychokinesthetic mote within her awareness! Jessica tried to reject it, but the mote swept closer . . . closer.
>
> They touched!
>
> It was like an ultimate simpatico, being two people at once: not telepathy, but mutual awareness.
>
> With the old Reverend Mother!
>
> —*Dune*

The Lady Jessica is a peculiar person. By drinking the last liquid breath of a drowned sandworm, she has absorbed her predecessors' living thoughts. She now stands as the latest link in an unbroken chain of consciousness that reaches back to the very first sayyadina, Raquella Berto-Anirul. As a newly initiated Reverend Mother, Jessica can remember the thoughts of all those who have suffered the Spice Agony. And her unborn daughter, the Abomination Alia, shares this dubious pleasure. She too has those same memories that reach from her mother back to the first Reverend Mother.

Jessica is understandably shaken by her ordeal. However, some solace might have come from knowing that, millennia before, a British philosopher named John Locke had tried to make sense of her situation. In his *Essay Concerning Human Understanding* Locke tries to understand exactly how memories and consciousness contribute to being a person. According to his theory of "personal identity," our Lady Jessica would be an extremely peculiar person indeed. With Shai-hulud's favor we'll understand why.

Who Is This Muad'Dib?

Who is the new religious leader on Arrakis? Enslaved by the Harkonnen barony, Thufir Hawat pondered this very question. Fremen attacks had increased on Arrakis, and they rallied to the cry of "Muad'Dib." Thufir couldn't have guessed, and would never have dared dream, that it was Paul Atreides, his most adept pupil, who "made drums from the skins of his enemies" (allegedly) and went by the name "Muad'Dib." The Fremen messiah is the same man as Paul Atreides. Paul Atreides is identical to Muad'Dib. (This identity relation doesn't half unnerve the old Baron when he finds out.)

Identity relations also hold *over time*. The older Paul "even-his-name-is-a-killing-word" Muad'Dib is also identical with the younger Atreides na-Duke, who lived on Caladan years before. Even though the toddler Paul looks nothing like the later Emperor Paul they are, we intuitively think, one and the same person. When Locke talks about "personal identity," he's investigating why, precisely, this is—what conditions a person must meet to stay the same person. We generally call these conditions "persistence conditions" because they determine what it takes to persist through time.

Locke thought, sensibly enough, that different things had different persistence conditions. Some things can stay the same over time simply by keeping the same atoms. Consider the Atreides signet ring—Leto's ring remains the same as Paul's so long as it's made of the same matter. But this doesn't satisfy all cases of identity. Consider what Locke says about living creatures (adapted from his *Essay*):

> In the state of living Creatures, their Identity depends not on a Mass of the same Particles; but on something else. For in them the variation of great parcels of Matter alters not the Identity: A tiny Worm grown up to a Shai-hulud, sometimes fat, sometimes lean, is all the while the same Worm . . .

True enough, but what makes it the same worm? It can lose matter (when it makes melange) and it can gain matter (eating sand-plankton)—so *mass* isn't important. Locke thinks an animal is a bunch of organs connected to perform certain processes, like respiration and digestion. As long as this *organization* continues to function—breathing, pumping blood, and so forth—the animal remains the same animal. Locke describes the continuation of these processes as "partaking of one Common Life," which comprises the condition for animal persistence.

Incidentally, Locke would've thought the same remained true for robot persistence. Obviously, he had no idea how fantastically complex robotics would become (he was pretty awe-struck by fob watches). And to a certain extent it doesn't matter since, by the time the Atreideses arrived on Arrakis, computers had been outlawed for ten thousand years. But generally, for Locke, machines differ from animals in only one respect—they need "external" motivation: they need to be wound up, programmed by us, and turned "on." Animal life, on the other hand, supposedly comes from "within."

We Bene Gesserit Sift People to Find the Humans

So rings, worms, and robots seem straightforward (kind of), but what about humans? And what about persons? Despite how we normally talk, "human" and "person" seem to apply to different things. (Locke wrote about 'men' rather than "humans," but since the Lady Jessica wouldn't have suffered this casual misogyny, we shan't either.) Now, as for a *human*'s persistence conditions—surely it's just a type of animal, right? *Homo sapiens* to be exact. Their parts are systematized in a certain way, and anything other than the body's organization, like rationality, becomes irrelevant to "humanhood." If, say, we met someone who had the intelligence of a worm but was biologically organized like us we would more than likely call it human (just a bit dim). But if we met a Guildsman, who was as intelligent as us (and then some), looking at their floating, bulbous bodies and their flappy little mouths, we might hesitate before calling them the same.

For Locke, being a *person* required something more than a coherent biological organization. To get a sense of the Lockean "conditions for personhood" let's turn to the twisted Mentat, Piter de Vries. Consider the following quotations:

> "You see, Baron, I know as a Mentat when you will send the executioner. You will hold back just so long as I am useful . . . To move sooner would be wasteful and I'm yet of much use." (*Dune*)

> A Person is a thinking intelligent Being, that has reason and reflection, and considers it self as it self, the same thinking thing in different times

and places; which it does only by that consciousness which is insepa-
rable from thinking, and as it seems to me essential to it. (Locke's
Essay)

The first citation provides a little snippet from one of Piter's many
squabbles with the Baron. Reflecting on his own utility, he can
intelligently predict how Baron Harkonnen will act. He's completely aware of himself (often talking creepily about "Piter" in the
third person while lusting over our Lady Jessica). He also thinks of
himself as existing over time. In fact, he helpfully demonstrates the
Lockean conditions for personhood (which appear in the second
quotation). They include reason, reflection, self-awareness, and
awareness that the self exists through time. Locke thinks *consciousness* proves essential to all of these.

Humans then constitute a kind of animal, and persons are thinking, rational, *conscious* beings. We'll get on to consciousness in a
second, but first a score needs to be settled with the Sisterhood.
The Bene Gesserit witches are anti-Lockeans—at least in their par-
lance. They think "people" refers to a kind of animal, and "human"
refers to a thinking, conscious being. That's the point of the Gom
Jabbar—to separate the special "humans" from the regular "people." For Locke, on the other hand, what Reverend Mother Gaius
Helen Mohiam *should've* said was: "We Bene Gesserit sift *humans*
to find the *people*." Not the other way round, Witch blood!

Now on to *consciousness*—it's a tricky concept, as slippery and
difficult to grasp as a hunter-seeker in a suspensor field.
Philosophers write mind-bending tracts devoted to understanding
what it means. For our purposes we only need to get the gist of
what Locke meant by it: my consciousness is my *thoughts* and my
recognition that these thoughts are *mine*, that they belong to "my
self," a self that exists over time. Personal Identity consists in this
consciousness, and consequently a person *remains* the same person so long as the same consciousness remains: "as far as this consciousness can be extended backwards to any past Action or
Thought, so far reaches the Identity of that *Person*; it is the same
self now it was then."

Despite writing hundreds of years ago, John Locke articulated a
highly influential theory of personhood. ("A Ghola of a Chance" in
this volume also looks at Locke's theory.) Indeed, his view still
affects how we think about persons today. Saying that consciousness (which includes self-awareness and rationality) makes up the

essence of being a "person" has strong intuitive appeal. And *extended* consciousness constitutes a person remaining the same over time. Now the significance of memories becomes clear. "Extended consciousness" sounds fancy, but it's basically what we experience when we remember performing actions. When Paul remembers leaving Caladan (the giant Heighliners, his father's heavy hand upon his shoulder . . .) he's aware of being the same person then as he is now—the same stream of consciousness links both of them. It's a way of stretching one thing through time.

The more perspicacious Mentats among you will have noticed some Harkonnen trickery afoot here. However, before testing for chaumas and chaumurky at Locke's table, another culinary matter needs attending to.

It's Said that the Fremen Scum Drink the Blood of Their Dead

Cannibals present a very real concern for Locke. Not that he'd ever (knowingly) met one—rather, they presented a curious obstacle for the principle of Christian resurrection. Locke's fellow-Christians believed that, when the Day of Judgment came, everyone who ever lived would be resurrected and reviewed by God. Locke and his friends often speculated on the specific details of resurrection. For example, would it be a complete *physical* resurrection? Presuming God were powerful enough to renew putrefied flesh, and remake decayed bodies, consider the physicist, Robert Boyle's quandary:

> far more impossible will this reintegration be, if we put the case that the dead man was devoured by cannibals; for then, the same flesh belonging successively to two different persons, it is impossible that both should have it restored to them at once, or that any footsteps should remain of the relation it had to the first possessor. (Boyle 1979, p. 198)

If you eat someone, you absorb that person's flesh into yours. So how's God going to separate everything out? This problem proved potentially worrisome for the descendants of *Dune Messiah*. Rumor spread by the city-dwelling Arrakeen's elite said that the Fremen drank the blood of their dead. And as Liet-Keynes pointed out, blood *is* an efficient energy source. This has similar consequences for what Boyle called "reintegration."

Okay, say we tried to resurrect a cannibalistic Fremen warrior. It would have been wholly possible given the techniques of the secretive Bene Tleilax. Following their lead, we would take some flesh from a Fremen cadaver and pop it in an "axolotl" tank. Leave it to simmer for a couple of days, and then hopefully we'd have cooked ourselves up a nice little clone or "ghola." (Needless to say this depends on our finding a Tleilaxian, and persuading these notoriously xenophobic puritans to help.) Excellent. But if this Fremen had eaten, in his past life, another Fremen (and maybe that Fremen ate another Fremen himself) what or *who* would we be cloning?

In their time, cannibals played a part in molding Locke's distinction between "humans" and "persons"—they gave him a very good reason to suppose that *humans* (as animals) wouldn't be resurrected on Judgment Day, while *persons* very well might. In turn, this contributed to Locke's belief that it's possible to *separate* a person from the human animal they are. Throughout the *Essay* he gave numerous examples of person transplantation where different bodies house the same person. For example (again, slightly adapted):

> For should the Soul of a Duke, carrying with it the consciousness of the Duke's past Life, enter and inform the Body of a Cymek as soon as deserted by his own soul, everyone sees, he would be the same Person with the Duke, accountable only for the Duke's Actions: But who would say it was the same Man?

Today we're more skeptical when it comes to souls flying in and out of bodies, and we generally think that consciousness, its causes and its effects, connect more closely to biology. Without going into detail, the insights of neuroscience suggest that what happens in our brain directly affects how we think, act, and reflect. Our brain is essential to our personhood. Consequently, when philosophers discuss persons swapping bodies today, they usually talk about it in terms of "brain transplantation" rather than the migration of immaterial souls.

And the cannibals? What if the Baron decides to eat a slaveboy's brain? To be honest, we have nothing to worry about here. They direct their cloning techniques at the molecular level—targeting and multiplying DNA sequences. Eating things doesn't normally change your genetic makeup.

These considerations present a revision to Locke's original distinction between humans and persons. We should stop thinking about immaterial souls popping in and out of bodies, and establish a closer connection between consciousness and our biology. Perhaps we should say that *brains* have some stake in Personal Identity. And were we to do this then consciousness would no longer be the only condition for a person's survival. . .

The Gallant Officer Gurney

Perhaps, given time, Locke could've been persuaded that keeping the same brain *was* necessary for staying the same person. But even if he had, he certainly wouldn't have thought it was *sufficient* for it. Memories and "psychological continuity" would still be an essential ingredient. However, these memories cause problems. We can see this if we take a closer look at the relation of identity.

Identity—the clever relation that attaches Muad'Dib to Paul, and the older Paul to the toddler Paul—has *special features*. First up, it's *symmetrical*—if Paul is identical to Muad'Dib, then Muad'Dib is identical to Paul. Secondly, it's *reflexive*—Paul is identical with Paul. And thirdly, the identity relation is supposed to be *transitive*. This means that the relation carries: if Paul the God-Emperor is identical to Paul the Fremen guerilla, and Paul the Fremen guerilla is identical to Paul the na-duke, then Paul the God Emperor is identical to Paul the na-duke. *Giudichar mantene*, no?

But hold up. According to Thomas Reid, one of Locke's contemporaries, memories don't accommodate this third essential feature of identity: *Transitivity*. Locke's model is wrong because personal identity based on memory is *not* transitive. He offers the "Gallant Officer" thought experiment to demonstrate why. Here's one version where Gurney Halleck can be seen to display the qualities of Reid's gallant officer:

> Gurney is undeniably a gallant officer. He could best Idaho six times out of ten, and plays a wicked tune on the baliset. The question is, how good is his memory? On Dune he may remember his trials with the Beast Rabban. The brutality that left him marked by the inkvine scar happened years before, yet he can quite vividly recall the stinging Harkonnen whip. But on Arrakis his memory falters. It troubles him that he cannot remember the color of his sister's eyes. The Harkonnens killed her and the rest of his family when he was a boy, but the sands of Dune have eroded those memories. In the slave pits he would have remembered every feature of her face, but as time passed he has forgotten.

And forgetfulness is a serious obstacle to the transitivity of Personal Identity. Gurney the Arrakeen smuggler can remember being tortured by Rabban, the Demon Ruler. According to Locke, the smuggler and the torture victim are identical persons. And in the slave pits of Giedi Prime, Gurney could remember his boyhood with his sister. So the victim and the boy are identical persons. *However*, Gurney the smuggler can't remember his boyhood—so Locke can't say that they are identical. Ya! Ya! Yawm!

Have You Tasted the Blessed Water?

Reid's objection highlights the difficulties of basing a person's identity on something as delicate as memories, which we're constantly losing. The Lady Jessica, however, faces another problem. She remembers *too much*.

The Water of Life—it has the distinctive cinnamon smell of melange, but is deadly poisonous. After drinking it, Jessica must alter it molecularly with her witch skills, and render it innocuous. "With her psychokinesthetic probing, she moved into it, shifted an oxygen mote, allowed another carbon mote to link, reattached a linkage of oxygen . . . hydrogen" (*Dune*). Way cool. Once this was done, the Reverend Mother Ramallo was brought to her, and, upon touching, their consciousnesses merged, "being two people at once." This had happened to Ramallo herself when she became a sayyadina, and so it had gone, reaching back to the first Fremen witches on Rossak. Undergoing this Spice Agony, Jessica received all of the accumulated tribe memories of her predecessors, called "the other memory." At this point we could quite plausibly say that her consciousness was extended backwards to many years before her own birth. For Locke this may mean that, as a *person*, she is identical to the very first Fremen Reverend Mother, Raquella Berto-Anirul (*and* all the others in-between).

Whoa! Take a breath. This truly is the Weirding way. Can Jessica really be the same person as Raquella Berto-Anirul? One of them is the concubine of Duke Leto Atreides, daughter of Baron Vladimir Harkonnen. The other is a doctor and co-founder of the Suk School, granddaughter of Vorian Atreides. On Locke's original model the identity of a person reaches as far back as their consciousness, so Jessica has to be. And yet . . . and yet . . . Raquella and Jessica are the same person only if extended consciousness is sufficient by itself for personal identity over time. We already suspected that this couldn't be the case (which is why brains were tentatively added to our account). Now, Jessica's Agony gives us another reason to reject the exclusivity of Locke's original criterion.

There are a few unknowns here. It's not obvious, for example, how Jessica experiences her new memories: does she remember them in the first person or in the third person? And are they really received or does she already have them, locked within her psyche? The answers are shrouded in the mystery and shadows of the Bene Gesserit sisterhood, so for our purposes, here's one possible, pared-down version:

Before the Spice Agony, Sister Jessica's consciousness extends back roughly to the time of her birth. Afterwards, it extends back to around 137 B.G., Raquella's birth date (thousands of years before Jessica's). After the Spice Agony, the Reverend Mother Jessica is identical to Raquella. But before it, as a Bene Gesserit sister whose consciousness is limited to her own life, she is certainly *not* identical to Raquella.

Mu Zein Wallah—have we forgotten about the *transitivity* of identity? Thomas Reid showed us one way that Lockean memory does not accommodate this transitivity, but Jessica has shown us another.

We have three persons: Jessica A, the adept, who hasn't yet drunk the water of life, Jessica B, the sayyadina who *has* drunk it, and Raquella C, the very first Fremen sayyadina.

- **Obviously–Jessica B can remember being Jessica A, so we have a case of Lockean personal identity.**

- **We can write this B = A.**

- **Similarly, thanks to the water of life, Jessica B can remember being Raquella C.**

- **So they're the same person too, which we'd write B = C.**

- **Now, Jessica B can remember being Jessica A leaving Caladan. And Jessica B can also remember being Raquella C leaving Rossak. Thus, according to the transitivity of identity the person Jessica A should be identical to the person Raquella C.**

- **That is, A = C.**

But according to Locke's model, she *isn't*! Jessica A can't remember being Raquella leaving Rossak! No consciousness links them, even though consciousness links Jessica A to Jessica B, and Jessica B to Raquella C. Therefore, we can quite confidently say that extended consciousness cannot be the solitary condition for a person's identity through time. This is true for Lady Jessica at the very least. If it weren't, then she would be both identical and not identical with Raquella Berto-Anirul, which is nonsense, cielago guano.

We can examine this difficulty from another angle, by looking at the Abomination, Alia. She too suffered the Spice Agony and received the Other Memory at the same time as her mother. Her consciousness—if she even possessed any—was also extended back to the deeds of Raquella Berto-Anirul. On Locke's model she will be the same person as Raquella. An unbroken memory link joins the two. But didn't we also think that Jessica had become the same person as Raquella? Surely this leads to gross contradictions. If both Jessica and Alia are Raquella, then they must be the same person! But this proves too bizarre. Here we have a situation where Alia and Jessica may be doing different things—Alia is happy, Jessica is not—and we will have to say "that person is both happy and not happy," or "that person is both killing Baron Harkonnen and not killing him."

Which Future Path to Take?

At the start it seemed that Locke might shed some light on Lady Jessica's predicament. But now it appears that she, and her daughter, have shed some light on his. Jessica has demonstrated another reason to think extended consciousness, as experienced in memories, is *not* enough for personal identity. Kull Wahad—I am *profoundly* stirred. However, *khala*, this isn't to say that we should discard Locke's model out-of-hand. Psychological continuity still, today, is regarded as a very important part of a person's persistence over time.

Modern philosophers disagree over exactly what *kind* of psychological continuity proves necessary. Some claim that we persist through time because of a relation of *mental contents*. Earlier psychological features *cause* the mental contents I have now. For example, Muad'Dib's decision to attack the Harkonnens was *caused* by his intention to revenge his father (formed on the news of the old duke's death). Other philosophers talk about mental *capacities*, the ability to do certain things. For instance, though Gurney Halleck forgets things (the color of his sister's eyes), he continues to make memories, think tactically and methodically, and have a penchant for the baliset.

However, not all contemporary philosophers think that our persistence depends on psychology. Another view is that our persistence conditions are just the same as a human animal's. Which is to say that, fundamentally, we're *animals* and not *persons*. A human animal lasts from the moment of conception to the moment of death, and consequently we do too. These "biological theorists" claim that one survives simply when one's animal functions (such as metabolism or respiration) continue. So, Jessica remains Jessica so long as the animal she is survives—she need not be conscious, she could even be in a vegetative state. Higher-brain functions are only required for personhood and we are not persons fundamentally. We—human animals—may become persons in much the same way that a Fremen may become a Waterman or an Atreides may become a Duke.

Choosing between these different options amounts to a tricky task. As we've seen, it's often a matter of presenting different 'thought experiments' and assessing our reactions to them. For example, brain transplant cases suggest that we're not, fundamentally, human animals. But, as Jessica demonstrated, extended consciousness alone cannot be sufficient for our survival. Following all these intuitions is like tracking worm-sign, and you may end up tying yourself in knots. Our common-sense beliefs often point in different directions and lead to contradictions—and this, in turn, undermines their authority. Consequently, some philosophers have decided that it is not so important for their model of Personal Identity to be "intuitive."

One such theorist is Daniel Dennett who, in his book *Consciousness Explained*, suggests that there are no such things as persons. He writes:

> The strangest and most wonderful constructions in the whole animal world are the amazing, intricate constructions made by the primate, *Homo Sapiens*. Each normal individual of this species makes a self. Out of its brain it spins a web of words and deeds, and, like the other creatures, it doesn't have to know what its doing; it just does it. This web protects it, just like the snail's shell, and provides for it a livelihood, just like the spider's web. (p. 416)

For Dennett, "person" is the centre of narrative gravity. Humans can talk—they refer to themselves and in doing so imply that there is some *thing* there, a being that is more than their body alone. But there is no real thing that persists over time, just a narrative that continues and is continually reinforced and embellished. Like Jessica we are no more than characters in externally constructed stories.

So, there are three future paths for you to choose between. Either you think that we stay the same over time by being the same person, some complex of psychological relations (like John Locke). If so, then Jessica will in some sense be the same as Raquella Berto-Anirul. Or perhaps you think that being a "person" is irrelevant and we stay the same simply by being the same animal (like Eric Olson) – so Jessica is just the animal who persists for as long as she is biologically able. Lastly, you may think that there's no such thing as a "person" (like Dennett). If this is the case, then we must be, like "Jessica," just characters in stories, and nothing but bundles of words.

Bi-la Kaifa.

Get Out of My Mind!

The deserts of Dune prove surprisingly fertile soil for discussions about personal identity, and an erg is needed for Locke to make his peace with Jessica. However, a few things must be said about the Abomination, St. Alia-of-the-Knife. She'd be upset if she weren't mentioned.

Alia is a little monster, no question. The old Truthsayer Mohiam calls for the destruction of this child who is not a child. "'Kill her! Kill her!' she cries from behind the Emperor's throne. 'Long were we warned against such a one and how to prevent such a birth'" (*Dune*). In the face of this unbridled venom, however, Alia would have found a stalwart ally in John Locke.

In Locke's day it was common for fetuses to be destroyed if they were "ill-shaped" (what the sisterhood might call "abominations"). However, in the *Essay*, Locke argues that as long as the baby will be able to think, the "human fetus should be preserved." If a child is different to the rest, as with Alia, then for Locke it simply showed that there are no fixed classes in nature. He demonstrates an inclusive attitude that allows for a very wide variation. Unlike members of her own sietch, Locke would not have thought Alia a freak, but simply an example of the variety within a species.

He would also have been fascinated by her status as a person. Having undergone the Spice Agony as a fetus she has no memories of her own, in the way that Jessica does. "One day I woke up," Alia said. "It was like waking from sleep except that I could not remember going to sleep. I was in a warm, dark place. And I was frightened" (*Dune*).

An Abomination is a fetus that has been completely overtaken by the memories of its ancestors. Mohiam fears such abomination in Alia, that she is wholly "other memory." She has no real memories of her own, not a droplet to add to the pool. Consequently, intriguingly, she must be identical with her mother Jessica, since they share every single memory. We've already touched on this thought, that Jessica and Alia are the same person, and the contradictions that result. It would be impossible for the same person to be in audience with the Emperor (as Alia) while at the same time being at counsel in a Fremen sietch (as Jessica). One person simply cannot be in two places at once! I'm sure the little troublemaker will take great pleasure in the difficulties she causes for our philosophers.

Unfortunately, as is often the case with philosophical studies, we are left with more questions than when we started. To begin with, our survival through time seemed pretty straightforward—but now! To be perfectly honest, I don't know whether I'm an animal or a person with psychological properties, I don't know if I can split into two or if I need bodily continuity to survive. In the hope that you may be more in tune to the Weirding Way, here are a few mind-bending puzzles of personal identity raised in the Duniverse.

- **Given that Paul Atreides himself distinguishes between Usul, Paul, and Muad'Dib, identifying different features in each—one as a lover, another as a duke, and as a religious leader—can we really say that they are identical?**

- **In *Children of Dune*, Leto II covers himself with sandtrout to merge with them and become a Shai-Hulud ("With a terrible singleness of concentration he achieved the union of his new skin with his body . . . *My skin is not my own*"). After this organic conversion, is the Shai-Hulud the same animal as Leto II?**

- **After drinking the Water of Life and undergoing the Spice Agony, is there an argument that Paul is the same**

person as Raquella Berto-Anirul, if he receives her memories?

• **Is the Other Memory, the entity received with the Water of Life, a person?**

The Duniverse forces us to ask curious and often unnerving questions about ourselves. By twisting and stretching what we see as 'natural'—human nature, and personhood—the stories of Arrakis encourage us to investigate our common, everyday intuitions. And in seeking answers to these questions, we should be open to any position. We shouldn't shy away from unappealing possibilities (that we're, for example, nothing more than insignificant vortices of "narrative gravity"), or be afraid to subject ourselves to thorough examination. In philosophy, perhaps more than any discipline, fear is the mind-killer—fear of our own insignificance, for instance, may easily cloud our judgment.

So assume the courageous stance of a Fremen warrior, perform some quick prana-bindu meditation, take a deep breath before approaching persons, and cry "Ya Hya Chouhada!" "Long Live the Debaters!"

Discovered by:
ADAM FERNER

Heroism of Muad'Dib

Paul Atreides the Nietzschean Hero

"I know my fate. One day my name will be associated with the memory of something tremendous—a crisis without equal on Earth, the most profound collision of conscience, a decision that was conjured up against everything that had been believed, demanded, hallowed so far . . . I do not want to be a holy man; sooner even a buffoon. — Perhaps I am a buffoon. —Yet in spite of that—or rather not in spite of it, because so far nobody has been more mendacious than holy men—the truth speaks out of me. —But my truth is terrible; for so far one has called lies truth. . . . For when truth enters into a fight with the lies of millennia, we shall have upheavals, a convulsion of earthquakes, a moving of mountains and valleys, the like of which has never been dreamed of. The concept of politics will have merged entirely with a war of spirits; all power structures of the old society will have been exploded—all of them are based on lies: there will be wars the like of which have never yet been seen on Earth. It is only beginning with me that the Earth knows *great politics . . . Where you see ideals I see what is human. Alas, all too human.*"

—FRIEDRICH NIETZSCHE, *Ecce Homo* (Preface)

As the *Dune* trilogy reaches its end, the "Lion of Atreides," the living messiah Leto II, runs and runs faster than any wind, "a blur atop the dunes." Leto runs in a physical sense, but also in a psychological sense as a way to run away from his very humanity, "Because the memory of being human is so rich in him." To be human or, in the case of Leto especially, to be "all-too-human" proves both a blessing and a curse. The trilogy maps out in a rich and complex way just how painful it can be to be human, and how cruelly human beings can act towards each other. In fact, such acts are not "cruel" as such, but *human* and this very human characteristic reaches its pinnacle in Leto. The life of Leto's father, and the man within Leto himself, Paul Atreides, expresses this characteristic most tragically.

Frank Herbert's great trilogy can be read on many levels. It qualifies certainly as a "fantasy," of course, but we aren't dealing here with beings so different from ourselves as to defy comprehension or empathy. These beings, on the whole, are very human: they suffer, they desire, they bleed, they die, they have ambitions, they have families, they have religion. Geographically, it operates in many different arenas, from palaces and sietches, to whole planets and the Imperium itself, but the physical geography in the sense of scale seems less relevant than the impact these environments have upon the psyche of those inhabiting it. A man can rule over thousands of planets, but he is still a man. As the Preacher, once ruler of those planets himself, points out to the Prince Farad'n in *Children of Dune*,

"Governments may rise and fall for reasons which appear insignificant, Prince. What small events! An argument between two women . . . which way the wind blows on a certain day . . . a sneeze, a cough, the length of a garment or the chance collision of a fleck of sand and a courtier's eye. It is not always the majestic concerns of Imperial ministers which dictate the course of history, nor is it necessarily the pontifications of priests which move the hands of God."

The "small" events are as important as the "big" events, in fact, as the Preacher also states, *"there are no intransigent opposites except in the beliefs of men and, sometimes, in their dreams."*

Muad'Dib: Sardonic, Illogical, Mythological

Greatness is a transitory experience. It is never consistent. It depends in part upon the myth-making imagination of humankind. The person who experiences greatness must have a feeling for the myth he is in. He must reflect what is projected upon him. And he must have a strong sense of the sardonic. This is what uncouples him from belief in his own pretensions. The sardonic is all that permits him to move within himself. Without this quality, even occasional greatness will destroy a man.

—From *The Collected Sayings of Muad'Dib* by the PRINCESS IRULAN *(Dune)*

Paul Atreides, Muad'Dib, is a hero—a god—to billions, but he sees the "small" and the "big" for what they really are. The great heroes of human history can lose themselves in their own greatness; they can believe in their own myth and this could destroy them. Many historical figures of the past would have done well to heed this psychological observation of the quality of being sardonic, of being prepared to mock oneself. Certainly, the German philosopher, Friedrich Nietzsche (1844–1900), recognized keenly the need for humor and self-mockery if one is to be both great and mentally stable. His "prophet," Zarathustra, represents for Nietzsche this kind of sardonic greatness:

> "This laughter's crown, this rose-wreath crown: I myself have set this crown on my head, I myself have canonized my laughter. I have found no other strong enough for it today. Zarathustra the dancer, Zarathustra the light, who beckons with his wings, ready for flight, beckoning to all birds, prepared and ready, blissfully light-hearted: Zarathustra the prophet, Zarathustra the laughing prophet, no impatient nor uncompromising man, one who loves jumping and escapades; I myself have set this crown on my head!" (*Thus Spoke Zarathustra,* "Of the Higher Man")

One should not take oneself too seriously, as Paul Atreides knows only too well. In *Dune,* the Baron Harkonnen observes that, *"They've a new prophet or religious leader of some kind among the Fremen . . . They call him Muad'Dib. Very funny, really. It means "the Mouse." I've told Rabban to let them have their religion. It'll keep them occupied."* The Baron, unwisely as it turns out, interprets the sardonic, the humorous, as therefore frivolous and contemptuous and so fails to appreciate the power of religion. While religion may well "keep them occupied" it's what they're occupied *with* that the Baron remains ignorant of. The Baron looks for the devious, for the cold logic of the Mentat Thufir Hawat, but religion doesn't follow logic.

   "Deep in the human unconscious is a pervasive need for a logical universe. But the real universe is always one step beyond logic" (*Dune*). As Nietzsche writes in *Beyond Good and Evil,* "Behind all logic, too, and its apparent tyranny of movement there are value judgments, or to speak more clearly, physiological demands for the preservation of a particular kind of life." Just because something doesn't follow logic, it doesn't mean that it's not important or powerful. Logic, science, "progress" can only provide us with

one understanding of the world, and not necessarily the "correct" one.

For Nietzsche, the important question, then, isn't whether something is "true" or not, but whether the values that it upholds are *life-enhancing ones* and have a place in his modern and increasingly secularizing world. To assume the value of truth for human beings is to assume a harmony between truth and our natures; we are naturally fitted for truth. The quest for "truth" has existed in philosophies and religions for thousands of years, but Nietzsche raises the question, What if truth is, not only unattainable, but not good for us? The values and beliefs that the Fremen live by aren't "true," but rather "heavily imprinted with our Bene Gesserit soothsay" to serve a particular purpose. "Truth," as such, is irrelevant. Power, however, is not: "My father once told me that respect for the truth comes close to being the basis for all morality. 'Something cannot emerge from nothing,' he said. This is profound thinking if you understand how unstable 'the truth' can be" (*Dune*).

When Nietzsche looks at Man, he sees the human being as "myth-less." We have lost the magic that a child experiences at the theater; we have become too cynical, too rational. When we look at history, we break it into parts and criticize it: what matters is what is "true," not what is "wonderful." Myths no longer have value because they aren't true. But, by presenting an objective, scientific, "Mentat" history we kill myth and religion, which is also "mythical," by accusing it of being false, crude, irrational and absurd. There is a place for science, but there is a place for myth too. Bernard Nightingale makes a wonderful remark in Tom Stoppard's Arcadia. "*Why does scientific progress matter more than personalities? . . . don't confuse progress with perfectibility. A great poet is always timely. A great philosopher is an urgent need. There's no rush for Isaac Newton. We were quite happy with Aristotle's cosmos. Personally, I preferred it. Fifty-five crystal spheres geared to God's crankshaft is my idea of a satisfying universe. I can't think of anything more trivial than the speed of light. . . .*"

Stagnation of Myth

In history we have, we *need*, role models which inspire us to greatness through imitation. For figures to be monumental they must be mythologized, not deconstructed and individualized. Our heroes need to be lacking specific detail, to be blurred around the edges, so that we can fill the gaps with our "poetic invention." That is, they have to be flexible in order to be relevant to our modern times. A healthy, thriving culture, for Nietzsche, consists in one which possesses the *"plastic power"* to *"incorporate . . . what is past and foreign,"* to *"recreate the moulds"* of the past in the language of the present (*Untimely Meditations*). In a sense, the mythologized figures act as our unwritten laws for a community. As Scytale observes in *Dune Messiah*, "Some say . . . that people cling to Imperial leadership because space is infinite. They feel lonely without a unifying symbol. For a lonely people, the Emperor is a definite place. They can turn towards him and say: 'See, there He is. He makes us one.' Perhaps religion serves the same purpose, m'Lord."

History must be creative and, to achieve that, it must be prepared to constantly examine itself and, as Nietzsche says in *Untimely Meditations*, "man must possess and from time to time employ the strength to break up and dissolve a part of the past" (p. 75). We're to judge this on the basis of what is life-fulfilling, what makes us grow. As Muad'Dib becomes a living god, he sees the dangers of religion, as well as its creative spirit: "I've had a bellyful of the god and priest business! You think I don't see my own mythos? Consult your data once more, Hayt. I've insinuated my rites into the most elementary human acts. The people eat in the name of Muad'Dib! They make love in my name, are born in my name—cross the street in my name. A roof beam cannot be raised in the lowliest hovel of far Gangishree without invoking the blessing of Muad'Dib!" (*Dune Messiah*).

When people start to idolize their figures, they stagnate. As Nietzsche states in his Preface to *Twilight of the Idols*, "This little essay is a great declaration of war; and regarding the sounding out of idols, this time they are not just idols of the age, but eternal idols, which are here touched with a hammer as with a tuning fork: there are altogether no older, no more convinced, no more puffed-up idols." Muad'Dib is afraid of becoming "puffed up," and of his creation, his universe, becoming soft and stagnant: "And always he fought the temptation to choose a clear, safe course, warning 'That path leads ever down to stagnation'" (*Dune*). He goes into the desert and becomes The Preacher, the second message of his "sermon on the mount" in *Children of Dune* sums up his new purpose: "The most dangerous of all creations is a rigid code of ethics. It will turn upon you and drive you into exile."

Muad'Dib had "shaken the safe cosmos and replaced security with his Jihad" (*Dune Messiah*) but at great expense to the Fremen of Arrakis. With the reign of Muad'Dib, the Fremen of old look back to the way things were before. "The Fremen longed for the old days and the old ways" Scytale observed in *Dune Messiah* wondering what had brought the Fremen Farok into the conspiracy against their Mahdi. Stilgar, in *Children of Dune* too, laments: "The Friendly Desert, which once had spread from pole to pole, was reduced to half its former size. The mystic paradise of spreading greenery filled him with dismay. It was not like the dream. And as his planet changed, he knew he had changed." The changes that Muad'Dib brought about only cause him to be sickened by what he created and the desire within him to "bring down the structure built on his name."

Religion and Suffering

There should be a science of discontent. People need hard times and oppression to develop psychic muscles.

—From *The Collected Sayings of Muad'Dib* by the Princess Irulan (*Dune*)

Nietzsche, the philosopher, is also philosophy's greatest critic. He prefers the findings of psychology to the supposed grand and abstract discoveries of philosophy. But, again, truth is not about the "small" or the "big," it's about people. Humans comprise troubled souls, their drives remain fragmented, their desires flit from one thing to another. In *Dune*, the Fremen, with the importance of their religion and the belief in the Mahdi—the Messiah—display a wholeness that seems missing amongst the trivialities, fragmentation, and decadence of the battling Houses. In the Nietzschean sense, the Fremen prove "healthier" than the Atreides or Harkonnen, despite being seen as primitive and insignificant by the Houses. In fact, the Fremen are far more complex and powerful than they are given credit for.

The same cannot be said for the new generation of Fremen, like Agarves in *Children of Dune*, "one of the new breed who had gone to water-fatness." The Preacher saw what he had created: "At the edge of the third landing The Preacher turned, and it was as though he looked about him, seeing with his empty eye sockets the foppish city-dwellers, some of them Fremen, with garments which simulated stillsuits but were only decorative fabrics" The Fremen had become "cultured," but they had lost the hardness and vitality of the desert-dwellers. Paul Atreides, Muad'Dib, represents this civilized-barbaric dichotomy. On the one hand, we have the Duke's son, educated at the best schools and learned in religion, philosophy, government, and the sciences. On the other hand, we have Muad'Dib, the desert-dweller who orders drums to be made from the skins of his enemies. The veneer between civilized and barbaric proves a very thin one indeed. Suffering makes you hard, but it can also make you more human.

It's no surprise that Frank Herbert looked to the Islamic culture for inspiration. As a model for myth-making, coupled with an appreciation of the horror and suffering that life can bring forth, he could probably find no better example from history. Herbert writes in the Appendix that,

> the Fremen were a desert people whose entire ancestry was accustomed to hostile landscapes. Mysticism isn't difficult when you survive each second by surmounting open hostility. . . . With such a tradition, suffering is accepted...their everyday existence required brutal judgments (often deadly) which in a softer land would burden men with unbearable guilt.

Nietzsche too saw the Muslims, the Arab desert-dwellers, as a special and noble breed:

> Christianity robbed us of the harvest of the culture of the ancient world, it later went on to rob us of the harvest of the culture of Islam. The wonderful Moorish cultural world of Spain, more closely related to us at bottom, speaking more directly to our senses and taste, than Greece and Rome, was trampled down (I do not say by what kind of feet): Why? Because it was noble, because it owed its origin to manly instincts, because it said Yes to life even in the rare and exquisite treasures of Moorish life! . . . Later on, the Crusaders fought against something they would have done better to lie down in the dust before—a culture compared with which even our nineteenth century may well think itself very impoverished and very 'late'. (*The Anti-Christ*)

Nietzsche attacked his own century for being soft. A society that called itself cultured, but was really nothing but a "fairground motley," a "chaotic jumble" of confused and different styles. Rather than taking part in life, we become spectators. In Nietzsche's *Untimely Meditations*, he says "Mankind must work continually at the production of individual great men—that and nothing else is its task" (p. 161). Humanity needs to create favorable conditions for great figures to thrive, rather as a plant thrives in the right soil. Edric astutely observes in *Dune Messiah* what has become of Muad'Dib's creation: "What is enduring about beauty and pleasure?" Edric demanded.

> "We will destroy both Atreides. Culture! They dispense culture the better to rule. Beauty! They promote the beauty which enslaves. They create a literate ignorance—easiest thing of all. They leave nothing to chance. Chains! Everything they do forges chains, enslaves. But slaves always revolt."

The old Fremen were no longer free in this new world, but felt trapped, whereas the new breed were soft and ignorant of their own chains. By creating a paradise on Arrakis, Muad'Dib realized he was recreating Caladan: "We came from Caladan—a paradise world for our form of life. There existed no need on Caladan to build a physical paradise of the mind—we could see the actuality all around us. And the price we paid for achieving a paradise in this life—we went soft, we lost our edge" (*Dune*). Muad'Dib needed to exile himself into the desert and preach against all this, in the same way he insisted that "our child will be born in the sietch" where the old, noble ways can still be found.

Muad'Dib created an ordered society that believed itself to be free, but as Paul says to Chani in *Dune*, "Too much freedom breeds chaos. We can't have that, can we? And how do you make despotism lovable? . . . What's law? Control? Law filters chaos and what drips through? Serenity? Law—our highest ideal and our basest nature. Don't look too closely at the law. Do, and you'll find the rationalized interpretations, the legal casuistry, the precedents of convenience. You'll find the serenity, which is just another word for death." The passion that is love is replaced by the death that is order and serenity. The people believe they live in a just society, but Vladimir Harkonnen rants "There's no such thing as equal justice anywhere. Decisions must be weighed only as to their merit in maintaining an orderly society. Past civilizations without number have foundered on the rocks of equal justice. Such foolishness destroys the natural hierarchies which are far more important. Any individual takes on significance only in his relationship to your total society. Unless that society be ordered in logical steps, no one can find a place in it – not the lowliest or the highest. Come, come, grandchild! You must be the stern mother to your people. It's your duty to maintain order" (*Children of Dune*).

The people may believe they are free, secure and equal, but they are really chained, and delude themselves that they are equal. The truly free belonged to the Fremen of the sietch who knew they were part of a necessary hierarchy that is by no means secure and at peace, but in a perpetual state of unease and war. As the dwarf Bijaz tells Hayt in *Dune Messiah*,

"War is useful because it is effective in so many areas. It stimulates the metabolism. It enforces government. It diffuses genetic strains. It possesses a vitality such as nothing else in the universe. Only those who recognize the value of war and exercise it have any degree of self-determination."

The Prophet

He was warrior and mystic, ogre and saint, the fox and the innocent, chivalrous, ruthless, less than a god, more than a man. There is no measuring Muad'Dib's motives by ordinary standards. In the moment of his triumph, he saw the death prepared for him, yet he accepted the treachery. Can you say he did this out of a sense of justice? Whose justice, then? Remember, we speak now of the Muad'Dib who ordered battle drums made from his enemies' skins, the Muad'Dib who denied the conventions of his ducal past with a wave of the hand, saying merely: "I am the Kwisatz Haderach. That is reason enough."

—From *Arrakis Awakening* by the Princess Irulan (*Dune*)

I have not been asked, as I should have been asked, what the name Zarathustra means in precisely my mouth, in the mouth of the first immoralist. . . . Zarathustra was the first to see in the struggle between good and evil the actual wheel in the working of things: the translation of morality into the realm of metaphysics, as force, cause, end-in-itself. . . . Zarathustra created this most fateful of errors, morality: consequently he must also be the first to recognize it. . . . His teaching, and his alone, upholds truthfulness as the supreme virtue—that is to say, the opposite of the cowardice of the "idealist," who takes flight in face of reality; Zarathustra has more courage in him than all other thinkers put together.

—*Ecce Homo*, "Why I Am Destiny"

"Religion unifies our forces. It's our mystique," says Paul Atreides. Muad'Dib created a religion to unify, then became The Preacher to destroy what he had created. Nietzsche brings back Zarathustra because this Persian prophet created a religion and has now come back to destroy the belief in a set of values, that "most fateful of errors." Zarathustra preaches of the coming of a new kind of man, what he calls the Superman. The emphasis on courage, on nobility and ability to face reality are considered the true virtues of the great man; rather than the "cowardice" of false idealism:

> I deny first a type of man who has hitherto counted as the highest, the good, the benevolent, beneficent; I deny secondly a kind of morality which has come to be accepted and to dominate as morality in itself— decadence morality, in more palpable terms Christian morality. (*Ecce Homo*, "Why I am a Destiny)

Zarathustra is the first prophet to claim that salvation can be obtained through moral behavior; thus personal responsibility comes to the forefront: one will be judged on the Day of Judgment. Time is perceived as linear, moving morally towards its final consummation in the struggle between good and evil. Nietzsche recognizes the Abrahamic tradition of prophetic religions that appeal to an authority higher than the ancestral or the civil, but he would argue that they originate much further back than that: to the work of Zarathustra. As Nietzsche says in *Ecce Homo*,

> Zarathustra, the first psychologist of the good, is—consequently—a friend of the wicked. When a decadent species of man has risen to the rank of the highest species of man, this can happen only at the expense of its antithetical species, the species of man strong and certain of life. ("Why I Am Destiny")

This portrayal of Zarathustra prefigures the character of Muad'Dib who has to kill if he is to lead.

Nietzsche talks of the future of humanity; a different kind of humanity. The human being is the rope tied between animal and the Superman: He must overcome himself; the opposite of which is the desire for self-preservation which characterizes the attitude of "the last man." Humanity has discovered happiness and contentment but, as a result, is no longer prepared to take risks, to experiment with potentiality.

This is not real happiness, as the old Fremen are only too aware, whilst the new generation of water-fat Fremen care less. Nietzsche's new Prophet is all-too-human. Zarathustra has rejected the belief in gods or an after-life and instead looks within himself to overcome obstacles and be self-disciplined. Muad'Dib characterizes this feature of self-discipline; whilst religion is important as a unifying force—a force both Muad'Dib and Zarathustra recognize— the self should not rely on divine intervention to achieve their own goals. With the notion of Nietzsche's Superman, his new prophet, we have someone who is prepared to put aside comfort and security in the quest for greatness, for to go beyond good and evil as understood by the masses is to take risks and even put their own life in danger.

The prophet Zarathustra, and the prophet Muad'Dib, both represent humans—and they are "only" human—who, despite doubts as to their own purpose, put aside the security of wealth and family. They become outcasts, mocked by many. All signs of the Superman will appear as signs of illness or madness to the human herd. *"Everyone wants the same thing, everyone is the same: whoever thinks otherwise goes voluntarily into the madhouse,"* says Zarathustra. Despite his attack on all idols, Nietzsche is also caught within an ideal: the Superman gives him hope for the future; an archetype that acts as a meditative force to guide one through the present and into the future. This, also, is Frank Herbert's Muad'Dib and, indeed, his incarnation Leto II for "What is the son but the extension of the father?" (*Dune*).

Recorded by:
ROY JACKSON

FROM: BENE GESSENT ARCHIVES
An Alternative View to Princess Irulan
By: Reverend Mother Bellonda
Date: 15210 A.G.

Friedrich Nietzsche Goes to Space

I make three bold claims about Frank Herbert and his *Dune* novels:

- Frank Herbert is a philosopher.

- He's a philosopher, not just in the way that everyone can have a "philosophy" of something or other, but an honest-to-goodness philosopher, and he uses novels to construct and communicate his philosophy.

- Herbert's *Dune* saga is a work of philosophy that interacts primarily with the ideas of Friedrich Nietzsche and the way in which Nietzsche's ideas about humanity could be understood in light of the horrors of the twentith century.

From Zarathustra to Muad'Dib

The most basic encyclopedia entry on Friedrich Nietzsche will tell you that he was a philosopher from Saxony, born in 1844, and died 1900. It might tell you that, after studying with the classicist Ritschl and being heavily influenced by the philosopher Schopenhauer's writing, Nietzsche was one of the youngest ever professors appointed to the chair of classical philology at the University of Basel—a fancy way of saying that he taught about the civilizations of Greece and Rome.

Nietzsche is, however, particularly known in modern popular culture—having enjoyed a particular revival in the 1960s—for his strange and wonderful 1883–85 work *Thus Spoke Zarathustra*. *Zarathustra* is a work of narrative and poetic philosophy whose

189

main concept concerns the maturing of humankind into *Über-mensch*. *Übermensch* is variously translated as "Over Man" or "Super Man," or sometimes just "superman." "Beyond-man" might also work. Very basically, the Superman is *not* a costumed comic-book character, nor is he or she the *best* or *strongest* human. In fact, though this is a typical misunderstanding of Nietzsche's idea, he addresses this directly in the opening pages of *Zarathustra*, calling this the "Ultimate Man." Because many readers of Nietzsche confuse "Ultimate Man" for Nietzsche's "superman" Herbert uses Nietzsche's ideas about these two concepts the way that he does.

Herbert also weaves into the *Dune* saga Nietzsche's concept of "eternal recurrence," which suggests that one must live as though one will repeat one's life over and over again for eternity. If you find this difficult to understand, don't worry, you're not alone. However, if you've ever seen the 1989 film, *Dead Poets Society*, John Keating's "*carpe diem*" ('seize the day') philosophy is a good place to start thinking about it. Reward, value, and sense for life must be derived *from* life, not from any external metaphysical world or system of morality and ethics.

Nietzsche's work as a whole can be seen as a reaction to the way in which Christian Europe (and, by extension, any culture with a religious background) had developed a system of morality and necessity that was linked in part or wholly to the existence, action and commands of a metaphysical "god." *The Gay Science* (1882) is a particularly obvious example of this sort of thinking, and lays the ground for the ambitious *Zarathustra* project. *Zarathustra* is unique among Nietzsche's works, not because it contains ideas of Nietzsche's that he hadn't discussed elsewhere or that he doesn't deal with in his later works, but because it links many of them together in a form that philosophy has always struggled with: the novel.

But, no matter how much academic philosophers might so struggle, every culture knows that storytelling is an incredibly effective way to motivate both understanding and action. Nietzsche, the great destroyer of religion and religious morality, understood this better than many think. His philosophical descendant, Frank Herbert, had both the talent and the ability to emulate and to extend Nietzsche's program to a twentieth-century setting, in the wake of events that confirmed the importance of what Nietzsche had sought to teach us.

Children of Nietzsche

Parallels

There are two kinds of parallels between Nietzsche's work and Herbert's: One is to do with ideas—the Nietzschean notions of Superman, Ultimate Man, and eternal recurrence are woven throughout the grand tapestry of the *Dune* saga. The other sort of parallel between Nietzsche's work and Herbert's relates to narrative structure—the way the story unfolds. Where we see parallel narrative structure, this highlights the ideas that Herbert takes from Nietzsche's *Zarathustra*.

Zarathustra: A Quick Re-cap

The plot of *Zarathustra* revolves around the "going down" of the prophet Zarathustra (modeled, roughly, upon the historical Persian religious reformer Zoroaster) from his mountain retreat—where he has been meditating for ten years—to the world of man once more. Along the way, he meets various people and groups, witnesses various events, preaching, commenting and musing upon what he sees and experiences. From near the beginning of the book, a demonic buffoon, that opposes him and acts in a fashion similar to a court jester, stalks Zarathustra, challenging his points-of-view.

The preface to the book outlines the basics of Zarathustra's position:

1. God is dead.

2. Man must overcome his dependence on codes of morality and ethics drawn from superstition.

3. Humanity will thus become the *Übermensch* or Superman, a stage of maturity that looks to man as a predecessor.

4. 'Man' is a stage of development like a tightrope between animal and Superman.

Some people have interpreted Nietzsche to be saying that some people can become Supermen, as if he's producing a self-help guide to success. The mistaken association of Nietzsche's ideas with the German National Socialist Party is in keeping with this interpretation, yet, even though Nazi theory is—at best—a misunderstanding of Nietzsche's argument, the association of his ideas

and those of the Nazis is one of the reasons that it is surprising that
Herbert uses Nietzsche the way that he does. Instead, the
Superman is what all of humanity must become if it is to overcome
its reliance upon superstition, and set its own course. In his preface, Nietzsche calls the sort of misinterpretation that the Nazis had
of his ideas—that one sort of human could become more important than another sort of human—"Ultimate Man."

Those familiar with the *Dune* saga may recognize here a similarity with the purpose of Leto II's program: taking humanity from
its reliance upon gods to a future in which, through the purpose of
the Golden Path, humanity will never again allow itself to be dom-
inated by a monolithic vision or single individual—whether economic, political, religious, or otherwise.

Parallel 1: The Preacher and Zarathustra Go to Town

Three very specific parallels exist between episodes in the Dune
cycle and *Zarathustra* that may help us to see what Herbert's narrative structure owes to *Zarathustra*. The first goes as follows: In
Children of Dune, the physically blinded yet presciently aware
Muad'Dib enters Arrakeen after an absence of nearly a decade (just
as Zarathustra enters the first town in his first *down-going*). "The
Preacher" mounts the stairs of Alia's temple, and observes the mar-
ketplace thronging with business:

> A sudden diversion rippled through the crowd on the landing. Sand
> Dancers had come into the plaza at the foot of the steps . . . teth-
> ered to each other by elacca ropes. They obviously had been danc-
> ing thus for days, seeking a state of ecstasy. Foam dribbled from
> their mouths as they jerked and stamped to their secret music. A full
> third of them dangled unconscious from the ropes, tugged back and
> forth by the others like dolls on strings. One of these dolls had
> come awake, though, and the crowd apparently knew what to
> expect.

The narrative of the *Book for Everyone and No One* (as
Zarathustra is sub-titled) parallels this, as Zarathustra, arriving at
the market square: "for it had been announced that a tight-rope
walker would be appearing," immediately begins his famous first
discourse on the *Übermensch*, saying:

> *I teach you the Superman.* Man is something that should be overcome. What have you done to overcome him?
>
> All creatures hitherto have created something beyond themselves: and do you want to be the ebb of this great tide, and return to the animals rather than overcome man?
>
> What is the ape to men? A laughing-stock or a painful embarrassment. And just so shall man be to the Superman: a laughing-stock or a painful embarrassment. (p. 41)

In both situations, there is an instance of something that is tied, spanning, and spectacle. In both, the preacher-prophet uses the crowd's gathering and reaction to this spectacle as occasion to introduce his teachings: Parallel to the *Zarathustra* material just quoted, in *Children of Dune*, answering the crowd's laughter at the Sand Dancer's vision of Arrakeen's eventual destruction, the Preacher shouts: "Silence! . . . Did you not hear that man? Blasphemers and idolators! All of you! The religion of Muad'Dib is not Muad'Dib. He spurns it as he spurns you!" Leaving, the Preacher turns and shows the assembled crowd something that he had been carrying in his purse: "a desert-mummified human hand," and says, "I bring the Hand of God, and that is all that I bring!"

Just before entering the town that is the main scene of events in the preface of *Zarathustra*, Zarathustra runs into an "old saint" in the forest, who had known Zarathustra before he retreated to the mountain. At this point in the narrative, after they have finished talking—just before entering the town and exclaiming "*I teach you the Superman*"—Zarathustra wonders to himself if it is possible that the "old saint has not yet heard in his forest that *God is dead!*" (p. 41). Herbert's Preacher and Zarathustra are performing equivalent functions, and their audiences are equally unimpressed and unconvinced.

When Zarathustra enters the town, the reader first meets the buffoon-devil character. The tightrope walker is a visual metaphor of Zarathustra's teaching of the *Übermensch* or "superman." Instead of merely telling us that Man is a stage between animal and Superman, Nietzsche draws a picture and lets us see that Man is a stage between animal and Superman. This tightrope walker is upset in his progress between the towers by a "brightly-dressed fellow like a buffoon" who comes behind him, urging him on and out of his way. Finally, with "a cry like a devil," the buffoon springs over the tightrope walker, and causes him to fall to his death (pp. 47–48).

Like Leto II, whose physical transformation into a sandworm-human hybrid begins just after the Preacher shakes the "Hand of God" at the crowd in Arrakeen, the devil-buffoon cares not at all for the individual life of the tightrope walker, and Leto cares only for his "Golden Path." Leto is, in this regard, the devil-buffoon and the Superman, but not because of his new-found strength and speed, but only because of his dedication to the Golden Path. The overcoming that Zarathustra preaches is not that of becoming a greater man, but in transcending man. Similarly, the personal development of Leto II into the sandworm-human hybrid is not one that he wishes any other human to undergo, though it is important to him acting as the goad to allow humanity to change itself into something that goes beyond humanity as Leto found it.

The events following the preacher's appearance in Arrakeen extend the comparison between the *Dune* saga and *Zarathustra*: Towards the end of *Children of Dune*, in the exchange between Assan Tariq and Leto in the meeting of "the Preacher" and his son in the desert, there is an otherwise difficult-to-understand passage. After calling Leto a demon several times, Tariq repeats: "You're a demon," to which Leto replies: "Your demon. . . . But you are my demon." This echoes the structure of Zarathustra's meeting with the devil and the idea of transformation into Superman, which itself acts as the devil-buffoon to spur change. Though there is much intervening material in *Children of Dune*, the events and discussions still roughly parallel the narrative structure of *Zarathustra*. The conceptual parallel, however, is exact.

Parallel 2: The Ultimate Man, the Religion of Muad'Dib, and Leto's Reign

Historical Background

The second narrative parallel will take more couching than the first one, for I am going to take some time here to try to understand why Herbert uses Nietzsche's work so extensively in the *Dune* saga. As such, the events of the decades that come between the period in which Nietzsche published and Herbert's initial and continuing publication of the *Dune* saga until his death in the 1980s must be taken into account. In much the same way that Nietzsche's insights were considered and reconsidered throughout this period, so too does Herbert place Nietzsche's claims for humanity in the context of events that had subsequently taken place.

In one of the chapter-heading quotations of *Chapterhouse Dune*, a "Zensufi Master" (hence a Tleilaxu Master, though this is not yet known in the narrative) states "the person who takes the banal and ordinary and illuminates it in a new way can terrify. We do not want our ideas changed. We feel threatened by such demands. "I already know the important things!" we say. Then Changer comes and throws our old ideas away."

The use of the word "banal" here recalls the work published almost concurrently with *Dune* by the philosopher Hannah Arendt: *Eichmann in Jerusalem: A Report on the Banality of Evil*. This much-discussed and often surprising book presents a portrait of Adolf Eichmann, the so-called "Architect of the Holocaust," that is counter-intuitively grotesque in its lack of grotesque features.

Beyond her judgment that Eichmann's "deeds were monstrous," Arendt considers that "the doer . . . was quite ordinary, commonplace, and neither demonic nor monstrous" (*Eichmann in Jerusalem*, p. 4). She states concerning his actions that, "if this is 'banal' and even funny, if with the best will in the world one cannot extract any diabolical or demonic profundity from Eichmann, that is still far from calling it commonplace" (p. 288).

Humanity, reacting to the events of World War II, has struggled with the problem that the en-storying propaganda of the subsequent decades by actors on all sides of this drama has failed to satisfy. The snowballing implications of the barbarity of events that overtook us in the twentieth century hardly seems like the what we should have expected after two wars 'to end all wars'. "Somehow," muses Margaret Atwood's main character in her book *Cat's Eye*, "the war never ended after all, it just broke up into pieces and got scattered" (p. 429).

Perhaps it would be simplest to take the work of a philosopher who actually seems to encourage humans to outstrip themselves, to become more than men, to become *Supermen*, and consign it to the garbage can of history. But Herbert understands Nietzsche far better than that. The "banality" of "evil" exactly describes Paul's attitude and Herbert's presentation of the sixty-five billion deaths attributable to his Fremen-led jihad, even though we are told repeatedly that a much worse situation lay on either side of the path that Paul saw. Still, all of this ignores that this path, for better or worse, is the result of human actions.

Herbert's Superheroes and the Myth Fabric of Society

As Herbert muses in the opening paragraphs of "Dune Genesis," his 1980 essay discussing the origins of this work (just prior to the publication of *God Emperor of Dune*), "Personal observation has convinced me that in the power area of politics/economics and in their logical consequence, war, people tend to give over every decision-making capacity to any leader who can wrap himself in the myth fabric of the society." Paul may result from the Bene Gesserit breeding program, but even the genetic heritage he receives passively can't absolve him of his subsequent actions and their results. On this reading, then, *Dune* provides its own report on the banality of evil—a mirrored image of the problems associated with taking action in our own world—a tapestry woven from strands of our own "myth-fabric" whose warp and weft we, lacking perspective, struggle to understand.

Herbert goes on in "Dune Genesis" to make clear that his original impetus was exactly such a mirroring. Having watched the USDA project in the dunes south of Florence, Oregon, attempting to freeze the marching sands in place using an invasive and foreign species of poverty grass, Herbert was struck by the potential for the structures of the early twentieth-century world to be transformed and altered, but nevertheless continued in the future:

> Demagogues, fanatics, con-game artists, the innocent and the not-so-innocent bystanders – all were to have a part in the drama. This grows from my theory that superheroes are disastrous for humankind. Even if we find a real hero (whatever – or whoever – that may be), eventually fallible mortals take over the power structure that always comes into being around such a leader.
>
> Enormous problems arise when human mistakes are made on the grand scale available to a superhero.

Herbert goes on to say that his "superhero concept filled me with a concern that ecology might be the next banner for demagogues and would-be-heroes, for the power seekers and others ready to find an adrenaline high in the launching of a new crusade." Despite our contemporary awareness of this and this issue's prevalence in both media and politics in the twenty-first century, Herbert's prescience is perhaps not as surprising and prophetic as it seems to be. Although Al Gore's *An Inconvenient Truth* makes us think that the ecological banner is a new one, the patterns that are now being addressed in popular (and populist) settings are those that were set in place during the last century.

Some sorts of philosophy take it as read that philosophers shouldn't or can't concern themselves with questions of history, unless it's to do with theory on *doing* history or the "history of philosophy." Other philosophers argue that ideas, theory and history can't be kept separate. Herbert's *Dune* saga falls definitely in the latter camp. It calls us, not only to avoid such separation, but also actively to put into practice the consideration of history for a philosophical modeling of humanity. So, while "Dune Genesis" outlines how Herbert's notion of the problems with "superhero" leaders (he lists Hitler, Roosevelt, Stalin, Churchill, Mussolini, JFK, and Patton) contributed to his literary project—"Heroes are painful, superheroes are a catastrophe—the mistakes of superheroes involve too many of us in disaster." The *Dune* saga is a story-based examination of Nietzsche's ideas in the light of the history that had transpired since Nietzsche first published.

When he began his project, not yet two decades had passed since the end of the Second World War. The US was becoming involved (and by the time the initial stories and book were published, had become firmly entrenched) in the civil rights movement. Korea—the first "UN" war—had ended in uncertainty, Vietnam was underway. When he talks of "disaster," Herbert knows only too well of what he speaks.

Spannungsbogen: The Span of the Bow, the Golden Path, and the Tightrope

Still, the question must be asked: Why continue to interact with the ideas of a philosopher whose possible misapplication had been associated with the twentieth century's touchstone of evil, banal or not? Well, Herbert's next parallel with Nietzsche might help us to understand this better: In one of *Dune*'s chapter-introducing quotations, drawn from *The Wisdom of Muad'Dib* by the Princess Irulan, we read: "The Fremen were supreme in that quality the ancients called "Spannungsbogen"—which is the self-imposed delay between desire for a thing and the act of reaching out to grasp that thing." This quotation plays into the generally building tension of *Dune* and underscores the way in which the first book of the cycle invites its readers to side with Paul Atreides and to yearn for his coming to power.

Despite the disquieting visions of jihad that Paul has throughout the book, we're given to believe that the Fremen (including Liet-Kynes, the Imperial Planetologist and Fremen leader) and the Atreides are the "good guys," while Imperial and Harkonnen forces wear the black hats. On this level, *Dune* can be read as what literary specialists call a *Bildungsroman*—a coming-of-age-novel. Herbert manipulates this reading as he develops the disappointing *Dune Messiah* and the new parallels in *Children of Dune* with *Dune*. Despite ourselves, we place our trust in Leto II (whose *Children of Dune* is also a sort of *Bildungsroman*) as we did with Paul. What Paul sees in his prescient vision and fears, Leto embraces intentionally, and our sheep-like following of the "hero" of the piece leaves us admiring the Tyrant.

On another level, the struggle to regain control of Arrakis is the stuff of war movies and James Bond films: we always know who's "in the right." Even the way that "Atreides" and "Fremen" sound to the ear (not to mention the overtones of freedom present in the latter) compared to "Harkonnen" and "Sardaukar" (not to mention the Russian derivation of "Vladimir," and the way in which this might be received in the thick of the Cold War) predisposes the reader to this binary judgment of good and evil.

But the reference to *Spannungsbogen* doesn't merely help to build tension. It also alludes to the continuing philosophical parallels between Nietzsche's work and Herbert's. In Nietzsche's understanding, "Man is a rope, fastened between animal and Superman": "A dangerous going-across, a dangerous wayfaring, a dangerous looking-back, a dangerous shuddering and staying-still" (p. 43). This idea is the source of the tension to which Herbert refers in Irulan's *Spannungsbogen* discourse: the Superman describes, in part, the tension of the drawn bow, the back-slung spear arm, the cloud pregnant with rain, hail and lightning. As Leto discovers during his vision of transformation at Jacarutu:

> Leto sensed that he had ventured across old boundaries into a new land which only the imagination had witnessed, and that he now looked directly through the very next veil which a yawning humankind called *Unknown*.
> It was bloodthirsty reality . . .
> "I've become pasigraphic. I'm a living glyph to write out the changes which must come to pass. If I do not write them, you'll encounter such heartache." (*Children of Dune*)

("Pasigraphic" refers to a language of concepts rather than words.)

Portraits of "Ultimate Men": Mirroring Our Own Reality in Fiction

Nietzsche's model draws a contrast between the Superman and what he calls "the most contemptible man: the *Ultimate Man*," and seeks to draw out for us the ground of difference between the two. There are clear parallels between these "Ultimate Men" and the state of the empire in *Dune Messiah* and under the regency of *Children of Dune*:

> Alas! The time is coming when man will no more shoot the arrow of his longing out over mankind, and the string of his bow will have forgotten how to twang!
>
> I tell you: one must have chaos in one, to give birth to a dancing star. I tell you: you still have chaos in you.
>
> Alas! The time is coming when man will give birth to no more stars. Alas! The time of the most contemptible man is coming, the man who can no longer despise himself.
>
> Behold! I shall show you the *Ultimate Man*.
>
> The Earth has become small, and upon it hops the Ultimate Man, who makes everything small. His race is as inexterminable as the flea; the Ultimate Man lives the longest. (*Thus Spoke Zarathustra*, p. 46)

Some of the characteristics of the Ultimate Men (and what I see as parallels in the Duniverse) are as follows (quotations from *Thus Spoke Zarathustra*, pp. 46–47):

- "They have left the places where living was hard." (Fremen have left the sietch life, or neglect water discipline, and eventually live as "Museum Fremen" in the later books.)

- "A little poison now and then: that produces pleasant dreams." (Reliance on spice for visions within the new religion of Muad'Dib, and the loss of spice in Leto's reign for all but the most important visionary and other purposes.)

- "They still work, for work is entertainment. But they take care the entertainment does not exhaust them." (Again, the constant references throughout particularly *Children of Dune* concerning the new decadence of Arrakis.)

- "Everyone wants the same thing, everyone is the same: whoever thinks otherwise goes voluntarily into the madhouse."
  (The development of the religion of Muad'Dib into a bloody
  orthodoxy, and the subsequent imposition of uniformity
  across Leto II's empire.)

- "They are clever and know everything that has ever happened: so there is no end to their mockery." (Alia's reliance
  on her inner memories that ends with possession by the
  Baron Harkonnen; the split within the Bene Gesserit concerning the import of history, personified in the factional attitudes towards the Duncan Idaho ghola project between the
  Reverend Mothers Taraza and Schwangyu in *Heretics of
  Dune*.)

This discussion ends Zarathustra's first discourse. His audience
responds. "The shouting and mirth of the crowd interrupted him.
"Give us this Ultimate Man, O Zarathustra'—so they cried—'Make
us into this Ultimate Man! You can have the Superman!'"

And so the jihad that hijacks Paul's vision leads to an empire
within which the Ultimate Man succeeds very well indeed, until the
longest living "man," Leto II, imposes the monotonous and eventually intolerable reality of "Ultimate Man" in his 3,500-year reign,
producing the Scattering.

The Fremen jihad, the religion of Muad'Dib, the empire of Alia
of the Knife—none of these fulfills a vision of the future that will
lead to the firm establishment of humanity in the face of any centralized adversity. But neither is Leto II's empire! Herbert continually dashes our narrative expectations of heroic victory and
therefore success because this is our own dedication to Ultimate
Man.

Although aspects of the empire that his father built will be transformed—and so preserved—by Leto II, the Golden Path will be
something fundamentally other. It will not be a Fremen-led jihad
that looks essentially to the past for its shape, but rather a tight-
rope-like, Golden-Path-monotony that will issue with a diversified,
dangerous set of possibilities that includes the removal of the entire
house of Atreides from the vision of anyone with prescience (as the
descendants of Sonia Atreides become).

The transformation of the male-dominated Fremen and
Sardaukar military forces into the female-only Fish Speakers, and

the subsequent creation of the Honored Matres from this and the liberated Tleilaxu females (or, axolotl tanks), will lead eventually to the united Sisterhood formed from the blending of the Honored Matres and already combined House Atreides–Bene Gesserit hybrid. Nothing of the previous orders that populate the universe of those striving to be "Ultimate Men" will be left untouched by Leto II's Golden Path.

"Uncanny is human existence and still without meaning: a buffoon can be fatal to it. I want to teach men the meaning of their existence: which is the Superman, the lightning from the dark cloud man" (*Thus Spoke Zarathustra*, p. 49). These oracular words could serve as the motto for the 3,500-year rule of the draconian Leto II. The tension in *Dune*, therefore, isn't related only to the internal plot between Atreides and Harkonnen, but also to Paul's visions of a very disturbing future, a future that becomes only too apparent in the opening pages of *Dune Messiah*.

The overt citation of the German concept-word *Spannungsbogen* proves a signpost that makes obvious the comparison between the *Dune* cycle and the philosophy of *Übermensch* that Nietzsche develops in *Zarathustra*. *Dune* and its sequels investigate the idea of leadership and the conceptual universe surrounding the desire to obtain and to use power in the political arena against the background of Herbert's own time. So Herbert sets Paul up as the tight-rope walker—the Kwisatz Haderach—in a manner that recalls Zarathustra.

> The spear which I throw at my enemies! How I thank my enemies that at last I can throw it!
> The tension [German: *Spannung*] of my cloud has been too great: between laughter-peals of lightning I want to cast hail showers into the depths. (*Thus Spoke Zarathustra*, pp. 108–09)

Paul, burnt and blinded—like the failed tight-rope walker from *Zarathustra*—becomes a living reminder of what Zarathustra says: "*if* there were gods, how could I endure not to be a god! *Therefore* there are no gods" (p. 110). And his son will show humanity that "God is a thought that makes all that is straight crooked and all that stands giddy. What? Would time be gone and all that is transitory only a lie?" The Atreides line becomes for humanity god, devil, buffoon, prophet, and message all wrapped up together as a goad to abandon belief in the "evil and misanthropic . . . teaching about the one and the perfect and the unmoved and the sufficient and the intransitory."

But it isn't simply a neat fiction. No, Herbert is testing and examining Nietzsche's ideas concerning the Superman in a thought experiment that far surpasses Nietzsche's own in *Zarathustra*. Taking into account the real-world events that Nietzsche's philosophy had helped to describe, Herbert recognizes that Nietzsche's modeling of humanity's potential progress has incredible value for a world that had become increasingly influenced by and afraid of the effects of charismatic leaders.

Herbert shows us that the hollow victory of *Dune* that resounds so boomingly in *Dune Messiah* is that of *Ultimate Man*. The Bene Gesserit produce on purpose the Kwisatz Haderach because they believe he is the *fulfillment* of humanity. In reality, they only produce the conditions for Superman—the outcome of Leto II's Golden Path. Both Paul's prescient vision and Leto's Golden Path point to something other: not the fulfillment of (and therefore ability to dominate) humanity (in this case, the political, economic and religious system of the original empire of *Dune*), but rather the destruction of the cultural and other limitations inherent in this system. As Paul says to his mother:

> "You're thinking I'm the Kwisatz Haderach," he said. "Put that out of your mind. I'm something unexpected."
> *I must get word of this to one of the schools*, she thought. *The mating index may show what has happened.*
> "They won't learn about me until it's too late," he said. . . .
> "If you're not the Kwisatz Haderach," Jessica said, "what—"
> "You couldn't possibly know," he said. "You won't believe it until you see it."
> And he thought: *I'm a seed* (*Dune*).

As with Nietzsche's *Übermensch*— "lightning from the dark cloud man," the spear thrown by Zarathustra against his enemies—so with Paul, who is the seed and the Coriolis wind, and Muad'Dib, "'the One Who Points the Way." His empire may be that of the *Ultimate* Man, but he and his son will show humanity how to become the *Superman*.

The transformation of the human race that takes place over the course of the *Dune* saga isn't to be remade in the image of Paul Atreides. Instead, through the agency of the Atreides line, the transformation of humanity becomes possible. While Leto II will undergo radical transformation himself, his actions are those, not of pattern, but patterner. Not lightning, but lightning rod.

Parallel 3: Prescience and Eternal Recurrence

Part of Nietzsche's ideas concerning the Superman revolves around the effect that externally-derived or imaginary metaphysical systems have on human behavior. In response to this, he employs what philosophers call a "thought experiment," in which he shows us how liberating it would be to imagine that this life is all that there is, and therefore holds its own value. Originally introduced in Nietzsche's book *The Gay Science*, this thought experiment of "eternal recurrence" plays an important role in *Zarathustra*. Eternal recurrence is also deeply connected to the importance of prescience in the Dune cycle. Leto realizes that

> the structures of Imperial society [are] reflected in [the] physical structures of its planets and their communities. Like a gigantic unfolding within him, he saw this revelation for what it must be: a window into the society's invisible parts. Seeing this, Leto realized that every system had such a window. Even the system of himself and his universe. (*Children of Dune*)

This passage echoes and interprets Nietzsche's treatment of eternal recurrence in *Zarathustra*, in the vision that Zarathustra describes of "the most solitary man." In this vision, he walks "A path that mounted defiantly through boulders and rubble . . . despite the spirit that drew it downward, drew it towards the abyss, the Spirit of Gravity, my devil and archenemy . . . half dwarf, half mole." He goes on.

> Then something occurred which lightened me: for the dwarf jumped down from my shoulder. . . . And he squatted down upon a stone in front of me. But a gateway stood just where we had halted.
> "Behold this gateway, dwarf!" I went on: "it has two aspects. Two paths come together here: no one has ever reached their end.
> "This long lane behind us: it goes on for an eternity. And that long lane ahead of us—that is another eternity.
> "They are in opposition to one another, these paths; they abut on one another: and it is here at this gateway that they come together. The name of the gateway is written above it: 'Moment'.
> "But if one were to follow them further and ever further and further: do you think, dwarf, that these paths would be in eternal opposition?

"Behold this moment!" I went on. "From this gateway Moment a
long, eternal lane runs *back*: an eternity lies behind us.

"Must not all things that *can* run have already run along this lane?
Must not all things that *can* happen *have* already happened, been
done, run past?" (pp. 176–78)

The fear that this vision inspires in Zarathustra is one side of the
coin: looked at from this perspective, the eternally recurring
Moment becomes a path with no escape. This perspective invites
gods and superheroes to explain (and thereby construct) the fated
destiny of humanity. This is the perspective of Muad'Dib and the
empire of Ultimate Men that his prescience engenders. From
another perspective, though, the gateway of Moment—Leto's "win-
dow into system"—allows a freedom from the notion of destiny
altogether.

Herbert shows us that value-systems that come from things that
are only apparently necessary and eternal are actually temporary
and reliant on our own decisions. As Herbert asks in "Dune
Genesis," "Do you want an absolute prediction? Then you want
only today, and you reject tomorrow. You are the ultimate conservative. You are trying to hold back movement in an infinitely
changing universe. The verb to be does make idiots of us all." The
Superman is a humanity freed from the force of apparent necessity
that pretends to be the glue of culture, but ends up acting more
like the flypaper of time.

Philosopher of the Dangerous Perhaps

Only a few pages into his book *Beyond Good and Evil*, Nietzsche
wonders

> if it might even be possible that *what* constitutes the value of those
> good and honored things resides precisely in their being artfully
> related, knotted and crocheted to these wicked, apparently antithetical
> things, perhaps even in their being essentially identical with them.
> Perhaps! But who is willing to concern himself with such dangerous
> perhapses? For that we have to await the arrival of a new species of
> philosopher, one which possesses tastes and inclinations opposite to
> and different from those of its predecessors—philosophers of the dan-
> gerous "perhaps" in every sense. —And to speak in all seriousness: I
> see such new philosophers arising. (p. 16)

Frank Herbert: Philosopher of the Dangerous Perhaps. Devil on the tight-rope, Zarathustra in Muad'Dib's clothing.

Discovered by:
BROOK W.R. PEARSON

FROM: DAR-ES-BALAT
Possible Authors: Siona and Duncan Idaho
Date: 13725 A.G.

Son of the Curse of the Golden Path

Does the prophet see the future or does he see a line of weakness, a fault or cleavage that he may shatter with words or decisions as a diamond-cutter shatters his gem with a blow of a knife?

—*Private Reflections on Muad'Dib* by the PRINCESS IRULAN (*Dune*)

Put yourself in Paul-Muad'Dib's stillsuit.

You are victorious. Your atomics and sandworms have breached the Shield Wall in the midst of the grandmother of all storms. Your hordes of Fremen have broken the Emperor's deadly legions of Sardaukar. You stand once more in the Great Hall at Arrakeen, beside your mother Jessica and your beloved Chani, your warrior-advisors Stilgar and Gurney Halleck, your chosen Fedaykin. The defeated Emperor and his retinue are brought before you to parlay for peace as you take the Lion Throne. The Known Universe awaits your every command.

So why do you call out Feyd-Rautha, na-Baron and Harkonnen, to duel, man to man, knife to knife? It's kanly, the sworn vendetta between your houses. Feyd is fast, cunning, blooded in hundred of gladiatorial bouts. He isn't exhausted from having just led an army into battle, he could well kill you.

Is it recklessness? Honor? Vengeance? Good reasons, perhaps. But . . . Paul is an oracle with the special gift of foresight. He fore-knows what will happen after this day, this hour, because he has prescient visions of the future where fanatic legions of Fremen under the Atreides banner will sweep out across the Known Universe in their holy war. So Paul has no good reason to risk his life in a knife-fight with Feyd because nothing he does can divert

207

the horrors he's foreseen. Whether he lives or he dies he cannot be praised for it as a hero-martyr or shamed for it as reckless or a coward, because his choice of a life-or-death risk makes no difference anyway. The consequences are inevitable.

I showed in "Curse of the Golden Path" that the Atreides oracles slip the trap of the prescience because their power of oracle works in a special way: it is a supercomputing predictive knowledge of the probabilities that future events or series of future events will occur. Paul-Muad'Dib and his son Leto II, thanks to their special attunement, stand in a unique position to try to manipulate what timelines happen to occur. When events have a zero probability of occurring, they fall out of prescient vision; when events have a probability closer to 1, they are seen on more timelines; and when the event is absolutely inevitable, it is seen on all timelines. But is this the stuff of freedom if we can't attribute praise and blame—that is, responsibility—to people whose choices are so stifled by overwhelming future inevitabilities?

We strongly associate moral responsibility and accountability with freedom of will. Put it like this: Heroes rightly attract praise and honors for their deeds. Can there be heroes in a Duniverse where there are seers who foreknow inevitabilities? Or are there just actors, agents making decisions, some with great consequences, and some—oracles—with great knowledge of those consequences?

The rule of a good sequel is that it ups the ante. In *Children of Dune*, we learn more about the Atreides oracles' prescience. To answer the question of whether an oracle can be a hero, Herbert uses the action in *Children of Dune* to engage in a very clever, indeed very philosophical, thought-experiment: What if there were not one but two oracles? What if they met? Does this give them more or less free will? Does it give Paul and Leto the chance to be heroes? Same as in a court of law, first we have to decide the facts, then make judgment. First we do the metaphysics: Who was free how and when? Then we make with the ethics: Who is the hero?

Paul's Terrible Purpose

Paul Atreides seems a hero for his time. No, Paul Atreides seems a hero for any time.

The son of a Duke and heir to House Atreides, his Bene Gesserit mother Jessica trains him in the Sisterhood's ways of prana-bindu metabolic control, heightened awareness, and the Voice. The great Warrior-Mentat Thufir Hawat trains Paul to become, like him, a human super-computer. The famous Gurney Hallack and the last Swordmaster of the Ginaz, Duncan Idaho, train him in weapons and battle tactics. He is a natural Truthsayer. Finally, Paul is also the product of a secret breeding program by the Bene Gesserit to produce a Kwisatz Haderach, "a male Bene Gesserit whose organic mental powers would bridge space and time" (*Dune*).

All of which would make for a very well-equipped (perhaps a little over-equipped) hero for any adventure story. Even after the betrayal of his family and the defeat of his father's army, Paul constitutes a formidable opponent to set against the schemes of House Harkonnen and their patron, The Padishah Emperor. Paul, he got the tools and he got the talent!

Except . . . Ever since he was a boy, Paul has had prescient dreams of future events that then really come to pass. On Arrakis, with a highly increased diet of the spice melange, noted for enhancing psychic powers, Paul manifests a powerful talent for prescience. "Without even the safety valve of dreaming, he focused his prescient awareness, seeing it as a computation of most probable futures, but with something more, an edge of mystery—as though his mind dipped into some timeless stratum and sampled the winds of the future" (*Dune*). He begins to see with increasing clarity of vision and in ever-increasing number the many possible futures leading forward from the onrushing present. He also sees the number of possible futures narrow down where actions taken in the present shift the weight of possibilities.

Paul's prescience seems like the talent to top all his other talents. Why then does he regard it as a curse and a trap? He can see down along most of the possible futures the sight of a bloody jihad of hundreds of planets. It will be committed in his name because of his powers and the legend surrounding him that will raise him up as a messiah. Paul's tragedy in the *Dune* saga is that he struggles fitfully, hopelessly against this vision. He does not want jihad, not in the Mahdi's name, in the Fremen messiah's name, in his name. He secretly struggles against everybody around him who is unknowingly working towards the holy war to come.

As a boy, Paul sensed that he had a "terrible purpose." Paul comes to realize that what he sensed was really just (just!) a precognitive sense of a pent-up species-wide consciousness. "The race of humans had felt its own dormancy, sensed itself grown stale and knew now only the need to experience turmoil in which the genes could mingle and the strong new mixtures survive. All humans were alive," to Paul's sense of it, "as an unconscious single organism in this moment, experiencing a kind of sexual heat that could override any barrier" (*Dune*). It cannot be brooked; it cannot be turned aside. Paul's struggle against it is futile.

The Truth Shall Not Set You Free

In *Dune Messiah*, prescience's trap becomes literal. In an assassination attempt against him, a stone-burner destroys Paul's eyes. Eerily, he can entertain his oracular vision simultaneous and concurrent with the real time it was a vision of, "vision-reality, tick for tick." This ability horrifies Stilgar, as a good Fremen. Paul says to him, "They've blinded my body, but not my vision. Ah, Stil, I live in an apocalyptic dream. My steps fit into it so precisely that I fear most of all I will grow bored reliving the same thing so exactly" (*Dune Messiah*).

We're horrified too, because Paul knows exactly where this thread of vision will lead him: the vision's end, blindness of inner and outer sight.

Paul is the first of two oracles in the Atreides family. His twin children Leto II and Ghanima are exposed to the Spice Agony in their mother's womb. They are pre-born. Like Reverend Mothers, in the Spice Agony Leto and Ghanima regain all their ancestor's memories, except as unborn fetuses. The twins are born as fully-aware adult human consciousnesses in the bodies of children.

Leto and Ghanima both share their father's memories, therefore memory of Paul's prescient visions. But Gurney Halleck forces an overdose of spice on Leto to test whether one of his ancestors possesses him. As we readers know, Leto is no Abomination. The overdose, though, forces Leto's own power of oracle to manifest.

When it does, we learn much more about how prescience works. Paul wasn't ready for foresight. Leto is. He had the memory-self of his father inside his consciousness to guide him. As Leto's vision absorbs him, time becomes for him something like a trinocular sight into past, present, and future. Leto observes that "Time is a measure of space, just as a range-finder is a measure of space, but measuring locks us into the place we measure" (*Children of Dune*).

As he looks out into the swell of possible futures, he sees two things: the universe will end in a Typhoon Struggle, Krazilec. This destruction shall mirror and magnify beyond compare the horrors of Paul's jihad. He also sees a path to safety. Secher Nbiw, he calls it in Fremen: the Golden Path. Krazilec is unavoidable. Yet if Leto leads humanity along the Golden Path, humanity might survive Krazilec.

The Golden Path has three goals. First, Leto wants humankind to survive the inevitability that is the Typhoon Struggle. Secondly, he's educating the racial consciousness, right down into the genes. Third, he wishes to scatter humanity beyond the reach of a single mind's prescient vision.

The Tyrant

The first goal of the Golden Path is easy enough to understand, but what is the lesson that Leto wants to teach humanity? He wants to breed a genetic predisposition for liberty. To achieve the Golden Path, Leto plans to assume the Lion Throne and establish a supremely oppressive but secretly benevolent tyranny that will last for thousands of years. He merges with sandtrout, larval sand-worms, to make himself a human-sandworm hybrid, virtually inde-structible and extremely long-lived. Long-lived enough to see his plan through. Leto sacrifices his humanity to the grand, moral necessity—where his father Paul, who also saw Krazilec and the Golden Path to safety, was afraid to.

After his millennia-long tyranny called Leto's Peace, and the Famine Times which follow the collapse of his empire, the Golden Path sees fruition in the Scattering, a collective diaspora to other universes. When his power of oracle is activated for the first time, Leto says, "Universal prescience is a myth. Only the most powerful local currents of Time may be foretold. But in an infinite universe, local can be so gigantic that your mind shrinks from it" (*Children of Dune*). In the Scattering, humanity expands so far that the local events a prescience mind sees cannot contain all of them.

Why is this Leto's goal? Oracles aren't constantly exercising their power. When they do exercise it, they do so from a particular pre-sent moment and as the particular person they are. Leto realizes that an oracle, by looking and seeing the possible futures from the present circumstances—the moment in time they choose to look, the person who looks—fixes the set of possible futures they hap-pen to see as the only set of possible futures.

When having their prescient visions, the oracles fold time somewhat as Guild Space Navigators fold space. When you fold something in space, such as the corner of favorite page in *Dune* (Guilty!), you bring the tip of the corner into contact with the flat of the page. When Guild Navigators fold space, they bring two distant points in space together, making instantaneous space travel possible. Oracles fold points in time. Their visions bring the future into contact with the present, connected via their foresight. The state of the present, the right-then moment at which Paul or Leto has an oracular vision, impresses onto the future its possibilities. In a strange way, Paul and Leto cause the set of possible futures to become fixed as the only set of possibilities precisely because those possibilities are being actively foreseen from the present. In the Duniverse, oracular vision frames, delimits and shapes what are the possibilities. It also reduces the number of possibilities. Before Paul or Leto look, the future may have contained fantastically many, perhaps even infinite possibilities; after they look, every time they look, the number of possibilities is fixed to less and again less.

We define tyrants as having dominion over space, over their territories and the peoples within them. The terrific power of oracles in the Duniverse is that they are tyrants with dominion over time, over the events they see and the people in them. Noble son of a noble father, Leto believes that with terrific power comes terrific responsibility. Leto feels responsible to make sure that humankind evolves so that there are humans who are invisible to prescience. So that anybody with the power of oracle – including Leto himself – has a weakness, a literal oracular blind-spot. The third goal of Leto's Golden Path is breed into humanity his hoped-for, to-him-invisible assassins. Leto meets with success in Siona Atreides: he can't foresee Siona or her plans in any of the possible futures his vision lights on. He meets with this success rather finally, given that Siona murders him.

Vision-Battle in the Desert

Frank Herbert is clearly well-versed in the philosophical issues regarding the potential incompatibility between free will and foreknowledge. He has woven them into the *Dune* saga in such a way that the danger that oracle presents gives the story, not a fatalistic air of doom, but its most thrilling points of high drama.

Now to the highest point of the drama, the (dare I say it?) fateful meeting in *Children of Dune* between the two Atreides oracles, father and son, Paul and Leto. It's the only time in the *Dune* saga when two powerful, prescience-adept oracles encounter each other. I think this meeting shows that maybe Paul and Leto are free-willed—and avoid foreknowledge's paradoxes as best they can. They are free just when they cannot foresee!

Years before, Paul Atreides submitted to Fremen law for the blind and walked out into the desert. Somehow he survived and he is now called The Preacher. He has been more or less held captive by the renegade Cast-Out Fremen at Shuloch, who have been feeding Paul heavy doses of spice in the hope of his having visions they can exploit. Paul might have regained his power of oracle or he might not. I think we should assume he has not, but that nevertheless Paul still retains full, vivid recollection of his original vision.

Deep in the desert of the Tanzerouft, Leto waylays Paul. Paul is surprised, indeed, doubly so—surprised that there is a boy in the path of his sandworm mount who halts the worm in its trail, and surprised that the boy here is in fact his son. Yes, Atreides, life can surprise you. Of course Paul is surprised: an oracle can't see another oracle, so this possible meeting was never something he could have presciently envisioned. Leto has access to his father's memories of his vision. He is sure therefore this meeting was nothing Paul has presciently foreseen.

Leto waylays him because he sees this as his chance to again open up the future to the possibility of the Golden Path, a possibility his father's turning away from it has almost closed off. However seemingly innocuous their conversation, the two of them know it for what it really is: a vision-battle. And the stakes are as upped as stakes get: humankind's outlasting the Typhoon Struggle or perishing. Can Leto establish the future timelines which include the Golden Path as stronger possibilities or will Paul's inferior vision prevail? Recall what Princess Irulan also reports Muad'Dib said about the nature of oracle.

> He tells us that a single obscure decision of prophecy, perhaps the choice of one word over another, could change the entire aspect of the future. He tells us "The vision of time is broad, but when you pass through it, time becomes a narrow door." And always, he fought the temptation to choose a clear, safe course, warning "That path leads ever down into stagnation" (*Dune*).

This is a half-truth from Paul. He too saw the Golden Path and its grave necessity. The price is to wear "a skin that is not his own," surrender his humanity, and to take on his shoulders the burden of control of the Known Universe. Paul quailed before it, balked in favor of something approaching a normal life. Where Leto is unafraid, Paul was afraid of the painful, lonely, terrifically responsible choice, and of sacrificing his humanity for monstrosity. Not always the clear, safe course away from stagnation for Muad'Dib, not always. . . .

A Single Word at the Future's Precipice

Paul describes prophecy as a decision. What does he mean by this? For oracles, once they gain control over when and how to exercise their power of foresight, when and how to exercise it is a decision they make. While they are presciently envisioning all the future possibilities, because they're especially attuned to the connectedness of all the possible futures to the changing present moment, oracles are also in a position to affect which possibilities become more or less impossible. The Atreides oracles can't choose the set of future possibilities once they foresee them. The set of possibilities remain to be seen (or foreseen). They can help choose which possible timelines among the set are more probable or less probable. By frequently observing the possibilities for the future as they live and act in the present, they manipulate what the future possibilities are. Krazilec is inevitable because every timeline leads unwaveringly to it. Which specific timeline out of all the foreseen possible futures will be the one timeline that actually leads to it, that is entirely evitable. Whether the specific actual future includes the Golden Path is yet to be decided. Decided by acts in the present moment.

Paul might not be an oracle anymore when he meets his son in the Tanzerouft. However, he was an oracle and a Mentat and he hasn't forgotten his original visions. He has not forgotten the sense that even the slightest movement, the slightest word out of place, means that at this moment his son's divergent vision will gain the upper hand over his own. The battle of the visions is so fraught, so minute, so intricate and focused, that neither man wants to move or speak if he needn't. "Leto felt the dissonance between them. . . . Either he or his father would be forced to act soon, making a decision by that act, choosing a vision" (*Children of Dune*).

Even the Preacher's guide, a young Cast-Out from Shuloch, senses the vision-battle. "It was a shadow play all around them, a projection of unconscious forms" (*Children of Dune*). The boy has his orders: destroy the Atreides if they become Kwisatz Haderachs. The boy sets off a pseudo-shield in the desert nearby. It will attract a maddened worm that will kill all three of them. Leto senses the pseudo-shield has been activated; he waits for a signal. Paul whispers, desperately, "Don't." With the signal, Leto springs, kills the boy and throws the pseudo-shield far away, saving them from the worm.

The "Don't" of Paul's is the precipitating decision which chooses for a vision: Leto's vision – and the Golden Path to humankind's safety. Why is it? Is it just a lapse in concentration in their vision-battle? Unlikely. Even after his long time in the desert, Paul still constitutes a formidable opponent, even for his own son.

Is that one word his acceptance that his son is steadfast and resolute in the path—the Path—he has chosen, so why resist him? Let him have his vision! Or is it one final example of Paul's all-too-human irresolution in the face of titanic responsibilities, one more mistake born of his too-human frailty? After all, Paul shares much of his character with his father, the Duke Leto I. There was certainly a man who, in dangerous times with deadly responsibilities, cannot stop longing for and trying to hold onto simpler happinesses. Is Paul's "Don't" a moral failure? What could only be judged in the final analysis as the gasp of a coward?

I may have been too hasty in calling the vision-battle in the desert the highest point in a drama. Perhaps the correct literary allusion is a tragedy. Herbert reminds us that Atreides oracles are not like the oracles of myth. They are not voices from beyond drawn out in moments of mad ecstasy. Gaining the power of future-vision doesn't turn them into a pure, transparent lens. Paul Atreides is a human being of a time and with a distinctive personality that, like anybody, he would be hard-pressed to ever fully rise above. For Paul, the vision-battle is the peak of a tragedy. Paul is its hero: a tragic hero, in the ancient Greek sense, a hero who shapes the action yet simultaneously cannot escape a doom because a flaw that defines his very character, is the flaw that brings the doom about. In Paul's case, his flaw is his humanity. He doesn't want to become a monster just to save the future.

Paul-Muad'Dib is a hero, a conflicted and fascinatingly ambiguous hero, since in and because of his weakness he lets go the reins of time into his son's hands. Without Paul's moment of weakness, Leto couldn't be the hero he is by taking up the reins of time and start history along the Golden Path. Remember, though, that Leto is as half-blind in his visions as his father is: he cannot see what another oracle might do or have seen. So in that meeting deep in the desert they are both as free as two oracles can be, blind to how their vision-battle will end, seeing that they must fight it.

Aftermath at Sietch Tabr

"A REVEREND MOTHER WILL READ MY WORDS!" Every time I read that line in *Heretics of Dune*, the fifth of the Dune novels, the hairs on the back of my neck rise. The words are etched deep into the rock walls of a secret chamber beneath Sietch Tabr by a lasgun. The man who wrote them is none other than Leto Atreides II, the God-Emperor, dead for one and a half thousand years. Yet he knew that a Reverend Mother would read his words. And so she does: Reverend Mother Darwi Odrade, Bene Gesserit Security Mother discovers the secret chamber.

It puzzled me mightily when I first read it that Leto does not name names. "A REVEREND MOTHER WILL READ MY WORDS!" he writes. Leto can see the future. Why does he not name the Sister? ("DARWI ODRADE . . . THIS IS YOUR LIFE!") The answer is that Darwi Odrade, herself Atreides, bears the mark of Siona, the gene that renders its bearer invisible to prescience.

If Leto hasn't presciently foreseen the discovery of his secret chamber by a Reverend Mother, then his message on the walls of the secret chamber, addressed specifically to the Sisterhood, enjoining them to continue the Golden Path since he is dead, is at best a highly educated guess. Who else but a Bene Gesserit would know how to ride a sandworm, recognize Sietch Tabr, and follow his clues in the ancient hunting language Chakobsa to the secret chamber? Just because he has not presciently foreseen it doesn't mean he doesn't know in other ways. At worst, though, it's a stupendously risky gamble on Leto's part.

Even if Leto has presciently foreseen the discovery of his secret chamber by a Reverend Mother, can he ever have been sure what the Sisterhood will do on reading his message to them? All of the Sisterhood bear the mark of Siona, so the oracle has effectively blinded himself to the Sisterhood's decision. To turn a phrase, for Leto, the price of freedom is an invigilance of eternity.

In The Land of the Blind, the One-Eyed Man . . .

Freedom, Herbert is trying to say, is predicated, not on knowledge, but on a mixture of knowledge and ignorance. Paul and Leto's visions of the future contain abysses. Although they know where the timelines will come back into sight, they don't know what events will occur in the blindness of the abyss. During those times, they must act as everybody else does, on the evidence of their senses, their experience, and other mundane forms of knowledge. Leto's secret, personal victory is that when he succeeds in breeding somebody with a gene for invisibility from prescience, he substantively lessens how much he can foresee of the future – hence, reducing how much his prescient foreknowledge threatens his own free will. In his own way, Leto frees himself by blinding himself.

The vision-battle is father and son's personal abyss because they are limited by the presence of the other oracle. So what do his Atreides heroes do? Like all good heroes, they act. No stoic calmness of mind and imperturbability for them. They foresee the possibilities for the future, they see also which are become more or less probable as they act, they try to steer the course of history in the direction they want. As oracles, they have a small amount of freedom, to raise the chances whichever possibilities they prefer to happen will happen. They have a spectacular sort of freedom to affect the chances of whether things could be otherwise in the far distant future. The vision-battle in the desert decides the possibility of the Golden Path and beyond. A Reverend Mother will read their words? No, every citizen of the Imperium will read Paul's and Leto's words, their deeds, their every choice, in every future event that follows. We too in every page that follows in the *Dune* saga.

Nonetheless, Paul's and Leto's freedom isn't much different to the freedom of ordinary, everyday people whose intentional actions are as creative and determinative as theirs. We might not have prescient foreknowledge, but there is still much we know and foreknow about the chances of where our lives are heading. On a less universal scale than Paul and Leto, we try to do just the same thing: steer the course of our histories in the direction we want. God is not the proper analogue of the Dune oracles; you and I are.

Discovered by:
SAM GATES-SCOVELLE

Appendixes

References

Frank Herbert

Dune
Dune Messiah
Children of Dune
God-Emperor of Dune
Heretics of Dune
Chapterhouse: Dune

"Dune Genesis," *Omni*, July 1980 (accessible in January 2009 at http://www.dunenovels.com/news/genesis.html—no longer accessible there)

With Max Barnard: *Without Me You're Nothing: The Essential Guide to Home Computers* (Pocket, 1983)

Herbert, Brian, and Kevin J. Anderson. 2008. *Paul of Dune*. A Tor Book.

Other References

Anscombe, G.E.M. 2000. *Intention*. Harvard University Press.
Appiah, Kwame Anthony. 2005. *The Ethics of Identity*. Princeton University Press.
Aquinas, Thomas. 1997. Basic Writings of Saint Thomas Aquinas: God and the Order of Creation. Edited by Anton Charles Pegis. Hackett.
Arendt, Hannah. 1963. *Eichmann in Jerusalem: A Report on the Banality of Evil*. Penguin.
Asprey, Robert B. 1975. *War in the Shadows: The Guerrilla in History*, Volume1. Doubleday.
Atwood, Margaret. 1998. Cat's Eye. Anchor.
Baggini, Julian. 2005. *What's It All About? Philosophy and the Meaning of Life*. Oxford University Press.

Belzer, Marvin. 2005. Self-Conception and Personal Identity: Revisiting Parfit and Lewis with an Eye on the Grip of the Unity Reaction. *Social Philosophy and Policy*.

Boethius. 1902. *The Consolation of Philosophy*. Translated by W.V. Cooper. Dent, www.exclassics.com/consol/cons8.htm.

Clausewitz, Carl von. 2009. *On War*. Wildside Press.

Cottingham, John. 2003. *On the Meaning of Life*. Routledge.

Dennett, Daniel. 1992. *Consciousness Explained*. Back Bay Books.

Dewey, J. 1996. Creative Democracy: The Task Before Us. In L.A. Hickman, ed., *The Collected Works of John Dewey: The Electronic Edition. Later Works* 14. Intelex.

DiTommaso, Lorenzo. 2007. The Articulation of Imperial Decadence and Decline in Epic Science Fiction. *Extrapolation* 48:2 (July).

Emerson, Ralph Waldo. 2008 [1841]. Self-Reliance. In K. Sacks, ed., *Political Writings*. Cambridge University Press).

Gaunt, Peter. 2003. *Essential Histories: The English Civil Wars 1642–1651*. Osprey.

Gibbon, Edward. 1776–1789. *The History of the Decline and Fall of the Roman Empire*. Strahan and Cadell.

Guevara, Ernesto. 1985. *Guerrilla Warfare*. University of Nebraska Press.

Habermas, Jürgen. 1984. *The Theory of Communicative Action*, Volume I. Beacon Press.

———. 1987. *The Theory of Communicative Action*, Volume II. Beacon Press.

Hick, John. 2007. *Evil and the God of Love*. Macmillan.

Hinman, Larry. 2005. Aristotle and Virtue Ethics. *Ethics Updates*, <http://ethics.sandiego.edu/theories/aristotle/index.asp>, 10/12/2005.

Hobbes, Thomas. 1996. *Leviathan*. Cambridge University Press.

Hursthouse, Rosalind. 1999. *On Virtue Ethics*. Oxford University Press.

Kant, Immanuel. 1996. *The Metaphysics of Morals*. Translated by Mary J. Gregor, Cambridge University Press.

———. 2002. *Groundwork for the Metaphysics of Morals*. Translated by Thomas E. Hill and Arnulf Zweig. Oxford University Press.

Kazez, Jean. 2007. *The Weight of Things: Philosophy and the Good Life*. Blackwell.

Kupperman, Joel. 2006. *Six Myths about the Good Life: Thinking about What Has Value*. Hackett.

Laplace, Pierre Simon. 1951. *A Philosophical Essay on Probabilities*. Translated by Frederick Wilson Truscott and Frederick Lincoln Emory. Dover.

List, Julia. 2009. 'Call Me a Protestant': Liberal Christianity, Individualism, and the Messiah in *Stranger in a Strange Land, Dune*, and *Lord of Light. Science Fiction Studies* #107 (March).

Locke, John. 1998. *An Essay Concerning Human Understanding*. Edited by Roger Woolhouse. Penguin Classics.

MacIntyre, Alasdair. 1984. *After Virtue: A Study in Moral Theory*. University of Notre Dame Press.

———. 1999. *Dependent Rational Animals*. Open Court.

Mackie, J.L. 1955. Evil and Omnipotence. *Mind* 64:254 (April).

Mill, John Stuart. 1993. *Utilitarianism; On Liberty; Considerations on Representative Government; Remarks on Bentham's Philosophy*. Edited by Geraint Williams. Everyman.

Moongadget. 2009. Dune. <http://moongadget.com/origins/dune.html>.

Nietzsche, Friedrich. 1975. *Untimely Meditations*. Translated by Daniel Breazeale. Cambridge University Press.

———. 1982a. *The Anti-Christ*. In *The Portable Nietzsche*, edited and translated by Walter Kaufmann (Penguin).

———. 1982b. *Thus Spoke Zarathustra*. In *The Portable Nietzsche*, edited and translated by Walter Kaufmann (Penguin).

———. 1992a. *Beyond Good and Evil*. In *Basic Writings of Nietzsche*, edited and translated by Walter Kaufmann (Modern Library).

———. 1992b. *Ecce Homo*. In *Basic Writings of Nietzsche*, edited and translated by Walter Kaufmann (Modern Library).

Nussbaum, Martha. 1999. *Frontiers of Justice: Disability, Nationality, and Species Membership*. Harvard University Press.

Parfit, Derek. 1984. *Reasons and Persons*. Oxford University Press (Chapters 10 and 11).

Palumbo, Donald. 2002. *Chaos Theory, Asimov's Foundations and Robots, and Herbert's Dune: The Fractal Aesthetic of Epic Science Fiction, Contributions to the Study of Science Fiction and Fantasy*. Greenwood Press.

Plato. 1996. *The Republic*. Translated and edited by Richard W. Sterling and William C. Scott. Norton.

———. 1987. *Theatetus*. Translated by Robin H. Waterfield. Penguin Classics.

Schechtman, Marya. 1996. *The Constitution of Selves*, Chapter 4. Cornell University Press.

———. 2005. Personal Identity and the Past. *Philosophy, Psychiatry, and Psychology* 12:1.

Singer, Peter. 2009. *The Life You Can Save: Acting Now to End World Poverty*. Random House.

Stoppard, Tom. 1994. *Arcadia*. Faber and Faber.

Swanton, Christine. 2003. *Virtue Ethics: A Pluralistic View*. Oxford University Press.

Taylor, Richard. 1974. *Metaphysics*. Prentice-Hall.

———. 1984. *Good and Evil: A New Direction*. Prometheus.

Tessman, Lisa. 2005. *Burdened Virtues: Virtue Ethics for Liberatory Struggles*. Oxford University Press.

US Department of Defense. August 2009. *Dictionary of Military and Associated Terms*.

Velleman, J. David. 2006a. The Self as Narrator. In *Self to Self: Selected Essays* (Cambridge University Press).

————. 2006b. Self to Self. In *Self to Self: Selected Essays* (Cambridge University Press).

Williams, Bernard. 1985. *Ethics and the Limits of Philosophy*. Harvard University Press.

The Almanak en-Ashraf

Matthew A. Butkus

Matthew is an avid photographer, and has co-founded a photography company. He has done photographic work for diverse clientele, from ballet and theatre companies to *Playboy Golf*, and web design for a variety of companies. He is currently playing with his cameras in the swamps of Louisiana, and despite his best efforts, he has yet to be eaten by the gators. Having earned his Black Belt in Tae Kwon Do, he reminds his students regularly to beware of his ninja skills.

Matthew is an assistant professor of philosophy at McNeese State University, where he teaches courses in introductory philosophy and applied ethics in medicine and the sciences. Additionally, he is a lecturer at Chatham University, teaching courses in research methodology, evidence-based practice, and current issues in health care. When he isn't teaching, he works with a research group in critical care medicine at the University of Pittsburgh.

Christopher Ciocchetti

An avid cook, Chris knows a great deal about spice despite his brown eyes and deep ignorance of worms. Before moving to Louisiana in the summer of 2000, Arrakis was his paradigm of a hot, inhospitable environment. Now, however, he'd like to remind the Arrakisians that it's not the heat. It's the humidity.

Chris is an associate professor of philosophy at Centenary College of Louisiana. He teaches courses on ethics, social and political philosophy, and the history of philosophy, and he's never taught a single course on Bene Gesserit ethics, foldspace technology, nor the coming of the Kwisatz Haderach. He earned his PhD at the University of Kentucky where he wrote his dissertation on justifications for private property. He's the author of several articles on the philosophy of punishment.

Eva Erman

After years of *Dune* harassment from her partner Niklas, who made Eva watch the *Dune* film and series, without any lasting impression whatsoever, she finally gave in to his plea that "the books are so much better" and read them . . . and has since been totally hooked by the powerful saga.

Eva is a senior lecturer in political theory at Stockholm University, Sweden. She is the author of the book *Human Rights and Democracy* (2005) and has published articles on moral conflict, discourse ethics and agency in philosophical scholarly journals such as *Political Theory* and *Philosophy and Social Criticism*, and on the democratic deficit of global governance in scholarly journals such as *Review of International Studies* and *Ethics & International Affairs*. She's the chief editor of *Ethics and Global Politics*.

Adam Ferner

Occasionally, while bicycling around London, he hums the war theme from *Dune* and pretends to be riding a sand-worm—this tends to be fun until the other cyclists at the traffic-lights start staring at him. Sadly, his name isn't a killing word, so he just grins nervously until the lights change. He tried the Water of Life once but it gave him wind.

Adam is currently researching his doctoral thesis in Philosophy at Birkbeck College. His research interests lie in personal identity, the philosophy of the self, and nihilism. He also works on the journals *Philosophy* and *Think*, and teaches art-history at University College London.

In his spare time he trains to become a world-class trapeze artist.

Sam Gates-Scovelle

Sam is a philosopher and sometime professional writer/t-shirt-designer/ haiku poet based in Melbourne, Australia.

On his tenth birthday he got hooked on the spice melange when a cool uncle gave him *Dune*. He read and re-read it . . . often, fascinated by how every character's perspective on the universe and themselves was contingent yet wildly different, each just one more attempt at solving the human predicament: how to live.

For thirteen years now he's taught philosophy variously at the University of Melbourne, Monash University, and the Centre for Adult Education. He develops courses that apply modern and ancient philosophy to current affairs and daily life. Topics have included capitalism, *The Matrix*, software piracy, stem-cell technology, creation science, Google, blogging, oh, and the meaning of life.

One of Sam's favorite philosophers is Albert Camus, who wrote, "There exists a fact which seems utterly moral: namely, that a man is always a prey to his truths." Frank Herbert would, Sam thinks, agree, and so would Paul Atreides. "My father once told me that respect for the truth comes close to being the basis for all morality," Paul tells us, "'Something cannot emerge from nothing,' he said. This is profound thinking if you understand how unstable 'the truth' can be." Even the Mentats and the Bene Gesserit, who know the limits of their truths to be arbitrary, a product of their schooling, can do no more than live within them.

Other cool gifts from this uncle include a gents hairbrush (still in use) and a chocolate pudding (no longer in use).

Roy Jackson

Roy first started reading the *Dune* books when spending a week on a virtually deserted island off the west coast of Australia. There were no giant worms, but plenty of very scary and large monitor lizards.

Roy is Senior Lecturer in Religion, Philosophy and Ethics at the University of Gloucestershire in the UK. He has lectured in philosophy and religion for over twenty years now. His publications include *Nietzsche and Islam*, *Mawdudi and Political Islam*, *Teach Yourself Nietzsche*, and *The God of Philosophy*. His research interests are in Nietzsche, Islamic ethics—particularly the concept of jihad—and Philosophy of Religion.

As Nietzsche once said: "Although the most acute judges of the witches and even the witches themselves, were convinced of the guilt of witchery, the guilt nevertheless was non-existent. It is thus with all guilt." The Bene Gesserit Guilt-casters might well disagree with this. Roy himself has indulged in a little Bene Gesserit technique: whenever he has to go to the dentist he recites to himself the litany against fear: "I must not fear. Fear is the mind-killer." It doesn't work.

Greg Littmann

"I am profoundly disappointed!". A sincere exclamation of disappointment common in the Imperium. (It is said of Muad'Dib that once he watched a desert hawk chick emerge from its shell only to be accidentally stepped on by a Fedaykin and whispered: "Greg Littmann!".)

Bene Gesserit historians maintain that the phrase was originally the name of a philosophy professor at Southern Illinois University, Edwardsville. They believe that he had a PhD in philosophy from the University of North Carolina at Chapel Hill, although they concede that it might have been a certificate in knife combat. The Caladani lay "Philosophers of Old Earth" states "Oh-h-h, Greg Littmann loved all philosophy but especially metaphysics, philosophy of logic, philosophy of mind, and ethics! Play that baliset! He taught Metaphysics, Philosophy of Mind, Media Ethics and Critical Thinking! Now we all drink wine!"

The Spacing Guild secretly knows that Greg Littmann published in the philosophy of logic and wrote philosophy and popular culture chapters for *Doctor Who and Philosophy, Dune and Philosophy, The Onion and Philosophy, Final Fantasy and Philosophy*, and *Terminator and Philosophy*. The Guild has seen no need to inform the emperor.

Kristian Lund

Kristian is not entirely sure exactly what he is, and this is one of the many things he blames on his philosophy degree. He blames his philosophy degree on Frank Herbert.

Wanting to be a Mentat from the tender age of thirteen, he still gets irritated whenever his mechanical computer beats him at Go. Sixteen years later, he is one generalist education richer and is trying to do that human thing of coming up with new ideas, helping to use computer technology in guiding and counseling vulnerable youths.

Rather than wage a war of extermination, he wants to learn more about our new silicon friends. Consequently, he wrote his thesis on "Ownership of Knowledge" to look into all this new electronic "stuff" people seem to think they can own, control, and commoditize. In learning about technology and computers, he has adopted the First law of Mentat: "A process cannot be understood by stopping it. Understanding must move with the flow of the process, must join it and flow with it." He suspects the answer may be, that we think with the machines, instead of letting them think for us.

Another bruise from philosophy, is that Kristian is still hopelessly in love with the Truth. He implores you to please ask her to return his calls if you see her.

Louis Melançon

Louis has spent some time in deserts but has never seen a Maker. He is a US Army officer with a variety of combat arms and intelligence experiences at the tactical, operational, and strategic levels. He has been awarded the Bronze Star Medal and holds masters degrees from the Joint Military Intelligence College and Kings College, London and has contributed to both *Battlestar Galactica and Philosophy: Mission Accomplished or Mission Frakked Up?* and *Anime and Philosophy: Wide-Eyed Wonder*.

Niklas Möller

Niklas is a philosopher, currently working as post-graduate fellow at Cambridge University, UK, on various topics in moral theory. His PhD thesis was concerned with normative aspects of risk and safety.

Among the many pieces of advice passed on by his older cousin, such as that Carl Barks was the only true Donald Duck artist, and anyone believing something else was just utterly and forever wrong, his *Dune* recommendation are among those that have made an irresistible mark. No matter the passing years, Herbert's master vision has kept its grip on Niklas. One reason for this, he believes, is the powerful dark and pessimistic side to the *Dune* saga, a strand that evokes resistance as well as lures him in. It strongly reminds him of Kafka, and he could hear Herbert's voice echoing in Kafka's reply to the question of whether there is really no hope: "Oh yes, there is hope," Kafka retorted, "plenty of hope, infinite hope. Only not for us."

Niklas has published articles in international journals such as *Journal of Applied Philosophy* and *International Journal of Risk Assessment and Management*, as well as in international and Swedish anthologies.

Jeffery Nicholas

Jeffery teaches as an Associate Professor of Philosophy at Mount Angel Seminary, a variety of courses in philosophy and Catholic social thought.

He knew that wanting to be a Mentat meant many hours of study in philosophy and logic, plus long hours of reading *Dune* over and over. This inevitably led him to want to write, and to write things stranger than life. His professional publications include "Eucharist and Dragon Fighting" in *Philosophy of Management*. He's also written two novels that hide in a drawer away from prying eyes, and is currently working on a third novel about a vampire seminarian.

He co-founded and serves as the Executive Secretary of the International Society for MacIntyrean Enquiry.

Brook W.R. Pearson

Brook is a multi-disciplinary philosopher living and teaching in Vancouver, where he teaches in the Humanities Department of Simon Fraser University.

Ranging across literature, history, religious studies, aesthetics, psychology and philosophy, recently, his courses have become a little stranger than usual. A course on Venice tried to prove that Venice doesn't really exist. A class on Roman literature had as its central thesis that "Rome is cyberspace," and one on classical Greek culture suggests that steampunk might be the best way to understand what's going on there.

He blames Frank Herbert for a lot of this: Once upon a time, on the recommendation of a friend, Brook went into a small library in the old morgue of a decommissioned Second World War Canadian Air Force Base in Saskatchewan, and found a battered copy of Frank Herbert's *Dune*.

Book by book, the series revealed itself to him, like archaeology in reverse—oldest layers seen first, echoes of the Duniverse's past recognizable in its fictional future.

And so, the *Dune* saga entered with him the chrysalis of higher education and grew there alongside degrees in theology and biblical studies, and eventually classics and philosophy. Studying languages, religions, philosophies, he realized that Herbert had already pushed him to see connections and developments in history and thought as part of an emerging pattern whose layers are never fully visible.

Shane Ralston

Shane is an assistant professor of philosophy at Pennsylvania State University,-Hazleton, a scholar of democratic theory and American philosophy as well as an aspiring Mentat. He is the 2008 winner of the American Philosophical Association's William James Prize for Best Paper in American Philosophy. He has published in *Transactions of the Charles S. Peirce Society*, *Review of Policy Research*, and *Education and Culture*.

Simon Riches

Simon Riches is Research Associate at the Institute of Psychiatry, King's College London, and teaches philosophy at Heythrop College, University of London. He holds a PhD in philosophy from University College London and has previously taught in its philosophy department. He also studied philosophy at the University of Southampton and psychology at the University of East London. He is editor of *The Philosophy of David Cronenberg* and a contributor to *The Philosophy of David Lynch*.

Stephanie Semler

Stephanie is a philosopher and erstwhile science-fiction author living in the bounty of the Blue Ridge of southwestern Virginia. Her love of science fiction and philosophy converges on the work of Frank Herbert, who in his infinite talent and wisdom, found a way to do both at the same time.

She has taught philosophy at Radford University, Virginia Military Institute, and Southern Virginia University, and is currently teaching at Virginia Tech. Her research interests are broad and centered in the history of philosophy. She has been primarily interested in personal identity and its related problems, particularly in the work of Aristotle and Kant. She holds a Doctorate in Philosophy from the University of California, Santa Barbara, and lives in Salem, Virginia, with her husband, Jim Baker.

Killing and Healing Words

CPSIA information can be obtained
at www.ICGtesting.com
Printed in the USA
JSHW022041021121
20091JS00001B/1